D1860371

A Dictionary of the Pathan Tribes on the North-West Frontier of India

A Dictionary of the Pathan Tribes on the North-West Frontier of India

By

Compiler: J. Wolfe Murray

GYAN

Published by

GYAN

Gyan Publishing House
5, Ansari Road
Daryaganj, New Delhi-110002
Phone: 011-47034999, 9811692060
E-mail: books@gyanbooks.com

Distribution Network
gyanbooks.com
India, USA, Canada, UK, Australia, France

ISBN : 978-81-212-6783-0 (PB)
First Published, 1899

2nd Impression 2022

Printed at: Gyan Press, Delhi.

A Dictionary of the Pathan Tribes on the North-West Frontier of India
Author: COMPILER: J. WOLFE MURRAY

A
DICTIONARY OF THE PATHAN TRIBES
ON THE
NORTH-WEST FRONTIER OF INDIA,

It is requested that any errors and omissions may be brought to the notice of—

The Assistant Quarter Master General,
Intelligence Branch,
Simla.

1899.

PREFACE.

THIS work has been compiled with a view to providing an index to the numerous ramifications of the Pathan tribes of the North-West Frontier, in such a form that any obscure sub-division may be easily referred to its proper tribal position: but all detailed particulars of the history and genealogy of the tribes, such as may be found in larger works of reference, have been excluded. In order also to diminish the bulk of the work without greatly decreasing its utility, certain cis-frontier Pathan tribes (including the divisions, etc., of the Bangash and Khaṭṭaks) have been omitted; the Turis, however, have been included.

J. WOLFE MURRAY, *Lieut.-Colonel,*
Assistant Quarter Master General,
Intelligence Branch.

SIMLA;
1st June 1899.

EXPLANATORY NOTE.

The classification adopted in this dictionary is as follows :—

1. The tribe.
2. The clan of the tribe.
3. The division of the clan.
4. The sub-division of the division.
5. The section of the sub-division.
6. Other minor fractions of the section.

The headings in the dictionary read from the lesser to the greater, thus ;—Dadu Khel are a minor fraction of the Dreplara section, of the Khusrogi sub-division, of the Nasruddin division, of the Zakha Khel clan, of the Afridi tribe.

Figures in brackets indicate the number of the fighting men of the fraction immediately preceding the figures.

The locality of the tribe, clan, or division, etc., is also given within brackets, where this is capable of accurate definition, and is not sufficiently indicated in the name of the tribe, clan, etc. In many cases the names of the headmen have been given.

"Gar" and "Samil."—These terms refer to the two political factions into which the tribes on the

Peshawar and Kohat borders are divided. At some remote period a bitter feud existed between the Gar and Samil branches of the great Bangash tribe, and all the neighbouring tribes appear to have joined one faction or the other; although the origin of the quarrel has been forgotten, the division still remains.

"SUNIS" AND "SHIAHS."—The vast majority of the frontier tribesmen belong to the former sect; and this may be assumed to be the case where not otherwise expressly stated.

"HAMSAYAS."—Vassal or dependent settlers, amongst an alien tribe.

A DICTIONARY OF THE PATHAN TRIBES ON THE NORTH-WEST FRONTIER OF INDIA.

A

ABA KHEL.—A minor fraction of Adam Khel, Nazar Khel, Ali Khan Khel, Sarki Khel, Madda Khel (1,600), Ibrahim Khel, Utmanzai, Darwesh Khel Wazirs.

ABA KHEL.—A sub-division of Nekpi Khel, Khwazazai, Akozai—Yusufzai Swatis.

ABA KHEL.—A section of Aka Maruf, Babuzai, Baizai, Akozai—Yusufzai Swatis.

ABA (or ABAO) KHEL.—A section of Makhozai, Nasuzai, Iliaszai, Bunerwals.

ABA KHEL (1,200).—A sub-division of Babuzai, Baizai, Akozai—Yusufzai Swatis.

ABA KHEL (2,000).—A sub-division of Kuz Sulizai, Baizai, Akozai—Yusufzai Swatis.

ABA KHEL.—A sub-division of Khadakzai, Khwazazai, Akozai—Yusufzai Swatis.

ABA KHEL.—A section of Ismailzai, Daolatzai, Malizai, Bunerwals.

ABA KHEL.—A sub-division of Nurizai, Malizai, Bunerwals.

ABA KHEL. (80; Dera Ismail Khan District).—Nomadic, a section of Isot Khel, Mian Khel, Lohana, Pawindahs. Headman; see Mian Khel.

ABA KHEL (Mohmand country).—A sub-division of Masaud, Safis, a vassal clan of the Mohmands.

ABA KHEL (Left bank of Mastura).—A section of the Fateh Khan Khel, Utman Khel, Daulatzai, Orakzais. Samil. Headman; Bayaz.

ABA KOR.—A sub-division of Maimana Khel, Khwaezai, Mohmands. Headman; Attai.

ABAS KHEL (80).—A minor fraction of the Panj Pilara, Abdullai, Aimal Khel, Bahlolzai, Mahsuds. Headman; Kamir.

ABAS KHEL (80).—A section of the Haibat Khel, Nana Khel, Bahlolzai, Mahsuds. Headmen; Shorang Khan, Asi.

ABAS KHEL (100).—A minor fraction of the Shumi Khel, Palli Khel, Manazai, Alizai, Mahsuds. Headmen; Magri, Mador, Imar, and Mirab.

ABAS KHEL (10).—A minor fraction of Gita Khel, Muhammad Khel, Malakh, Mallizad, Dawaris. Headman; Mad Azam.

ABAZAI (1,000).—A division of Khwazazai, Akozai—Yusufzai Swatis. NOTE.—The Abazai division are now dependents of the Khan of Dir.

ABBA KHEL (200).—A division of Tatta, Battannis. Headmen; Kota (Alladadi), Sarang Khan (Shakar).

ABBAS KHEL.—A minor fraction of Aba Khel, Ismailzai, Daulatzai, Malizai, Bunerwals.

ABDAL KHEL.—A division of Kuki Khe (4,500) Afridis. Gar. Headmen; Mulla Anwar Shah, Gulrur, Said Ali, Mulla Lajbar, Mulla Amir, Gulsam, Sherulla, Budai.

ABDI KHEL.—A minor fraction of Shugai, Tori Khel (2,670) Ibrahim Khel, Utmanzai, Darwesh Khel Wazirs. Headmen; Allahyar and Ghalbal.

ABDULANI.—A sub-division of Mekhiani, Spin, Tarins. Headman; Azim.

ABDULAZAI (2,000; Zhob).—A division of (Northern) Sanzar, Kakars. Headman; Sultan Muhammad (Pakhezai).

ABDUL AZIZ KHEL (80; Mastura valley).—One of the four divisions of the Muhammad Khel Orakzais; are called the "Khans of the Muhammad Khel." Gar. Shiah.

ABDUL KHEL (340; North of Kharmana river).—A minor fraction of the Mastu Khel, Khwaja Khel, Masuzai, Lashkarzai, Orakzais. Gar. Headman; Ashraf Khan.

ABDUL KHEL.—A minor fraction of Bora Khel (1,000), Mohmit Khel, Utmanzai, Darwesh Khel Wazirs. Headmen; Sheikh, Khoja Mir, and Pahlwan.

ABDUL KHEL (50).—A section of the Kasim Khel, Badanzai, Shaman Khel, Mahsuds. Headmen; Jani Khan and Mir Janai.

ABDUL KHEL.—A sub-division of Urmuz Khel, Sipah (1,200), Afridis. Samil. Headmen; Sher Jan, Jumma, Daud, Shibran, Chimnai.

ABDUL KHEL (? IDAL KHEL) (25).—A minor fraction of Chuttan, Zira Khel, Amzoni Mallizad, Dawaris. Headman; Gumal Khan.

ABDUL KHEL (21).—A minor fraction of Umarzai, Zira Khel, Amzoni, Mallizad, Dawaris. Headmen; Amir, Sheikh Musa, Niaz.

ABDULLAI (1,158).—A subdivision of the Aimal Khel, Bahlolzai Mahsuds. Headman; Azim Khan.

ABDUL MIRZI.—(410; North of Kharmana river).—A section of the Landaizai, Masuzai, Lashkarzai, Orakzais. Gar.

ABDUL RAHIM KHEL.—A sub-division of Landi Khel, Sipah (1,200), Afridis. Samil. Headmen; Amir Wali.

ABDUL RAHMAN KHEL (Tirah).—A sub-division of the Bazid Khel, Sheikhan, "Hamsayas" of the Orakzais. Samil. Headmen; Ahmad Gul.

ABDUL RAHMAN KHEL (340).—A minor fraction of the Sher Khel, Haibat Khel, Nana Khel, Bahlolzai, Mahsuds. Headman; Guldad.

ABDUL RAHMAN KHEL.—A minor fraction of Idar Khel, Ali Khel, Khaddar Khel (770), Mohmit Khel,

Utmanzai, Darwesh Khel Wazirs. Headmen: Nur Muhammad, Ahmad Din.

ABDUL RAHMAN KHEL (50).—A minor fraction of Abdul Rahman Khel, Muhammad Khel, Malakh, Mallizad, Dawaris. Headmen; Fazil-din, Kasim, Salam Khan, Zar Muhammad.

ABDUL RAHMAN KHEL (100).—A section of Muhammad Khel, Malakh, Mallizad, Dawaris. Headmen; Fazil Din, Hakim Khan, Gul Kadam.

ABDUL WIDANAI (50).—A section of the Malik Dinai, Manazai, Alizai, Mahsuds. Headman; Shawagar.

ABDUR RAHMAN KHEL (200).—A section of the Musa Khel, Mamuzai, Lashkarzai, Orakzais. Gar.

ABRAHIM KHEL (560; See Mamuzai).—A section of the Alikaran, Mamuzai, Lashkarzai, Orakzais. Gar.

ACHAKZAIS (13,000; Both sides of the Peshin border).—A large tribe, an off-shoot of the Barakzai Duranis, divided into the Gujanzai and Badinzai clans. The leading division of the former clan is the Ahmadzai, said to be distinct from the Hamidzai division. Headmen; Haji Ghulam Haidar Khan, *Khan Bahadur*, is the leading man; others are Ayaz Khan (Hamidzai), Akbar Khan (Ghaibzai), etc. The clans, divisions, etc., of the Achakzais are not separately indexed in this Dictionary.

ACHAR KHEL (20).—A section of Maryam Khel, Darka Khel, Mallizad, Dawaris. Headmen; Didar, Yar Muhammad, Mazal.

ACHARS or ATSARS (200—Kazha Valley, North Waziristan).—A colony of Yusufzai Saiads, now settled amongst the Madda Khel Wazirs of the Tochi. Headmen; Dingai, Mirbaz, Rastam Khan, Sadim.

ADAR KHEL (Bannu; Chapri, etc., Kuram).—A minor fraction of Said Khel, Umarzai (600). Shin Khel, Ahmadzai, Darwesh Khel Wazirs.

ADALA KOR.—A minor fraction of Behram Kor, Dildar Khel, Mohmand Khel, Kattia

Khel, Hassan Khel. Mitha Khan Khel, Kuki Khel (4,500), Afridis. Gar. Headmen; Ghanni and Torbaz.

Adal Kor.—A sub-division of Hassani Khel, Burhan Khel, Mohmands. Headman; Shahlai.

Adam Khel (5,900; A small wedge of hills, jutting out between the Peshawar and Kohat Districts, surrounding the Kohat Pass and including the Turki valley.) One of the two non-Khyber Afridi clans. They do not migrate to any extent in summer. Headmen; Babri, Jowaki, in British territory.

Adam Khel, Madda Khel.—A minor fraction of Nazar Khel, Ali Khan Khel, Sarki Khel, Madda Khel (1,600), Ibrahim Khel, Utmanzai, Darwesh Khel Wazirs. Headmen; Kadam Khan of Pashai, and Nabbi Khan of Sanjalai.

Adam Khel.—A sub-division of Wargare, Dana, Battannis.

Adamzai (9; Laki).—A sub-division of Malezai, Kakanwal Lunis.

Adda Khel.—A minor fraction of Jamaldin Khel. Wadin, Khazzar Khel, Ali Khan Khel, Sarki Khel, Madda Khel (1,600). Ibrahim Khel, Utmanzai, Darwesh Khel Wazirs.

Adili Khel—A minor fraction of Mirghat Khel, Basi Khel, Kamal Khel, Saib Jan, Aka Khel (1,800), Afridis. Samil.

Adinazai (90).—A minor fraction of Mulazai, Panizai, Harun Khel, Sanatia, Kakars. Headman; Mushkai.

Adinzai (?,000; Uch, Shawa, and Ramora valleys).—A division of Khwazazai, Akozai—Yusufzai Swatis. Headman; Nasrullah Khan of Uch.

Adinzai (390).—A section of Sarangzai, Harun Khel. Sanatia, Kakars. Headmen; Mir Ahmad (Amadun); Wahab (Amadun).

Adinzai (North Zhob).—A section of Badsuzai, Alizai, Sanzar, Kakars.

Adris (100).—A section of Arozai, Ahmad Khel, Sen Khel, Sheranis.

Adu Khan Kor.—A section of the Umar Khan Khel, Alisherzai, Lashkarzai, Orakzais. Samil.

Adu Khel (600).—A section of the Ali Karan, Mamuzai, Lashkarzai, Orakzais. Gar. Headman; Mulla Nur Badshahi.

Adwani (34).—A sub-division of Ismailalagh, Spin, Tarins. Headman; Biland.

Afridis (26,500; Lower and easternmost spurs of the Sufed Koh range, west and south of Peshawar, including the Bazar and Bara valleys, and all the northern part of Tirah). There are 6 so-called Khyber clans of Afridis, *viz.*, Kuki Khel, Kambar Khel, Kamar Khel, Malikdin Khel, Sipah, and Zakha Khel; also two outside clans, *viz.*, Aka Khel, dwelling on the Orakzai border, and Adam Khel, who occupy a mountainous tract projecting into British territory between Peshawar and Kohat. With the exception of the Adam Khel, the whole of the Afridi tribe is migratory, remaining in the highlands of Tirah in summer, and descending to the Kajuri, Bazar, and Khyber valleys in winter. The Khyber and Kohat passes are commanded by the tribe.

Afza Khel.—A minor fraction of Umar Khel, Ali Khel, Khadar Khel (770), Mohmit Khel, Utmanzai, Darwesh Khel Wazirs.

Afzal Khel (Gumatti and Wana).—A minor fraction of Ali Khel (10), Bomi Khel, Nasra Din, Kalu Khel, Ahmadzai, Darwesh Khel Wazirs.

Afzal Khel.—A minor fraction of Mandi Khel, Mad Khozhai, Khaddar Khel (770), Mohmit Khel, Utmanzai, Darwesh Khel Wazirs. Headman; Amzalla.

Afzal Khel (Samana range and south side of Khanki valley).—A sub-division of the Rabia Khel, Ismailzai, Orakzais. Samil. Headmen; Muhammad, Khairulla, Halim, Aziz.

Aggai Khel (Bajaur).—A sub-section of Ilal Khel, Salarzai, Tarkanis.

Aghzan (90).—A section of Zira Khel, Amzoni, Mallizad,

Dawaris. Headmen; Muhammad Alam, Shahmurad.

Agzar Khel.—A sub-division of Niamat Khel, Tatta, Battannis. Headman; Marwut.

Ahad Kor.—A sub-division of Dawat or Dauta Khel, Khwaezai, Mohmands.

Ahmad Khel.—A minor fraction of Ismail Khel, Makhozai, Nasuzai, Iliaszai, Bunerwals.

Ahmad Khel (2,000).—A subdivision of Targhari, Sanzar, Kakars. Headmen; Piro, Rahim, Kamat, Pir Mahi.

Ahmad Khel (1,242).—A division of Oba Khel, Sheranis.

Ahmad Khel (850).—A division of Sen Khel, Sheranis.

Ahmad Khel (120).—A section of the Sultanai, Shabi Khel, Alizai, Mahsuds. Headmen; Nilgar, Daur.

Ahmad Khel (40).—A section of the Umar Khel, Nana Khel, Bahlolzai, Mahsuds. Headman; Faujdar.

Ahmad Khel.—A minor fraction of Nikki Khel, Hassan Khel, Pakhai (1,000), Budai, Zakha Khel, Afridis. Samil. Headmen; Gulbadam, Wali, Tirakai, Khairulla, Morad, Ghorzi.

Ahmad Khel (38).—A section of Zira Khel,i Amzoni, Mallizad, Dawaris. Headmen; Shandai, Channi, Shahnawaz.

Ahmad Khel (30).—A section of Taiota, Idak, Tappizad, Dawaris. Headmen; Daisal, Halim Shah.

Ahmadzai (11; Laki).—A subdivision of Malezai, Bakanwal, Lunis.

Ahmadzai (11,960; Left bank of Kuram river and British territory, Wana, Shakai, etc., Mahsud country). A clan of the Darwesh Khel Wazirs. Headmen; Mani Khan, Sperkai, is the most influential; see also the two divisions of the Ahmadzais, *viz.*, Kalu Khel and Sain or Sani Khel.

Ahmadzai.—(West of Dera Ghazi Khan District.)—A sub-division of Mangizai, Laharzai, Musa Khels. Headman; Mir Baz.

AHMADZAI (1,000; West of Dera Ghazi Khan District).—A sub-division of Balil Khel, Musa Khels. Headmen; Jala, Rahman, Lawan, Gai, Wadan (Malizai), Bahadur, Gulan (Husenzai), Halim Sardar Khan Lat, Jamal Balu Khan (Maghduzai), Khan Muhammad, Fateh Khan, (Mahmadzai), Lal Khan. Dost Muhammad (Kudizai).

AHMADZAI. (450).—A clan of the Ushtaranas. The divisions, etc., of the Ahmadzais are not separately indexed in this Dictionary.

AHMAKZAI (Bori valley, Zhob).—A section of Mirzai, Alizai, Sanzar, Kakars.

AHMEDAI KOR.—A section of Muhammad Khan Kor, Burhan Khel Pandiali, Mohmands. Headmen; Namdad, Nasir, Narai.

AHMEDAKZAI (Basawal, Kabul river).—A division of the Kukozai, who are affiliated with the Mohmand clans.

AHMED BEG KHEL.—A minor fraction of Mohib Khel, Shekhai, Annai (1,000), Budai, Zakha Khel, Afridis. Samil. Headmen; Akbar Din, Aliakai, Mohiuddin, Shahzada, Arsala, Aligul.

AIB KHEL (Western Buner).—A sub-division of Salarzai, Iliaszai, Bunerwals.

AIB KHOR.—A minor fraction of Shaikh Khel, Aib Khel, Salarzai, Iliaszai, Bunerwals.

AIDAL KHEL (50).—A section of the Birri Khel, Galeshahi, Shaman Khel, Mahsuds. Headmen; Alizai, Gul Azad.

AIDU KHEL (Left bank of Mastura). A section of the Yarkulli Khel, Bazoti, Daulatzai, Orakzais. Samil. Headman; Daim.

AIKAM KHEL (80).—A subdivision of the Band Khel, Bahlolzai, Mahsuds. Headmen; Kalandar Shah's son, Mehtar.

AIMAL KHAN KHEL.—(Mastura river) A sub-division of the Zanka Khel, Ali Khel, "Hamsayas" of the Orakzais. Gar. $\frac{1}{3}$ Shiah.

AIMAL KHAN KOR.—A section of the Umar Khan Khel, Alisherzai, Lashkarzai, Orakzais. Samil.

AIMAL KHEL.—A minor fraction of Hati Khel, Mali (or Muli) Khel, Salarzai, Iliaszai, Bunerwals.

AIMAL KHEL (1,743).—A division of the Bahlolzai, Mahsuds.

AIMAL KHEL.—A minor fraction of Tor Khel, Asad Khel, Mitha Khan Khel, Kuki Khel (4,500), Afridis. Gar. Headmen; Razai and Islamdin.

AIMAL KHEL.—A minor fraction of Tashi Khel, Sharaki (200). Galai, Adam Khel, Afridis.

AIMAL KHEL.—A minor fraction of Kasim Khel (250), Kimat Khel, Jawaki, Adam Khel, Afridis.

AIMAT KHAN KOR (300).—A minor fraction of the Ali Karan, Sipah, Mamuzai, Lashkarzai, Orakzais. Gar. Headman; Mohibulla.

AIMAT KHEL.—A minor fraction of the Ash Khel, Nasrazai, Masuzai, Lashkarzai, Orakzais. Samil. Headman; Ismail.

AIPAI KOR.—A sub-division of Hassan Khel, Dawezai, Mohmands. Headman; Sandan.

AIZEKACHKAI. (70).—A section of the Malik Dinai, Manazai, Alizai, Mahsuds. Headman; Shahabuddin.

AJAB KHEL (19).—A sub-division of Zerakki, Mallizad, Dawaris. Headmen; Rozam Shah, Ghain Shah.

AKA KHEL (Bajaur).—A sub-division of Nur Khel, Samilzai, Tarkanis.

AKA KHEL.—A sub-division of Khadakzai, Khwazazai, Akozai—Yusufzai Swatis.

AKA KHEL.—A section of Ismailzai, Daolatzai, Malizai, Bunerwals.

AKA KHEL.—A section of Panjpai, Nasuzai, Iliaszai, Bunerwals.

AKA KHEL (75).—Dera Ismail Khan District).—Nomadic, a section of Isot Khel, Mian Khel, Lohana, Pawindahs. Headman; see Mian Khel.

AKA KHEL (Goshta, Kabul river).—A sub-division of

Dawat or Dauta Khel, Khwaezai, Mohmands. Headmen; Zaman Shah, Akram.

Aka Khel.—A section of Khalil Khel, Kasim Khel, Tarakzai, Mohmands. Headman; Khaista.

Aka Khel (45).—A section of the Salimkai, Khalli Khel, Shaman Khel, Mahsuds. Headman; Masta Khan.

Aka Khel (1,800).—The hills south-west of Peshawar, the Bara and Waran valleys). One of the two non-Khyber Afridi clans. Samil.

Aka Kor.—A section of Khalil Khel, Kasim Khel, Tarakzai, Mohmands. Headman; Sher Ali.

Akali.—(Bannu and Shawal.) A minor fraction of Sardi Khel, Bakka Khel (1,000), Wali Khel, Utmanzai, Darwesh Khel, Wazirs.

Akai Kor.—A minor fraction of Asaf Khel, Dalkha Kor, Dadu Khel, Tarakzai, Mohmands.

Aka Maruf (1,500).—A subdivision of Babuzai, Baizai, Akozai—Yusufzai Swatis.

Akazai (1,165.—Black Mountain). A division of Isazai, Yusufzais. Headmen; Zirif Khan, Saidwali, Shahbakht Khan, Dad Khan.

Akazai (125; Mahaban).—A sub-division of Utmanzai, Mandan, Yusufzais.

Akbar Khel (Bar Yakhdand.)—A division of Utmanzai Mohmands.

Akhel (Ibrahim Khel; 600).—One of the six divisions of the Ismailzai, Orakzais. Samil. Headman; Abdul Azim.

Akhorwal.—See Tator Khel.

Akhtarzai (Zhob).—A section of Ibrahimzai, Shadzai, Alizai, Sanzar, Kakars.

Akhtarzai (500; Zhob).—A section of Shadzai, Ali Khel, Sanzar, Kakars.

Akhun Khel (980).—A clan of the Allaiwals.

Akhund Khel (Black Mountain).—Headman; Amir Khan.

Akhund Khel (400; Chagarzai portion of Buner).—A

religious body, not belonging to any particular clan.

Akhundan (12).—A section of Tarota, Idak, Tappizad, Dawaris. Headman; Israfil.

Akhundan (9).—A section of Barim Khel, Amzoni, Mallizad, Dawaris. Headmen; Channi, Majib Shah.

Akhundzada.—The descendant of an Akhund, or spiritual chief of renown.

Akhti Khel (9).—A section of Maryam Khel, Darpa Khel, Mallizad, Dawaris. Headmen; Pachi, Zerdast.

Akka Khel.—A section of the Aimal Khan Khel, Zanka Khel, Ali Khel, "Hamsayas" of the Orakzais. Gar. ⅛ Shiah. Headman; Darya Khan.

Akozai (70; Black Mountain).—A section of Tasan Khel, Akazai, Isazai, Yusufzais.

Akozai-Yusufzais (40,400;* Swat Valley from the Panj kora junction to Kohistan).—A large tribe of Pathans, inhabiting both banks of the Swat river, sometimes known as Upper and Lower Swatis; see also "Swatis."

Akri Khel.—A minor fraction of Karim Khel, Jamal Khel, Malik Shahi (400), Wali Khel, Utmanzai, Darwesh Khel, Wazirs. Headman; Sarjamal.

Aladadzai (146).—A minor fraction of Bulozai, Panizai, Harun Khel, Sanatia, Kakars. Headman; Sher Shah.

Aladadzai (100; Zhob).—A section of Jalalzai, Alizai, Sanzar, Kakars.

Alafdin Khel.—A minor fraction of Misri Khel, Bosti Khel (156), Galai, Adam Khel, Afridis.

Alam Khan Khel (250).—A minor fraction of the Machi Khel, Shumi Khel, Palli Khel, Manazai, Alizai, Mahsuds. Headmen; Alibat, Aka Khel, Suleman, Musa, Shazoo and Khamtuni.

Alam Khan Khel (110).—A minor fraction of the †Nasi Khel, Haidar Khel, Tor, Tappizad, Dawaris. Headmen; Lalo Khan, Wali Khan.

* Note.—This does not include Mians, Gujars, and other "Fakirnama."

† See also Appendix I.

ALAM KHAN KHEL (12).—A section of Alizai, Darpa Khel, Mallizad, Dawaris. Headmen; Najib, Isa Khan.

ALAM KHEL.—A section of Kanezai, Kattagarm, Tatta, Battannis.

ALAM KHEL.—A minor fraction of Feroz Khel, Tor Sapar (350), Galai, Adam Khel, Afridis.

ALAZAIS (50; North of Torbela).—A division of Utmanzai, Yusufzais.

ALI AHMAD KHEL —A minor fraction of Baghdad Khel, Keimal Khel, Urmuz Khel, Sipah (1,200), Afridis. Samil. Headman; Nabat.

ALI BEG KHEL (Bajaur).—A division of Isazai Tarkanis.

ALI KARAN.—(Head of Khanki river.) One of the two subdivisions of the Mamuzai, Lashkarzai, Orakzais. Gar.

ALIKHANAI.—A minor fraction of Khushalai, Tori Khel (2,670), Ibrahim Khel, Utmanzai, Darwesh Khel Wazirs. Headman; Fateh Mir.

ALI KHAN KHEL.—A section of the Ali Karan, Mamuzai, Lashkarzai, Orakzais. Gar. Headman; Mosadi.

ALI KHAN KHEL (30).—A minor fraction of the Garri Khel, Baran Khel, Chabar Khel, ShamanKhel, Mahsuds. Headmen; Belak, Zarpiyao.

ALI KHAN KHEL.—A minor fraction of Bash Khel (150), Sharaki, Galai, Adam Khel, Afridis.

ALI KHAN KHEL.—A minor fraction of Kasim Khel (250) Kimat Khel, Jawaki, Adam Khel, Afridis.

ALI KHAN KHEL.—A minor fraction of Sarki Khel, Madda Khel (1,600), Ibrahim Khel, Utmanzai, Darwesh Khel Wazirs. Headmen :—

Sadda Khan.
Alambe Khan.
Shadam Khan.
} Ger Madda Khels,

also Sabir of Inzar Kach, Nur Shah of Sanzala, and Umar Khel of Inzar Kach. See also Star Ali Khan Khel, and Waruka Ali Khan Khel. The latter are frequently alluded to as the "Ali Khan Khel" simply.

ALIKHANZAI (West of Dera Ghazi Khan district).—A section of the Kudizai, Ahmadzai. Balil Khel, Musa Khels. Headman; Dost Muhammad.

ALI KHEL (3,000—Source of Mastura river).—One of the four "Hamsaya" clans of the Orakzais. Gar. ⅓rd Shiah. Headman; Hamid Khan.

ALI KHEL (Mastura, Bara, Khanki, and Miranzai valleys).—A sub-division of the Samozai, Sheikhan, "Hamsayas" of the Orakzais. Samil. Headman; Hamid Khan.

ALI KHEL (26).—A sub-division of the Khalli Khel, Shaman Khel, Mahsuds. Headman; Haji Muhammad.

ALI KHEL.—A minor fraction of Mast Ali, Shaikh Khel, Aib Khel, Salarzai, Iliaszai, Bunerwals.

ALI KHEL.—A section of the Makhozai, Nasuzai, Iliaszai, Bunerwals.

ALI KHEL.—A section of Khan Khel, Kuz Suliza, Baizai, Akozai—Yusufzai Swatis.

ALI KHEL (2,000; Opposite Chakdara main Swat valley).—A division of Bar Ranizai, Akozai—Yusufzai Swatis. Headmen; Saadat Khan, Saifullah Khan, Shirin Khan, all of Aladand.

ALI KHEL (or ALIZAI) (9,800. Zhob—and Khaisor).—A division of Sanzar, Kakars.

ALI KHEL.—A sub-division of Bobak, Dana, Battannis.

ALI KHEL (600).—A section of Shadzai, Alizai, Sanzar, Kakars.

ALI KHEL.—A minor fraction of Idia Khel, Jani Khel (1,000), Wali Khel, Utmanzai, Darwesh Khel Wazirs.

ALI KHEL.—A section of Khaddar Khel (770), Mohmit Khel, Utmanzai, Darwesh Khel Wazirs. Headmen; Nur Muhammad, Makach, Liarai, Sakhe Man, Akhmad, Nambuti, Salih Din, Nazarka, Zarak.

ALI KHEL.—A minor fraction of Shugai, Tori Khel (2,670), Ibrahim Khel, Utmanzai, Darwesh Khel Wazirs. Headmen; Gul Baid, Gulli, Guland.

Ali Khel.—A section of Manyar Khel (360), Ibrahim Khel, Utmanzai, Darwesh Khel Wazirs. Headmen; Zira Khan, Mihrab Khan, Kabal, Nawaz Khan, Adal Baz Muhammad, Niaz Gul.

Ali Khel. (Bannu District).—A section of Musa Khel, Shin Khel (3,400), Ahmadzai, Darwesh Khel Waziris.

Ali Khel (10).—A minor fraction of Bomi Khel, Nasra Din, Kalu Khel, Ahmadzai, Darwesh Khel Wazirs.

Ali Khel (100).—A section of Ashu Khel, Hassan Khel, Adam Khel, Afridis.

Ali Khel.—A minor fraction of Tor Khel, Asad Khel, Mitha Khan, Khel, Kuki Khel (4,500), Afridis. Gar. Headmen; Razai and Islamdin.

Ali Khel.—A section of Jowakai, Babakri, Sipah (1,200), Afridis. Samil. Headman; Ali Shah.

Ali Khel.—A sub-division of Landi Khel, Sipah (1,200), Afridis. Samil. Headman; Ali Shah.

Ali Khel (178).—One of the five sections of the Haidar Khel, Tor, Tappizad, Dawaris. Headmen; Mad Alam, Alif Khan, Abizar, Azad Khan.

Ali Khel.—A section of Sheikhmal, Kambar Khel, (4,500), Afridis. Gar. Headmen; Ahmad Shah, Hikmat, Alla Khan, Mirshak, Shahzada, Khairulla, Mir Hussan Shero, Nurai, Nur Ali, Shuja Gul, Munir.

Ali Kwaja Khel.—A section of Panjpai, Nasuzai, Iliaszai, Bunerwals.

Alikzai (21; Thal Chotiali).—A division of Drigzai, Lunis. Headmen; Agar, (Shikar Khanzai), Anmar, (Hassan Khanzai), Adam, (Nura Khanzai), Sado, (Baranzai).

Alim Khan Kor.—A minor fraction of Sultan Khel. Hassan Khel, Pakhai (1,000), Budai, Zakha Khel, Afridis. Samil. Headmen; see Sultan Khel.

Ali Muhammad Khel (100).—A minor fraction of the Nikarrab Khel, Khoidad Khel, Gidi Khel, Manazai, Alizai, Mahsuds. Headman; Surkamand.

ALI SHER KHEL.—A minor fraction of Babur Khel, Keimal Khel, Urmuz Khel, Sipah (1,200), Afridis. Samil. Headman; Khanezaman.

ALI SHER KHEL.—A sub-division of Gadaizai, Iliaszai, Bunerwals.

ALI SHER KHEL.—A minor fraction of Warkham Khel, Aib Khel, Salarzai, Iliaszai, Bunerwals.

ALI SHER KHEL (Buner).—A sub-division of Nurizai, Iliaszai, Yusufzais.

ALI SHER KHEL (3,120; Loargai, Peshawar border).—A clan of Shinwaris. The remaining three clans of Shinwaris are Afghan subjects. Headmen; Kamran, Saiad Ghulam, Nadir Khan, Zarin, (Khwaja Khel), Nawak (Pirwal Khel), Abdul Karim, Saiad Amir, Abdul Rahman (Shekmal Khel), Badzin (Ash Khel).

ALISHERZAI (3,000; Khanki and Kuram rivers, and sides of Zawaghar, up to Kharmana stream).—One of the three divisions of the Lashkarzai, Orakzais. Samil.

ALIZAI (1,000; Kuram).—A sub-division of Landizai, Chardai, Turis.

ALIZAI or STURI KHEL (500; About 16 miles from source of Mastura).—One of the divisions of the Daulatzai, Orakzais. Samil.

ALIZAI (50; South of Kharmana river).—An unimportant sub-division of the Masuzai, Lashkarzai, Orakzais, Samil. Headman; Landai.

ALIZAI (4,042).—One of three clans of the Mahsud Waziri tribe. Headmen; Badar Din, Muhammad Afzal, Badshah Khan, Shah Salim, Siman.

ALIZAI (18; Chotiali).—Nomadic, a section of Walainai, Rakanwal, Lunis. Headmen; Ali, Umr.

ALIZAI (1,000; North of Koh-i-Mohr peak).—One of eight clans of the Utman Khels.

ALIZAI (Zhob).—A sub-section of Badsuzai, Alizai, Sanzar, Kakars.

ALIZAI (9,800; Zhob).—The largest division of Sanzar, Kakars. Headmen; Shah Karez (Mirzai), Ghimdah (Batozai), Sirdar Shah Jehan (Jalalzai).

Alizai (Zhob).—A section of Ibrahimzai, Shadzai, Alizai, Sanzar, Kakars.

Alizai (66).—A sub-division of Darpa Khel, Mallizad Dawaris. Headmen; Ghazal, Gul Azam, Pir Azam, Shermon, Sheikh Muhammad Din, Niazpur.

Alladad Khel (South of Kharmana river).—A section of the Mandu Khel, Nasrozai, Masuzai, Lashkarzai, Orakzais. Samil. Headman; Azad Khan.

Alladad Khel.—A section of Sen Khel, Abba Khel, Tatta, Battannis.

Alladadi Khel.—A subdivision of Shah Khel, Tatta, Battannis.

Allahdad Khel.—(Mastura valley).—A sub-division of the Bar Muhammad Khel, Muhammad Khel, Orakzais. Gar. Shiah. Headman; Sarandaz.

Allahi Khel.—A section of Kemal Khel, Abazai, Khawazai, Akozai—Yusufzai Swatis.

Allaiwal (8,720; Allai valley, north of Nandibar and south of Kohistan).—A considerable tribe, of Swati origin. See "Swatis." The principal Alla village is Pokal. Headmen; Khairullah Khan and Arsala Khan.

Allia Khel.—A sub-division of Karna Khel, Malikdin Khel (4,000), Afridis. Samil. Headmen; see Yar Muhammad Khel.

Alli Khel (25).—A section of Malli Khel, Idak, Tappizad, Dawaris. Headmen; Mokhsein, Malli, Ismail Khel, Salak.

Alli Khel (64).—A section of Barim Khel, Amzoni, Mallizad, Dawaris. Headmen; Lar, Shahba Din, Namballi Khan, Patita Khan, Bakhtamir, Piya Khan.

Almar Khel (20).—A minor fraction of the Khoidadai, Malikshai, Aimal Khel, Bahlolzai, Mahsuds. Headmen; Surkamand, Ali Khan, Suleman.

Alrabi Khel (Mahaban).—A section of Bazid Khel, Mada Khel, Isazai, Yusufzais. Headmen; see Bazid Khel.

AMADDI KHEL.—A section of Mullah Khel, Bahram-ka-Khel, Bar Ranizai, Akozai—Yusufzai Swatis.

AMAZAI (2,000; Mahaban).—A division of Usmanzai, Yusufzais. Headman; Manza Khan.

AMBABA KHEL. (Mastura valley).—A sub-division of the Sipah, Muhammad Khel, Orakzais. Gar. Shiah.

AMBABA KHEL.—A minor fraction of Samzal or Sunyal Khel, Kamal Khel, Sahibjan, Aka Khel, (1,800), Afridis. Samil.

AMBAR KHEL.—A sub-division of Mat Khan Khel, Kambar Khel (4,500), Afridis. Gar. Headmen; Sher Khan, Hamid and Nurai.

AMINA KHEL.—A section of Alisher Khel, Gadaizai, Iliaszai, Bunerwals.

AMIN KHAN KOR.—A minor fraction of Durar (300), Khusrogi, Nasruddin, Zakha Khel, Afridis. Samil. Headman; see Bucha Khel.

AMIN KOR.—A section of Rasul Kor, Wali Beg Kor Gandab, Halimzai, Mohmands. Headmen; Gulabdin, Umardin, Shams-uddin.

AMROHI (Mohmand country).—A sub-division of Kandahari Safis, who are one of the vassal clans of the Mohmands. Headman; Abbas.

AMZAL KHEL (40).—A minor fraction of the Faridai, Khamar Khel, Gidi Khel, Manazai, Alizai, Mahsuds. Headmen; Nazar Shah, Gul Amir.

AMZONI (738).—One of the eight divisions of Mallizad, Dawaris. Headmen. Malik Wazirgai is the most influential Amzoni; see also Zira Khel, Ibrahim Khel, and Taib Khel.

ANAM (Barang).—A minor fraction of Madak, Bada, Asil, Ismailzai, Utman Khels.

ANDAK KHEL (40).—A minor fraction of the Nekzan Khel, Sher Khel, Haibat Khel, Nana Khel, Bahlolzai, Mahsuds. Headman; Maisera.

ANDAR KHAN KHEL.—A sub-section of the Panjpai, Musa Khel, Nurizai, Malizai, Bunerwals.

Andars (1,000; Ghazni, Kalat-i-Ghilzai.)—One of the Pawindah trading clans.

And Khel (25).—A sub-division of the Alizai (or Sturi Khel), Daulatzai, Orakzais. Samil. Shiah. Headmen; Gul Khan, Ahmad Sher.

Anezai (North Zhob).—A section of the Badsuzai, Alizai, Sanzar, Kakars.

Angur Kor.—A minor fraction of Muradi Khel, Dalkha Kor, Dadu Khel, Tarakzai, Mohmands.

Anizai (80).—A minor fraction of Land, Amand, Ahmad Khel, Oba Khel, Sheranis.

Anjani Khel (25).—A sub-division of the Alizai (Sturi Khel), Daulatzai, Orakzais. Samil. Headman; Zain Khan.

Anjra Khel.—A clan of the Zmarais. Headmen; Ghairat Khan, Mazhi Khan, Aku Khan, Alu Khan.

Anki Khel.—A minor fraction of Ismail Khel, Makhozai, Nasuzai, Iliaszai, Bunerwals.

Annai (1,000).—A sub-division of Budai, Zakha Khel, Afridis. Samil. Headmen; see Shekhai, Bash Khel, and Umar Khel.

Anniadin Khel.—A minor fraction of Dawar Khel, Ismail Khel, Bozi Khel, Madda Khel (1,600), Ibrahim Khel, Utmanzai, Darwesh Khel Wazirs.

Aoliazai (140).—A minor fraction of Shadozai, Bulozai, Panizai, Harun Khel, Sanatia, Kakars. Headman; Ali Muhammad.

Arab Khel.—A section of Ghaibi Khel, Bahram-ka-Khel, Bar Ranizai, Akozai—Yusufzai Swatis.

Arabi Khel (Bori, Zhob).—A sub-division of Sanzar, Kakars.

Arabzai (West of Dera Ghazi Khan District).—A section of Mahmadzai, Ahmadzai, Balil Khel, Musa Khels. Headman; Fateh Khan.

Ara Khel.—A minor fraction of Ghulam Khel (300), Haibat Khel, Jawaki, Adam Khel, Afridis.

Aramiya Khel.—A minor fraction of Mir Khan Khel, Asat Khel, Wuzi Khel (800), Utmanzai, Darwesh Khel, Wazirs. Headman; Jama Gul.

Aram Khel (Khasora and Shawal valleys).—A minor fraction of Bachagoi, Tor, Jani Khel, Wali Khel, Utmanzai, Darwesh Khel Wazirs. Headman; Shalamir.

Arbu Khel (2,000; Bori, Zhob).—A division of (Southern) Sanzar, Kakars.

Arghund (56).—One of the eight divisions of Mallizad, Dawaris. Headmen; Hakim Khan, Niamai.

Arghund (16).—A sub-division of Arghund, Mallizad, Dawaris. Headman; Hakim Khan.

Arozai (600).—A sub-division of Ahmad Khel, Sen Khel, Sheranis.

Asad Khel.—A sub-division of Mitha Khan Khel, Kuki Khel (4,500), Afridis. Gar.

Asaf Khel (400).—A section of Dalkha Kor, Dadu Khel, Tarakzai, Mohmands. Headmen; Jang, Abdullah, Lalo, Nawab, Sardaro.

Asaf Khel.—A minor fraction of Mawal Khel, (760), Haibat Khel, Jawaki, Adam Khel, Afridis.

Asai Khel.—A section of Wuzi Khel (800), Mohmit Khel, Utmanzai, Darwesh Khel Wazirs. Headman; Jama Gul.

Ash Khel (580).—A section of the Nasruzai, Masuzai, Lashkarzai, Orakzais. Samil. Headman; Hakim.

Ash Khel (200; Loargai).—A division of the Ali Sher Khel, Shinwaris. Headman; Badzin.

Asha Khel.—A sub-division of Abba Khel, Tatta, Battannis.

Asha Khel.—A sub-division of Nekpi Khel, Khwazazai, Akozai—Yusufzai Swatis.

Ashak Khel (25; Dera Ismail Khan District).—Nomadic, a minor fraction of Shapi Khel, Isot Khel, Mian Khel, Lohana, Pawindahs. Headman; see Mian Khel.

Ashant Khel.—A division of Kamrai, or Kamar Khel (600), Afridis. Samil.

Ashazai (1,300; Centre of Buner).—One of the four divisions of the Iliaszai, Bunerwals.

As Khel.—A sub-division of Usman Khel, Bar Banizai, Akozai—Yusufzai Swatis.

Ashrab Khel.—A minor fraction of Ismail Khel, Bozi Khel, Madda Khel, (1,600), Ibrahim Khel, Utmanzai, Darwesh Khel Wazirs.

Ashraff.—A minor fraction of the Ali Karan, Saiad Khan, Nmasi, Manugai, Lashkarzai, Orakzais. Gar.

Ashraf Khan (Bannu District and Shawal).—A minor fraction of Sheikbudin, Sardi Khel, Bakka Khel (1,000), Wali Khel, Utmanzai, Darwesh Khel Wazirs.

Ashraf Khel.—A section of Kamal Khel, Sahib Jan, Aka Khel, (1,800), Afridis. Samil.

Ashral (225).—A clan of the Allaiwals.

Ashtors (200; North of Agror).—One of the leading clans of the Tikriwals. See also "Swatis."

Ashu Khel (1,400).—A sub-division of Hassan Khel, Adam Khel, Afridis.

Asil.—A division of Ismailzai, Utman Khels.

Askandi Khel.—A minor fraction of Ali Khel, Manzar Khel (360), Ibrahim Khel, Utmanzai, Darwesh Khel Wazirs. Headmen; Baz Muhammad and Niaz Gul.

Askandi Khel (Bannu and Shawal).—A minor fraction of Morib Khel, Usman Khel, Takhti Khel, Bakka Khel (1,000), Wali Khel, Utmanzai, Darwesh Khel Wazirs. Headman; Mozalmir.

Askari Khel (160).—A minor fraction of the Ali Karan, Abrahim Khel, Mamuzai, Lashkarzai, Orakzais. Gar.

Aspani.—A sub-division of Mekhiani, Spin, Tarins. Headman; Ahad.

Astanai (510).—A sub-division of the Shabi Khel, Alizai, Mahsuds. Headmen; Siman, Shahzur, Mawul, Lalgul, Alif Shah, Khari.

Asu Kor.—A sub-division of Babazai Kor, Dawezai, Mohmands. Headmen; Moza Khan, Khan Zada.

Atam Khel.—A minor fraction of Mawal Khel (769), Haibat Khel, Jawaki, Adam Khel, Afridis.

Atarzai (120).—A section of Bazai, Harun Khel, Sanatia, Kakars. Headman; Aslam Khan (Kasim Kala).

Atlak.—A minor fraction of Nekzam Khel, Tor Sapar, (350), Galai, Adam Khel, Afridis.

Atman Khel.—A section of Kesu, Woruke, Dana, Battannis.

Ato Khel (200).—A section of Busha Khel, Kamali, Halimzai, Mohmands. Headmen; Tor Khan, Zarin, Rahim Dad.

Atrap Khel.—A division of Samilzai, Tarkanis.

Atsars.—See Achars.

Auli Khel.—A section of Abdul Khel, Urmuz Khel, Sipah (1,200), Afridis. Samil. Headman; Sher Jan.

Ausa Khel (600; On both banks of the Panjkora river, below the Nasrudin Khel).—One of the four clans of Yusufzais of Dir.

Awad Khel.—A section of Adizai, Boba, Dana, Battannis.

Awad Khel (40).—A section of Taru Khel, Boba, Dana, Battannis.

Awal Khel (70; Black Mountain).—A section of Painda Khel, Akazai, Isazai, Yusufzais.

Awar Khel.—A minor fraction of Mira Khel, Mad, Khozhai, Khaddar Khel (770), Mohmit Khel, Utmanzai, Darwesh Khel Wazirs. Headman; Watanzai.

Aya Khel.—A sub-division of As-azai, Iliaszai, Bunerwals.

Ayaz Khel (Dir).—A section of Painda Khel, Sesada, Malizai, Yusufzais.

Ayaz Khel—(Samana and Khanki valleys).—A sub-division of the Rabia Khel, Ismailzai, Orakzais. Samil. Headmen; Mustakim, Mastan, Saigul, Ghanni, Idar Shah, Shiraz Beg.

Aymena Kor.—A minor fraction of Hyatai Kor, Shah Mansur Khel, Dadu Khel, Tarakzai, Mohmands. Headman; Babu Jan.

Ayub Khel. (25; Dera Ismail Khan District).—Nomadic, a minor fraction of Baloch Khel, Isot Khel, Mian Khel, Lohana, Pawindahs. Headman; see Mian Khel.

Ayub Khel.—A sub-division of Yar Ali Khel, Kamrai Khel (600), Afridis. Samil. Headman; Azam Din.

Azad Khel (120).—A section of Tatu Khel, Boba, Dana, Battannis.

Azad Khel.—A section of Sultan Khel, Sher Gulla, Aka Khel, (1,800), Afridis. Samil.

Azad Khel or Sipah (*Not the Daulatzia Sipah*) (610).—A section of the Alikaran, Mamuzai, Lashkarzai, Orakzais. Gar.

Azam Khel (6).—A sub-division of Khaddi, Mallizad, Dawaris. Headman; Shahzaman.

Azar Khel.—A section of Durbi Khel, Kambar Khel, Kambar Khel, (4,500), Afridis. Gar. Headmen; Muhammad Sher, Khwaja Ali, Yaro, Nurai.

Azar Mir Khel.—A minor fraction of Sikandar Khel, Abdul Khel, Bora Khel (1,000), Mohmit Khel, Utmanzai, Darwesh Khel Wazirs.

Azdi Khel (200).—A minor fraction of the Shamak Khel, Abdullai, Aimal Khel, Bahlolzai, Mahsuds. Headman; Azim.

Azi Khel (2,100).—A sub-division of Bar Sulizai, Baizai, Akozai—Yusufzai Swatis. Note.—Above numbers include 1,200 men living outside Swati limits.

Azi Khel.—A sub-division of Ali Khel, Bar Ranizai, Akozai—Yusufzai Swatis.

Azim Khan Kor.—A section of the Umar Khan Khel, Alisherzai, Lashkarzai, Orakzais. Samil.

Aziz Khel.—A section of Alisher Khel, Gadaizai, Iliaszai, Bunerwals.

Aziz Khel.—A minor fraction of Karu Khel, Mali (or Muli) Khel, Salarzai, Iliaszai, Bunerwals.

Aziz Khel (250; Black Mountain).—A sub-division of Akazai, Isazai, Yusufzais. Headmen; Shah Bakht Khan, Nam Khan

Aziz Khel. (Mastura valley, down to near Hangu).—A sub-division of the Mamozai, Mishtis, "Hamsayas" of the Orakzais. Samil. Headman; Khani Alam.

Aziz Khel. (Near Hangu).—A division of the Mada Khel (800), "Hamsayas" of the Orakzais. Samil. Headman; Maoz.

Aziz Khel (230).—A section of the Nazar Khel, Aimal Khel, Bahlolzai, Mahsuds. Headman; Bramat Khan.

Aziz Khel.—A section of Durbi Khel, Kambar Khel, Kambar Khel (4,500), Afridis. Gar. Headmen; Muhammad Sher, Khwaja Ali, Yaro, Nurai.

Aziz Khel.—A minor fraction of Ali Sher Khel, Bahmr Khel, Keimal Khel, Urmuz Khel, Sipah (1,200), Afridis. Samil. Headman; Khanizaman.

Aziz Khel.—A minor fraction of Shadi Khel, Bora Khel (1,000), Mohmit Khel, Utmanzai, Darwesh Khel Wazirs.

Azmat Khel (19).—A sub-division of Zerakki, Mallizad, Dawaris. Headmen; Bandi and Said Akbar.

B

Baba.—A section of Khakizai, Ashazai, Iliaszai, Bunerwals.

Babadar Khel.—A minor fraction of Kui Khel, Tor Sapar (850), Galai, Adam Khel, Afridis.

Babakar Khel.—A minor fraction of Alisher Khel, Musa Khel, Nurizai, Malizai, Bunerwals.

Babakar Khel (766.)—A division of Khodad Khel, Zaimukhts.

Babakar Khel.—A section of the Shadi Khel, Boba, Dana, Battannis.

Babakar Khel (West of Dera Ghazi Khan District).—A sub-division of Hamzazai, Balil Khel, Musa Khels. Headman; Sanjar.

Babakar Khel (10; Dera Ismail Khan District);—Nomadic, a minor fraction of Pasani, Isot Khel, Mian Khel, Lohana, Pawindahs. Headman; see Mian Khel.

Baba Khel (300.)—The principal section of the Datti Khel, Galeshahi, Shaman Khel, Mahsuds.

Baba Khel.—A section of Fatteh Khel, Abazai, Khwazazai, Akozai—Yusufzai Swatis.

Baba Khel.—A *faqir* section of Khaddar Khel (770), Mohmit Khel, Utmanzai, Darwesh Khel Wazirs. Headmen; Wadin Shah and Idagai.

Baba Khel (10).—A minor fraction of Malik Khel, Miri Khel, Land, Malakh, Mallizad, Dawaris. Headman; Pir Shah Alam.

Babak Khel.—A minor fraction of Ali Khel (100), Ashu Khel, Hassan Khel, Adam Khel, Afridis.

Babakki, (520).—A section of Hassu Khel, Tor, Mallizad, Dawaris. Headmen; Faujdar, Mad Afzal, Karar, Gul, Hassan, Gul Raihan, Badar, Mir Kazam, Diwana Khan, Niazgai.

Babakri,—A division of Sipah (1,200), Afridis. Samil. Headmen; see Suran Khel, Ghaibi Khel, and Jawakai.

Baba Nmasi (Mastura valley).—A sub-division of the Bar Muhammad Khel, Muhammad Khel, Orakzais. They are in reality Ali Khels. Gar. Shiah.

Babar (20).—A division of Spin, Tarins.

Babar Khel (16).—A minor fraction of the Khoidadai, Malikshai, Aimal Khel, Bahlolzai, Mahsuds. Headman; Mukhtar.

Babar Khel.—A minor fraction of Kalla Khel (700), Ashu Khel, Hassan Khel, Adam Khel, Afridis.

BABAR KHEL (8).—A minor fraction of Ahmad Khel, Zira Khel, Amzoni, Mallizad, Dawaris. Headman: Shahnawaz.

BABAR (700; Dera Ismail Khan District).—A tribe of the same race as the Sheranis. Headmen; Akhmedzada Muhammad Gul, Mulla Mir Khan, Dur Muhammad Khan, Ali Muhammad Khan, Muhammad Husen.

BABAT KHEL (18).—A minor fraction of the Mirdad Khel. Abdul Rahman Khel, Sher Khel, Haibat Khel, Nana Khel, Bahlolzai, Mahsuds. Headman; Hassan.

BABAZAI (Pipal).—A division of the Dawezai, Mohmands. Headmen; Hazur Khan, Jafar, Kochai, Moza Khan, Mohmandai.

BABAZAI (West of Dera Ghazi Khan District).—A sub-division of Land Palai, Laharzai, Musa Khels. Headman; Ali Khan.

BABI KHEL.—A section of the Hamza Khel, Gandab, Halimzai, Mohmands. Headmen; Seth, Saiad Alam, Saiad Akbar, Painda Khan.

BABI KHEL—A section of Hamza Khel, Kamali, Halimzai, Mohmands. Headmen; see Hamza Khel, Kamali.

BABI KHEL.—A section of Hamza Khel, Kamali, Halimzai, Mohmands. Headmen; see Hamza Khel.

BABI KHEL (Samana and Khanki valleys).—One of the six sub-divisions of the Rabia Khel (700), Ismailzai, Orakzais. Samil. Headmen; Said Muhammad, Said Nazir, Abbas Khan, Mazid Arsala Khan.

BABRI KHEL (25).—A section of the Pir Muhammad Khel, Haidrai, Chahar Khel, Shaman Khel, Mahsuds. Headman; Ramzan.

BABU (43; Anambar Gap).—A division of Palao, Lunis. Headmen; Malik Mir Khan (Duranizai), Hazik (Nimakai), Safar (Bazai.)

BABU KHEL.—A sub-division of Adinzai, Khwazazai, Akozai—Yusufzai Swatis.

BABU KHEL.—A section of Maddi Khel, Utmanzai Bar Ranizai, Akozai—Yusufzai Swatis.

BABU KHEL.—A minor fraction of Sherga Khel, Utmanzai, Adinzai, Khwazazai, Akozai—Yusufzai Swatis.

BABULZAI (5).—A sub-division of Salezai, Rakanwal, Lunis. Headman ; see Salezai.

BABUR Khel.—A section of Keimal Khel, Urmuz Khel, Sipah (1,200), Afridis. Samil. Headman ; Khanezaman.

BABUZAI (5,200 ;* Left bank of Swat).—A division of Baizai, Akozai—Yusufzai Swatis. Headmen ; Nasrullah Khan, Firoz Khan, Pasand Khan.

BABUZAI (105).—A section of Narozai, Dumar, Sanzar, Kakars. Headman ; Muhammad Gul of Chilez.

BABUZAI.—Another name for the Sepah division of Baezai, Mohmands.

BACHAGAI.—A minor fraction of Tor, Jani Khel (1,000), Wali Khel, Utmanzai, Darwesh Khel Wazirs. Headmen ; Mirbosh, Shadamir, Kaimal, Gulbaz.

BACHA KHEL (55).—A section of the Pathanai, Shabi Khel, Allzai, Mahsuds. Headmen ; Titai, Rahmdin.

BACHI KHEL.—A minor fraction of Zakho Khel, Janakhori (800), Hassan Khel, Adam Khel, Afridis.

BADA.—A sub-division of Asil, Ismailzai, Utman Khels.

BADANZAI (313).—A division of the Shaman Khel, Mahsuds. Headman ; Sayad Akbar Shah.

BADAR KHEL (60)—A minor fraction of the Walidad Khel, Palli Khel, Abdullai, Aimal Khel, Bahlolzai, Mahsuds. Headmen ; Bayak, Musa, Razamdin.

BADAZA KHEL (Mastura river).—A sub-division of the Mani Khel, Muhammad Khel, Orakzais. Gar. Shiah.

BADDA KHEL.—A minor fraction of Saifali, Kabul Khel (2,600), Wali Khel, Utmanzai, Darwesh Khel Wazirs. Headman ; Kotan Khan.

BADDA KHEL (10).—A section of Utman, Miram Shah, Tappizad, Dawaris. Headman ; Sarak Shah.

* NOTE.—This includes 700 men of this division not living in Swat limits.

BADDAR KHEL.—A minor fraction of Bar Khozhai, Khaddar Khel (770) Mohmit Khel, Utmanzai Darwesh Khel, Wazirs. Headman; Saiyid Ali.

BADI KHEL (7).—A minor fraction of Umarzai, Zira Khel, Amzoni, Mallizad, Dawaris. Headman; Gulapir.

BADI KHEL.—A minor fraction of Dardoni, Wuzi Khel, Mohmit Khel, Utmanzai, Darwesh Khel Wazirs.

BADIN KHEL.—A minor fraction of Nahaki or Yusaf Kor, Ibrahim Khel, Kamali, Halimzai, Mohmands. Headmen; Saimal, Gulshah, Zai Khan, Post Khan, Gul Hamesh.

BADINZAI.—A section of Abdulazai, Sanzar, Kakars.

BADINZAI (150).—A section of Shabazai, Dumar, Sanzar, Kakars. Headman; Abdul.

BADIWAI (186).—A sub-division of the Khalli Khel, Shaman Khel, Mahsuds.

BADNI KHEL.—A minor fraction of Karim Khel, Jamal Khel, Malik Shahi (400), Jani Khel, Wali Khel, Utmanzai, Darwesh Khel Wazirs. Headman; Jumazan.

BADR KHEL (15; Dera Ismail Khan District).—Nomadic, a minor fraction of Aka Khel, Isot Khel, Mian Khel, Lohana, Pawindahs. Headman; see Mian Khel.

BADSUZAI (Zhob).—A minor fraction of Ali Khel, Sanzar, Kakars.

BADU KHEL (Mahaban).—A section of Hasan Baz Khel, Mada Khel, Isazai, Yusufzais. Headman; Bara Khan.

BADWAN.—A section of Hani, Panezun, Sanzar, Kakars.

BADZAI.—A sub-division of Kattagarm, Tatta, Battannis. Headmen; Nawaz (Kallandar Khel), Saiad Khan and Baram (Bazid Khel).

BAEKZAI (Hazarnao, Kabul river).—One of the three divisions of the Kukkozai, who are one of the affiliated Mohmand clans.

BAEZAI (8,000).—The most powerful of the Mohmand clans. Headmen; Wahid

Khan, Saiad Azam, Ghairat, Sultan Said, Paind Khan, Payo, Tola, Pirai, Amin Khan, Yad Gul.

BAGHBAN KHEL.—A minor fraction of Sudan Khel (350), Isperka, Kalu Khel, Ahmadzai, Darwesh Khel Wazirs. Headmen; Jalandar Shah, Mani Khan.

BAGHDAD KHEL.—A section of Keimal Khel, Urmuz Khel, Sipah (1,200), Afridis. Samil. Headmen; Khanezaman, Lal Muhammad, Sher Jan.

BAGHDADZAI (West of Dera Ghazi Khan District).—A section of Inzai, Hasan Khel, Balil Khel, Musa Khels. Headman; Salavi.

BAHADUR KHEL.—A section of Abdul Khel, Urmuz Khel, Sipah (1,200), Afridis. Samil. Headman; Shibran.

BAHADUR KHEL.—A minor fraction of Khojal Khel (600 in Wana), Shadi Khel, Nasra Din, Kalu Khel, Ahmadzai, Darwesh Khel Wazirs.

BAHADUR KHEL (Left bank of Mastura river).—A section of the Mir Kulli Khel, Bazoti, Daulatzai, Orakzais. Samil.

BAHADUR KHEL (70).—A section of the Shumi Khel, Palli Khel, Manazai, Alizai Mahsuds. Headman; Awal Khan.

BAHADUR KHEL (Dakka, Girdi, and Peshawar valley in winter, Upper Helmand in summer).—Nomads, a sub-division of Utmanzai Kuchi (Mohmand).

BAHADUR SHAH KHEL.—The head division of Samilzai, Tarkanis.

BAHARZAI (West of Dera Ghazi Khan District).—A section of Husenzai, Ahmadzai, Balil Khel, Musa Khels. Headman; Bahadur.

BAHLOL KHEL (15).—A minor fraction of the Bizodai, Malikshai, Aimal Khel, Bahlolzai, Mahsuds. Headman; Ahmad Khan.

BAHLOLZAI (4,078).—One of the three great clans of the Mahsuds.

BAHRAM-KA-KHEL (800; From Malakand to Swat river).—A division of Bar

Ranizai, Akozai—Yusufzai Swatis. Headman; Gujar Khan.

BAHRAM KHEL (Samana and Khanki valleys).—A subdivision of the Rabia Khel, Ismailzai, Orakzais. Samil.

BAHRAM KHEL.—A minor fraction of Sherga Khel, Utmanzai, Adinzai, Khwazazai, Akozai—Yusufzai Swatis.

BAIANZAI (200).—A section of the Mareghutzai, Kebzai, Sanzar, Kakars. Headman; Basharat.

BAIKAN KHEL.—A minor fraction of Zakho Khel, Janakhori (800), Hassan Khel, Adam Khel, Afridis.

BAI KHEL (30—Dera Ismail Khan District).—Nomadic, a sub-section of Aba Khel, Isot Khel, Mian Khel, Lohans, Pawindahs. Headman; see Mian Khel.

BAI KHEL.—A section of Firozai, Chagarzai, Malizai, Bunerwals.

BAIK KHEL (Bannu District).—A minor fraction of Khandar Khan Khel, Hathi Khel (2,000), Shin Khel, Ahmadzai, Darwesh Khel Wazirs.

BAI KOR.—A minor fraction of Durba Khel, Hamza Khel, Gandab, Halimzai, Mohmands. Headmen; see Durba Khel.

BAIN KHEL (Right bank of Khanki, and Kuram up to Kharmana river).—A subdivision of the Alisherzai, Lashkarzai, Orakzais. Samil. Headman; Alam Khan.

BAIRAM KHEL (124).—A division of Chuar Khel, Sheranis.

BAIZAI (19,400;* Left bank of Swat River from Kohistan down to and including Thana).—One of three clans of the Akozai—Yusufzai Swatis.

BAIZAI (Zhob).—A minor fraction of the Badsuzai, Ali Khel, Sanzar, Kakars.

BAJID KHEL.—A section of Hasan Khel, Gadaizai, Iliaszai, Bunerwals.

BAJIZAI (16).—A sub-division of Mirzai, Rakanwal, Lunis. Headman; see Mirzai.

---

* NOTE.—This number includes 5,000 men of the Babuzai and Bar Sulizai divisions living outside Swat limits.

BAKAR KHEL.—A minor fraction of Bakar Khel, Idal Khel, Hathi Khel (2,000), Shin Khel, Ahmadzai, Darwesh Khel Wazirs.

BAKAR KHEL.—A minor fraction of Bash Khel (150), Shoraki, Galai, Adam Khel, Afridis.

BAKAR KHEL (Bannu District, Shakai, Birmal and Wana). A sub-section of Idal Khel, Hathi Khel (2,000), Shin Khel, Ahmadzai, Darwesh Khel Wazirs. Headmen; Bander Khan, Sheikh Piyao, Landai, Kasim Shah.

BAKAR KHEL (10).—A minor fraction of Malik Khel, Miri Khel, Land, Malakh, Mallizad, Dawaris. Headman; Sheikhband.

BAKHAL KHEL.—A minor fraction of Feroz Khel, Tor Sapar (350), Galai, Adam Khel, Afridis.

BAKHI KHEL.—A minor fraction of Mir Ali Khel, Idia Khel, Jani Khel (1,000), Wali Khel, Utmanzai, Darwesh Khel Wazirs. Headmen; Akaldin.

BAKHIL.—A minor fraction of Takhmal Khel, Nazar Khel, Ali Khan Khel, Sarki Khel, Madda Khel (1,600), Ibrahim Khel, Utmanzai, Darwesh Khel Wazirs.

BAKHMALI KHEL.—A section of Kulla Khel, Malikdin Khel, Malikdin Khel, (4,000) Afridis. Samil. Headmen; Akbar, Dostai, Sher Gul, Zarif, Shams-ud-din.

BAKHSHAI.—A minor fraction of Datta Khel, Abdul Khel, Bara Khel (1,600), Mohmit Khel, Utmanzai, Darwesh Khel Wazirs.

BAKHSHI KHEL.—A section of Madda Khel, (1,600) Ibrahim Khel, Utmanzai, Darwesh Khel Wazirs. Headmen; Gulli of Stara, and Alam Shah.

BAKHTA KHEL (Bannu District).—A minor fraction of Khanbeg Khel, Tori Khel, Musa Khel, Hathi Khel (2,000), Shin Khel, Ahmadzai, Darwesh Khel Wazirs.

BAKHTAWAR KOR.—A minor fraction of Hyatai Kor, Shahmansur Khel, Dadu Khel, Tarakzai, Mohmands. Headman; Multan.

BAKHTIARZAI.—A division of Anjra Khel, Zmarais. Headman; Mazhi Khan.

BAKHTI KHEL (100).—A minor fraction of the Baba Khel, Datti Khel, Galashahi, Shaman Khel, Mahsuds. Headmen; Khalil, Ghazai, Ghanim Shah, Kaim.

BAKI KHEL (60).—A minor fraction of Ipi, Haidar Khel, Tor, Tappizad, Dawaris. Headmen; Fatteh Khan, Wali Khan, Saleh Khan.

BAKI KHEL (8).—A minor fraction of the Ali Khel, Haidar Khel, Tor, Tappizad, Dawaris. Headman; Jamal Sahib.

BAKI KOR (South of Khurmana river).—A section of the Alizai (50), Masuzai, Lashkarzai, Orakzais. Samil. Headman; Mir Ahmad Shah.

BAKIR KHEL (800; Shamil valley, Khost).—A clan of Khostwals.

BAKKA KHEL (1,000; Wana and Bannu Districts).—A sub-division of Wali Khel, Utmanzai, Darwesh Khel Wazirs. Headmen; see Takhti Khel, Sardi Khel, and Narmi Khel.

BAKKA KHEL (25).—A minor fraction of Ipi, Haidar Khel, Tor, Tappizad, Dawaris. Headmen; Kashmir, Zirak, Zarbat.

BAKOH KHEL.—A minor fraction of Sudan Khel (350), Isperka, Kalu Khel, Ahmadzai, Darwesh Khel Wazirs. Headmen; Jalandar Shah, Mani Khan.

BAKSHAI (25).—A section of the Ozbakai, Shingi, Bahlolzai, Mahsuds. Headmen; Sanjan, Najib.

BAKSHI KHEL.—A minor fraction of Mandi Khel, Wuzi Khel (800), Mohmit Khel, Utmanzai, Darwesh Khel Wazirs.

BAKSHOZAI (West of the Dera Ghazi Khan District).—A sub-division of Hamzazai, Balil Khel, Musa Khels. Headman; Shadak.

BALAJKOI.—A sub-division of Shanai (750), Zakha Khel, Afridis. Samil. Headman; Said Khan.

BALAL KHEL.—A section of Hassan Khel (400), Mohmit Khel, Utmanzai, Darwesh Khel Wazirs. Headmen; Gholam Jam, Malakdin, Khan (?), Niyaz Muhammad, Payao Khan, Baddi Fakir, Khan Ghazat.

BALEL KHEL (60).—A minor fraction of Aghzan, Zira Khel, Amzoni, Mallizad, Dawaris. Headmen; Muhammad Alam, Pir Gholam.

BALI KHEL (16).—A minor fraction of Poi Khel, Muhammad Khel, Malakh, Mallizad, Dawaris. Headman; Suleman.

BALIL KHEL (3,500; West of Dera Ghazi Khan).—A clan of the Musa-Khels. Headmen; see Ahmadzai, Hamzazai, and Hasan Khel.

BALIL KHEL (15).—A minor fraction of Chuttan, Zira Khel, Amzoni, Mallizad, Dawaris. Headman; Gholam Khan.

BALI KHEL.—A section of Ibrahim Khel, Utmanzai, Bar Ranizai, Akozai—Yusufzai Swatis.

BAL KHEL.—A minor fraction of Kharmanj Khel, Khwaja Khel, Miamai, Kabul Khel (2,600), Wali Khel, Utmanzai, Darwesh Khel Wazirs.

BALLA KHEL (Bannu District).—A minor fraction of Taos Khel, Pirba Khel, Hathi Khel, (2,000), Shin Khel, Ahmadzai, Darwesh Khel Wazirs.

BALLI KHEL.—A minor fraction of Shadi Khel, Bara Khel (1,000), Mohmit Khel, Utmanzai, Darwesh Khel Wazirs. Headman; Kipat Khan.

BALO (Laman).—A sub-division of Asil, Ismailzai, Utman Khels.

BALOCH KHEL (215, Dera Ismail Khan District).—Nomadic, a sub-division of of the Isot Khel, Mian Khel, Pawindahs.

BALOE KHEL (20).—A minor fraction of the Ipi, Haidar Khel, Tor, Tappizad, Dawaris. Headmen; Andaram Khan, Mihrdin Khan, Mir Baz Khan, Gulshadin.

BALOLZAI (60).—A division of Kapip, Sheranis.

BAMI KHEL (800).—A subdivision of Babuzai, Baizai, Akozai—Yusufzai Swatis.

BAM KHEL (780).—A clan of Khudu Khels.

BAMUT KHEL (Dir).—A section of Painda Khel, Sesada, Malizai, Yusufzais.

BANAIR KHEL.—A section of Kulla Khel, Malikdin Khel Malikdin Khel (4,000) Afridis; Samil. Headman; see Bakhmali Khel.

BANDA (77).—A division of Tappizad, Dawaris. Headmen; Shabal, Shadak, Ayaz Khan, Ghonsamir, Sur Kamand.

BAND KHEL (260).—The smallest of the four divisions of the Bahlolzai, Mahsuds.

BANGA KHEL (100).—A minor fraction of the Kharmach Khel, Nazar Khel, Aimal Khel, Bahlolzai, Mahsuds. Headman; Nikarrab.

BANGAL KHEL (15).—A section of the Kasim Khel, Chahar Khel, Shaman Khel. Mahsuds. Headmen; Masid, Yargul, Azad.

BANGASH (3,000;* Kohat, Miranzai and Kurram valleys).—A great tribe of Pathans, the main clans of which are Miranzai, Baizai and Samalzai. Gar. Shiah. The divisions, etc., of the Bangash are not indexed in this Dictionary.

BANGASH KHEL (100).—A section of Astanai, Shabi Khel, Alizai, Mahsuds. Headman; Siman. Lalgul.

BANGASH KHEL (60).—A section of the Taru Khel, Bobak, Dana, Battannis.

BANGASH KHEL (25).—A subdivision of Tapiai, Tappizad, Dawaris. Headman; Zara.

BAO KHEL.—A minor fraction of Mir Asan Khel, Badu Khel, Adinzai, Khwazazai, Akozai—Yusufzai Swatis.

BAOLA KHEL.—A sub-division of Sarsa, Tatta, Battannis.

BARA KADDAM.—(Lower Mastura river).—A sub-division of the Abdul Aziz Khel, Muhammad Khel, Orakzais. Gar. Shiah.

BARA KHEL (Mastura river).—A minor fraction of the Bazid Khel, Sturi Khel, Alizai, Daulatzai, Orakzais. Samil.

*The numbers here given are based on the Census returns of 1891. Slightly older authority, however, gives the fighting strength of the Bangash, including those of Kuram, as 7,500, taking one in five of the total number of souls to be fighting men.

BARA KHEL.—A minor fraction of Must Ali, Shaikh Khel, Aib Khel, Salarzai, Iliaszai, Bunerwals.

BARA KHEL.—A sub-division of Sepah, Baezai, Mohmands. Headmen; Paind Khan, Shirin, Mujim Khan,

BARA KHEL (Mahaban).—A section of Hasanbaz Khel, Mada Khel, Isazai, Yusufzais.

BARAKZAI (West of Dera Ghazi Khan District).—A section of Kabalzai, Nokuzai, Labarzai, Musa Khels. Headman; Momin.

BARAKZAI (160).—A subdivision, of Yahia Khel, Sen Khel, Sheranis.

BARAKZAI (890).—A subdivision of the Targhari, Sanzar, Kakars.

BARAM KHEL.—A minor fraction of Ali Khel, Manzar Khel (360), Ibrahim Khel Utmanzai, Darwesh Khel Wazirs. Headman; Adal.

BARAM KHEL (Bannu District).—A minor fraction of Khanbeg Khel, Tori Khel, Musa Khel, Hathi Khel (2,000), Shin Khel, Ahmadzai, Darwesh Khel, Wazirs.

BARAM KHEL (9).—A section of Hakim Khel, Mubarak Shahi, Mallizad, Dawaris. Headman; Shandai, Ahmad Shah.

BARAM KHEL (60).—A section of Manderi, Idak, Tappizad, Dawaris, Headmen; Janai Khan, Gandalai.

BARAN KHEL (Bannu District).—A minor fraction of Ali Khel, Musa Khel, Hathi Khel (2,000), Shin Khel, Ahmadzai, Darwesh Khel Wazirs.

BARAN KHEL (85).—A subdivision of the Chahar Khel, Shaman Khel, Mahsuds. Headman; Kelak.

BARANZAI or MIAN KHANZAI (600).—A sub-division of Kebzai, Sanzar, Kakars.

BARAT KHEL (250; Black Mountain).—A sub-division of Akazai, Isazai, Yusufzais. Headmen; Saidwali Hassan Khan, Zota Khan, Kalai Khan, Awal Khan.

BARAT KHEL.—A minor fraction of Alisher Khel, Musa Khel, Nurizai, Malizai, Bunerwals.

BARAT KHEL. (1,000).—A subdivision of Babuzai, Baizai, Akozai—Yusufzai Swatis.

BARAT KHEL (Bannu District).—A minor fraction of Balk Khel, Khandar Khan Khel, Hathi Khel (2,000), Shin Khel, Ahmadzai, Darwesh Khel Wazirs.

BARAT KHEL.—A minor fraction of Sudan Khel, Isperka (1,350), Kala Khel, Ahmadzai, Darwesh Khel Wazirs.

BARAT KHEL (2,000; Zhob).—A division of (Northern) Sanzar, Kakars.

BARAKZIAS.—See Duranis.

BARAKZAI.—A division of Anjra Khel, Zmarais. Headman; Aku Khan.

BARBAR KHEL.—A section of Aya Khel, Ashazai, Iliaszai, Bunerwals.

BAR DURANIS.—A name sometimes applied to the Pathan tribes who inhabit the north-eastern part of Yaghistan, enclosed between the range of the Hindu Kush, the Indus, the Salt Range and the range of Suliman, and first applied to them by Ahmad Shah. The name applies to the Yusufzai Utman Khels, Tarkanis, Mohmands, Afridis, Orakzais, Shinwaris, the tribes of the plains of Peshawar, and those of Bangash and Khatak.—(*Elphinstone.*)

BARGA KHEL. (Bannu, Chapri, and Gurang in Kuram).—A section of Kundai, Tor Khel, Umarzai (600), Shin Khel, Ahmadzai, Darwesh Khel Wazirs. Headman; Niazye.

BARHAN KHEL (80; North-east of Buner).—A minor fraction of Ismail Khel, Makhozai, Nasozai, Iliaszai, Yusufzais.

BARI KHEL.—A minor fraction of Aba Khel, Ismailzai, Daulatzai, Malizai, Bunerwals.

BARI KHEL (15).—A minor fraction of Sogi Khel, Muhammad Khel, Malakh, Malizad, Dawaris. Headman; Pira Khan.

BARI KHEL (4).—A minor fraction of Khuttay, Taib Khel, Amzoni, Mallizad, Dawaris. Headman; Zakam Khan.

BARI KHEL (15).—A minor fraction of the Adi Khel, Haidar Khel, Tor, Tappizad, Dawaris. Headmen; Azad Khan, Sherdala.

BARID KHEL (Mastura).—A section of the Sturi Khel, Alizai, Daulatzai, Orakzais.

Barkai Khel.—A minor fraction of Mian Khel, Janakhori (800), Hassan Khel, Adam Khel, Afridis.

Bar Kaum (78).—A section of Hassu Khel, Tor, Mallizad Dawaris. Headmen; Badil, Dini, Painda Khan, Nizam Gul, Gulsohil, Pir Ahmad Shah, Baki, Badrang.

Barkazai.—A sub-division of Daulatzai, Malizai, Bunerwals.

Bar Khani.—A minor fraction of Badi Khel, Dardoni Wuzi Khel (800) Mohmit Khel, Utmanzai, Darwesh Khel Wazirs.

Barim Khel (191).—A division of Amzoni Dawaris. Headmen; Juma Shah, Mina Shah, Channi, Majib Shah, Lar, Shabba Din, Namballi Khan, Pátila Khan, Bokhtamir, Piya Khan, Gubzir.

Barim Khel.—(10), A minor fraction of Poi Khel, Muhammad Khel, Mallizad, Dawaris. Headman; Kadam.

Bariwal (19).—A sub-division of Zerakki, Mallizad, Dawaris. Headmen; Shahzada, Haibat Khan.

Barkhan Khel.—A section of Musa Khel, Kuz Sulizai Baizai, Akozai—Yusufzai Swatis.

Bar Khan Kor (280; Khanki river).—A minor fraction of the Umar Khan Khel, Ali Karan, Mamuzai, Lashkarzai, Orakzais. Gar. Headman; Amir Shah.

Bar Khozai.—A section of Khaddar Khel (770), Mohmit Khel, Utmanzai, Darwesh Khel Wazirs. Headmen; Sadirai, Hukam Shah, Saidigai, Said Ali.

Barki Khel (35).—A minor fraction of Dur Khel, Babakki, Hassu Khel, Tor, Mallizad, Dawaris. Headmen; Badar, Mir Kazam.

Bar Killa (30).—A minor fraction of Dangar Khel, Piran Dangar Khel, Muhammad Khel, Malakh, Mallizad, Dawaris. Headman; Badrana, Said Akbar.

Bar Makazai.—A sub-division of Wara, Mamund, Tarkanis.

Barmast Khel.—A section of the Tari Khel, Shakhi, Waraspun, Battannis.

Barmi Khel (Bannu District).—A minor fraction of Sardi Khel, Bakka Khel (1,000), Wali Khel, Utmanzai, Darwesh Khel Wazirs.

Barmi Khel (Bannu District).—A minor fraction of Khandar Khan Khel, Hathi Khel (2,000), Shin Khel, Ahmadzai, Darwesh Khel Wazirs. Headman; Shah Tamoz.

Barmi Khel.—A minor fraction of Mushakki, Macha, Madda Khel (1,600), Ibrahim Khel, Utmanzai, Darwesh Khel Wazirs.

Barmi Khel.—A division of Kamrai, or Kamar Khel, (600), Afridis, Samil. Headmen; Hafiz Samandar, and Azam Khan.

Bar Muhammad Khel (1,000; Mastura valley).—One of the four divisions of the Muhammad Khel, Orakzais. Gar. Shiah. Headmen; Usman Khan, Muhammad Akbar Khan.

Baro Khel (60).—A section of the Haidar Khel, Tor, Tappizad, Dawaris. Headmen; Khan Sahib Nasir Khan, Tor Khan.

Baromai (125).—A sub-division of the Shabi Khel, Alizai, Mahsuds. Headman; Muhammad Ayaz.

Barozai.—A sub-division of Hamzazai, Sanzar, Kakars.

Barozai.—A sub-division of Wara, Mamund, Tarkanis.

Baru Khel.—A section of Hamza Khel, Gandab, Halimzai, Mohmands; with them go the Taru Khel. Headmen; Lal Dad, Jallat Amir Baz, Fattehullah.

Baru Khel.—A section of Hamza Khel, Kamali, Halimzai, Mohmands.

Barumi Khel (86).—A section of the Khoidad Khel, Gidi Khel, Manazai, Alizai, Mahsuds. Headman; Shali.

Bar Sulizai.—(8,350;* North Swat, left bank, to Kohistan).—A division of the Baizai, Akozai—Yusufzai Swatis.

Baryam (45).—A section of the Pathanai, Shabi Khel, Alizai, Mahsuds. Headmen; Lal Khan, Azim, Tumazan.

---

* This includes 4,950 men of the Azi Khel and Jinki Khel sub-divisions, living outside Swat limits.

BASHAMZAI.—(West of Dera Ghazi Khan District).—A sub-division of Nozai, Laharzai, Musa Khels. Headman; Sheran.

BASHAR KHEL.—Bannu District).—A minor fraction of Bozi Khel, Ali Khel, Musa Khel, Hathi Khel (2,000), Shin Khel, Ahmadzai, Darwesh Khel Wazirs.

BASH KHEL.—A section of Annai (1,000,) Budai, Zakha Khel, Afridis. Samil. Headmen; Pir Gul, Safar, Dost Hak, Khanezaman, Zeb Jan, Rahmatulla, Madaki.

BASH KHEL (150).—A section of Sharaki, Galai, Adam Khel, Afridis.

BASH KHEL.—A minor fraction of Sher Khan Khel, Umar Khan Khel, Malikdin Khel, 4,000), Afridis. Samil. Headmen; see Umar Khan Khel.

BASH KHEL.—A sub-division of Mat Khan Khel, Kambar Khel (4,500), Afridis, Gar. Headmen;. Sher Khan, Hamid, and Nurai.

BASHMIRI (8).—A section of Zira Khel, Amzoni, Mallizad, Dawaris. Headman; Khonai.

BASID KHEL.—(Mastura river to Hangu.)—A sub-division of the Mamuzai, Mishti, "Hamsayas" of the Orakzais. Samil.

BASI KHEL.—(Cis-Indus, and Duma mountain).—A sub-division of Ghagarzai, Malizai, Yusafzais.

BASI KHEL, (Bara valley).—A section of Kamal Khel, Sahib Jan, Aka Khel (1,800), Afridis. Samil.

BASRAON, (Bannu District).—A minor fraction of Tori Khel, Musa Khel, Hathi Khel (2,000), Shin Khel, Ahmadzai, Darwesh Khel Wazirs.

BASSIA KHEL.—A sub-division of Niamat Khel, Tatta, Battannis. Headman; Raddat.

BASSI KHEL.—A minor fraction of Painda Khel (200), Shadi Khel, Nasra Din, Kalu Khel, Ahmadzai, Darwesh Khel Wazirs. Headman; Sawar Khan.

Bassu Kor.—A minor fraction of Makki Khel, Kattia Khel, Hassan Khel, Mitha Khan Khel, Kuki Khel (4,500), Afridis. Gar. Headmen; see Makki Khel.

Bata Khel (25).—A section of Zhao Khel, Tapiai, Tappizad, Dawaris. Headman; Ahmad.

Batak Khel (40).—A minor fraction of the Nekzam Khel, Sher Khel, Haibat Khel, Nana Khel, Bahlolzai, Mahsuds. Headmen; Titi, Muhammad Afzal.

Battannis (4,060; country between Waziristan and Dera Ismail Khan District).—A Pathan tribe, some of whom also live in British territory. Headmen; Bangi, Kushal Khan, Mir Azim, Kota, Nawaz, Miani, Sher Khan, Dillasa Khan, Razza Khan, Jabari, Batur, Gula Khan, Morad Khan, Ahmad Shah.

Batkai (60).—A sub-division of the Gidi Khel, Manazai, Alizai, Mahsuds. Headman; Azmat.

Batozai or Batzai, (1,000).—A sub-division of Alizai, Sanzar, Kakars.

Battai Khel.—A minor fraction of Walli Khel, Ali Khel, Sheikhmal Khel, Kambar Khel, (4,500), Afridis. Gar. Headmen; Miro, Ali Khan, Gauhar, Feroz.

Batti Khel (40).—A minor fraction of the Faridai, Khamar Khel, Gidi Khel, Manazai, Mahsuds. Headmen; Zulfikar, Baghdad.

Bawla Khel (Bannu, Wana, and Birmal).—A section of Sirki Khel (800 [400 in Wana]), Shin Khel, Ahmadzai, Darwesh Khel, Wazirs. Headmen; see Sirki Khel.

Bawlai.—A minor fraction of Dani Khel, Matkai, Malik Shahi (400), Jani Khel, Wali Khel, Utmanzai, Darwesh Khel, Wazirs. Headman; Pirwal.

Baya Khel (40).—A section of the Baromai, Shahi Khel, Alizai, Mahsuds. Headmen; Kutal, Zindai.

Bayuks or Khoidad Khel, (Eastern) Zaimukhts (1,741).—One of the two Zaimukht clans.

Bazai or Banza (1,359).—A sub-division of Harun Khel, Sanatia, Kakars. Headman; Mulla Baidula.

Bazanai.—A sub-division of Mekhiani, Spin, Tarins.

Bazar Khan Khel (Mastura).—A sub-division of the Utman Khel, Daulatzai, Orakzais. Samil.

Bazid Khel.—A section of the Badzai, Kattagarm, Tatta, Battannis.

Bazid Khel (British territory).—A sub-division of Jawaki (1,200), Adam Khel, Afridis.

Bazid Khel (450; Mahaban).—A sub-division of Mada Khel, Isazai, Yusufzais. Headmen; Shahdad Khan, Sarfaraz Khan, Saiad Kalam, Shah Mardan, (Alrabi Khel), Muhammad Ali Khan, Baz Khan, (Tata Khel).

Bazid Khel.—A minor fraction of Mian Khel, Janakhori (800), Hassan Khel, Adam Khel, Afridis.

Bazid Khel.—(Mastura, Khanki, and Miranzai valleys).—A division of the Sheikhan, "Hamsayas" of the Orakzais. Samil.

Bazid Khel.—See Tor (or Bazid) Khel.

Bazi Khel.—A section of Khan Khel, Kuz Sulizai, Baizai, Akozai—Yusufzai Swatis.

Bazoti (500; Mastura).—One of the four divisions of the Daulatzai, Orakzais. Samil.

Behram Kor.—A minor fraction of Dildar Khel, Mohmand Khel, Kattia Khel, Hassan Khel, Mitha Khan Khel, Kuki Khel (4,500), Afridis. Gar. Headmen; Ghanni and Torbaz.

Bejal, (19).—A minor fraction of Bar Kaum, Hassu Khel, Tor, Mallizad, Dawaris. Headman; Pir Ahmad Shah.

Bengali Khel.—A section of Sen Khel, Abba Khel, Tatta, Battannis.

Beror (100; Black Mountain).—A division of Deshiwal, Swatis. Headman; Sadar Ali of Kabal.

Betani (Mastura).—A section of the Kambar Khel, Bazoti, Daulatzai, Orakzais. Samil.

Bezazai (13).—A section of Isa Khel, Ahmad Khel, Oba Khel, Sheranis.

BHANGI KHEL.—A minor fraction of Umar Khel, Ali Khel, Khadder Khel (770), Mohmit Khel, Utmanzai, Darwesh Khel Wazirs. Headman: Salih Din.

BHAI KHEL (28).—A section of Barim Khel, Amzoni, Mallizad, Dawaris. Headmen; Juma Shah, Mina Shah.

BIAZ KHEL (30; Dera Ismail Khan District).—Nomadic, a minor fraction of Zakoki, Sein Khel, Mian Khel, Lohana, Pawindahs. Headman; see Mian Khel.

BIBA KHEL (60; Black Mountain).—A section of Barat Khel, Akazai, Isazai, Yusufzais.

BIBAL THOR (770).—A clan of Allaiwals.

BIBIZAI (120.)—A sub-division of the Shabi Khel, Alizai, Mahsuds. Headman; Dinak Khan.

BIBLAI (40).—A section of the Malai, Shingi, Bahlolzai, Mahsuds. Headmen; Gul Muhammad, Mahmud.

BIDA KHEL.—A minor fraction of Gangi Khel (400 in Wana), Bomi Khel, Nasra Din Khel, Kalu Khel, Ahmadzai, Darwesh Khel Wazirs.

BIJAL KHEL.—A minor fraction of Ali Khel, Manzar Khel (360), Ibrahim Khel, Utmanzai, Darwesh Khel Wazirs. Headman; Zira Khan.

BIJAL KHEL.—A minor fraction of Khojal Khel (600 in Wana), Shadi Khal, Nasra Din, Kalu Khel, Ahmadzai, Darwesh Khel Wazirs.

BIJJAL KHEL (13).—A section of the Zarri Khel, Chahar Khel, Shaman Khel, Mahsuds. Headman; Fattehmir.

BIJJI KHEL (70).—A section of the Malai, Shingi, Bahlolzai, Mahsuds, Headmen; Salelim, Khan Zaman, Nasajam.

BILAL KHEL.—A sub-division of Shan Khel, Tatta, Battannis. Headman; Mir Azim.

BILALZAI (West of Dera Ghazi Khan District).—A section of Kabalzai, Nokuzai, Laharzai, Musa Khels. Headman; Hasan.

BILAND KHEL (35).—A minor fraction of the Gurri Khel, Dachi Khel, Palli Khel, Manazai, Alizai, Mahsuds. Headmen; Azam, Diwar.

BILAZAWI KHEL.—A division of Khani Khel, Chamkannis.

BIMBARAI (300; Kuz Totai).—One of the eight clans of the Utman Khels.

BINDAN KHEL.—A minor fraction of Warkam Khel, Aib Khel, Salarzai, Iliaszai, Bunerwals.

BIN KHEL (Mahaban).—A section of Hasan Khel, Mada Khel, Isazai, Yusufzais. Headmen; Sherdad Khan, Ahwan Khan.

BIRRI KHEL (71).—One of the sub-divisions of the Galeshahi, Shaman Khel, Mahsuds. Headman; Piya Shah.

BIZAZAI (West of the Dera Ghazi Khan District).—A sub-division of Hamzazai, Badil Khel, Musa Khels. Headman; Bakar.

BISEN KHEL (700; British territory and Badar).—A minor fraction of Shadi Khel, Nasra Din, Kalu Khel, Ahmadzai, Darwesh Khel Wazirs. Headmen; Jalal Khan, Timur Khan, Nazir Khan, Gul Adam, Sahib Khan.

BIZODAI (81).—A section of the Malikshai, Aimal Khel, Bahlolzai, Mahsuds.

BOBA (980).—A division of Dana, Battannis. Headmen; Dillasa Khan (Azad Khel), Nazar Khan (Tajbi Khel), Ashraf (Dadi Khel), Chandan Khan (Paia Khel), Azim (Bagh), Toti (Rasul Khel).

BOBAI (25).—A section of Hakim Khel, Mubarak Shahi, Mallizad, Dawaris. Headmen; Khan Samand and Landai.

BOBAK (650).—A division of Dana, Battannis.—Headmen; Jabari (Ali Khel), Batur (Shadi) Khel, Gula Khan (Wargare), Morad Khan (Waruke).

BOBALAI.—A minor fraction of Dre Pillari, Tori Khel (2,670), Ibrahim Khel, Utmanzai, Darwesh Khel Wazirs. Headmen; Miandin Khan.

BOBALLI (Gumatti and Wana).—A minor fraction of Ali Khal (10), Bomi Khel, Nasra Din Khel, Kalu Khel, Ahmadzai, Darwesh Khel Wazirs.

BOBAR KHAN (Bannu District).—A minor fraction of Wadigai, Musa Khel, Hathi Khel (2,000), Shin Khel, Ahmadzai, Darwesh Khel Wazirs.

BOBAR KHEL.—A minor fraction of Khojal Khel (6.0 in Wana), Shadi Khel, Nasra Din Khel, Kalu Khel, Ahmadzai, Darwesh Khel Wazirs. Headman; Sarwar Khan.

BODARZAI (Gomal).—A division of Miani, Sheranis.

BOIASAI.—A sub-division of Ladu, Rakanwal, Lunis. Headman; see Ladu.

BOI KHEL.—A minor fraction of Bakar Khel, Idal Khel, Hathi Khel (2,000), Shin Khel, Ahmadzai, Darwesh Khel Wazirs.

BOI KHEL (50).—A minor fraction of the Garerai, Shumi Khel, Palli Khel, Manazai, Alizai, Mahsuds. Headmen; Dawagar, Mira Khel.

BOI KHEL (40).—A section of the Issuri, Tor, Tappizad, Dawaris. Headmen; Khwaja Muhammad Khan, Shah Nur, Auladin.

BOI KHEL (110).—A section of the Mamdai, Shingi, Bahlolzai, Mahsuds. Headmen; Mamak, Ghaisal, Muhammad Yar, Libas, Momindar.

BOKI KHEL.—(Bannu District). A minor fraction of Rozi Khel, Ali Khel, Musa Khel, Hathi Khel (2,000), Shin Khel, Ahmadzai, Darwesh Khel Wazirs.

BOLAKI KHEL.—A section of Tatar Khel or Akhorwal, (300), Hassan Khel, Adam Khel, Afridis.

BOMI KHEL (5,410; 3,400 in Wana).—A section of Nasra Din, Kalu Khel, Ahmadzai, Darwesh Khel Wazirs.

BONIYA KHEL (Bannu District).—A minor fraction of Barmi Khel, Khandar Khan Khel, Hathi Khel (2,000), Shin Khel, Ahmadzai, Darwesh Khel Wazirs. Headman; Shah Tamoz.

Bora Khel (1,000).—A sub-division of Mohmit Khel, Utmanzai, Darwesh Khel Wazirs. Headmen; Kipat Khan is the chief; others are Sheikh, Khoja Mir, and Pahlwan.

Bosi Khel.—A minor fraction of Musakki, Wuzi Khel, (800), Mohmit Khel, Utmanzai, Darwesh Khel Wazirs.

Bosti Khel (150).—A sub-division of Galai, Adam Khel, Afridis.

Boya (78).—A division of Tappizad, Dawaris. Headman; Gulbar Khan.

Boyakai (12).—A section of the Tappi Khel, Badanzai, Shaman Khel, Mahsuds.

Boza Khel (Bannu, Chapri and Gurang in Kuram).—A sub-section of Tor Khel, Umarzai (600), Shin Khel, Ahmadzai, Darwesh Khel, Wazirs.

Bozi Khel.—A section of Madda Khel (1,600), Ibrahim Khel, Utmanzai, Darwesh Khel Wazirs. Headmen; Namwar Khan (Khoji Khel) of Maizar, Nazar Khan of Zuram, and Rahman Shah (Ismail Khel).

Bozi Khel (25).—A section of, Shujawal, Mubarak Shahi, Mallizad, Dawaris.

Brahim Khel (25; Dera Ismail Khan District).—Nomadic, a minor fraction of Shadi Khel, Isot Khel, Mian Khel, Lohana, Pawindahs. Headman; see Mian Khel.

Brahimzai (West of Dera Ghazi Khan District).—A section of Kabalzai, Nokuzai, Laharzai, Musa Khels. Headman; Mulla Nadar.

Brahimzai (345).—A minor fraction of Khanozai, Panizai, Harun Khel, Sanatia, Kakars. Headman; Didan.

Brahimzai (West of Dera Ghazi Khan District).—A section of Maghduzai, Ahmadzai, Balil Khel, Musa Khels. Headman; Sardar Khan.

Brahimzai (West of Dera Ghazi Khan District).—A sub-division of Mangizai, Laharzai, Musa Khels. Headman; Dadu.

Brahimzai (240).—A section of Sarangzai, Harun Khel, Sanatia, Kakars. Headmen; Majid (Kwas), Daoran (Spezand).

Brahimzai (15).—A section of Yahia, Ahmad Khel, Oba Khel, Sheranis.

Brahimzai (200).—A sub-division of Yahia Khel, Sen Khel, Sheranis.

Brahimzai Bari (60).—A section of Isa Khel, Ahmad Khel. Oba Khel. Sheranis.

Brahozai (100).—A section of Shabozai, Dumar, Sanzar, Kakars, Headman; Khwast.

Bucha Khel.—A minor fraction of Durar (300), Khusrogi, Nasruddin, Zakha Khel, Afridis. Samil. Headmen; Arsal, Sultan Muhammad, Saadat Khan, Awalgul, Dilawar, Bazai, Amir, Gulmast, Gholai, Tor, Mir Hassan, Said Hassan.

Bucha Khel (Bajaur).—A sub-division of Kalut Khel, Samilzai, Tarkanis.

Buch Khel.—A minor fraction of Ranra Khel, Shati Khel, Wali Beg Kor Gandab, Halimzai, Mohmands. They are closely allied to the Ghunda Khel. Headman; Ghafar.

Budai (2,200).—A division of Zakha Khel, Afridis. Samil.

Budai Khel.—A minor fraction of Ali Sher Khel Babur Khel, Keimel Khel, Urmuz Khel, Sipah (1,200), Afridis. Samil. Headman; Khanezaman.

Budal Khel.—A minor fraction of Maruf Khel, Basi Khel, Kamal Khel, Sahib Jan, Aka Khel, (1,800), Afridis. Samil.

Budin Khel (100; British territory).—A minor fraction of Shadi Khel, Nasra Din, Kalu Khel, Ahmadzai, Darwesh Khel Wazirs. Headman; Mir Alam.

Buha Khel.—A minor fraction of Maddu Khel, Asad Khel, Mitha Khan Khel, Kuki Khel (4,500), Afridis. Gar. Headmen; Mir Khan, Gul Khan, Zalmai.

Bukki Khel.—A minor fraction of Painda Khel, Manak Khel, Bakhshi Khel, Madda Khel (1,600), Ibrahim Khel, Utmanzai, Darwesh Khel Wazirs.

Bulfarat or Bulfarad (80).—A clan of Isots. Headman; Nagashai Khan.

BULOZAI (1,384).—A section of Panizai, Harun Khel, Sanatia, Kakars. Headmen; Ali Muhammad, Ramzan, Faiz Mahamad.

BUNDI KOR.—A minor fraction of Sikandar Khel, Kandai, Isa Khel, Pandiali, Mohmands. Headman; Majlum.

BUNERWALS (9,700).—The name Bunerwal strictly applies only to those Iliaszai and Malizai Yusafzais who live in the basin of the Barandu, the principal river of the Buner country. The Firozai section of the Chagarzais may, however, be included in the term.

BURHAN KHEL (50).—A minor fraction of Dreplara, Khusrogi, Nasruddin, Zakha Khel, Afridis. Samil. Headmen; Arsal, Sultan Muhammad, Sa'adat Khan, Awalgul, Dilawar, Bazai, Amir, Gulmast, Gholai, Tor, Mir Hassan, Said Hassan.

BURHAN KHEL.—A minor fraction of Ismail Khel, Makhozai, Nasuzai, Iliaszai, Bunerwals.

BURHAN KHEL (500).—A division of Pandiali, Mohmands. Headmen; Sayad Gul, Badshah, Namdad, Khan Mir, Lal, Sayad Dal, Nasim Gul, Ghulam Shah, Muhammad Umar. The Burhan Khel is one of the "Assured" clans. *

BURHAN KOR.—A sub-division of Babazai, Dawezai Mohmands. Headmen; Kochai, Ghilzai.

BURZAI, or BURAZAI; (100; Zarghun mountain, east of Quetta).—A division of Dumar, Kakars.

BUSA KHEL.—A minor fraction of Pira Khel, Marjan Khel, Utmanzai, Adinzai, Khwazazai, Akozai—Yusufzai Swatis.

BUSHA KHEL (320).—A subdivision of Kamali, Halimzai, Mohmands.

BUT KHEL.—A division of Ismailzai, Utman Khels.

BUZR KHEL.—A section of Abdul Khel, Urmuz Khel, Sipah (1,200), Afridis. Samil. Headman; Jumma.

---

* Those Mohmand clans to which the British Government has given assurances that they shall not lose or suffer by the severance of their ancient connection with the Afghan State. The other "Assured" clans are the Dawezai, Halimzai, Isa Khel, Tarakzai and Utmanzai.

C

Chagai.—A minor fraction of Jambai Khel, Waruka, Ali Khan Khel, Sarki Khel, Madda Khel (1,600), Ibrahim Khel, Utmanzai, Darwesh Khel Wazirs.

Chagarzai (4,890; Along both banks of the Indus and on the Duma mountain, and (1,000) in the north-east of Buner).—A division of Malizai, Yusafzai, Pathans. The Firozai sub-division live in Buner; the other two sub-divisions, *viz.*, Nasrat Khel and Basi Khel, hold land on Duma, and on both sides of the Indus. Headmen; Kudrat Khan and Mirdad, who lead rival factions.

Chagarzai, Basi Khels (200; Black Mountain).—A division of the Pariaris.

Chahar Khel (30).—One of the three sections of the Kikarai, Nana Khel, Bahlolzai, Mahsuds. Headmen; Khost, Didari.

Chahar Khel (582).—One of the four divisions of the Shaman Khel, Mahsuds.

Chakmanis.—A tribe of Northern Khost, between the Mangals and Makbals, bordering Upper Kurram.

Chalak Khel.—A section of Tari Khel, Shakhi, Waraspun, Battannis.

Chalak Khel.—A minor fraction of Dre Nami, Balal Khel, Hassan Khel (400), Mohmit Khel, Utmanzai, Darwesh Khel Wazirs. Headman; Khan.

Chalgari.—See Mekhiani, Spin, Tarin.

Chamba Khel (80; Black Mountain).—A section of Barat Khel, Akazai, Isazai, Yusufzais.

Chamkannis (1,500; West of Tirah, and east of Kurram).—A small tribe of Pathans of doubtful origin.

Chamlawals (1,000).—The name applied to the mixed Mandan clans who inhabit the Chamla valley, south-east of Buner.

Chandan Khel.—A minor fraction of Marjan Khel, Utmanzai, Adinzai, Khwazazai, Akozai—Yusufzai Swatis.

Chandar Khel (Bajaur.)—A sub-division of Ilat Khel, Salarzai, Tarkanis.

Chandar Khel.—A minor fraction of Adam Khel, Nazar Khel, Star Ali Khan Khel, Sarki Khel, Madda Khel (1,600), Ibrahim Khel, Utmanzai, Darwesh Khel Wazirs.

Channi (15).—A minor fraction of Bar Kaum, Hassu Khel, Tor, Mallizad Dawaris. Headmen; Bedil, Dini.

Chapla (400).—A sub-division of Muia, Waraspun, Battannis. Headmen; Ahmad Shah, Mir Sultan and Daulat (Mandi), Didari (Dari), Janei and Rehman (Umar).

Chardai (8,600; Kuram)—The larger of the two clans of the Turis.

Charghal Khel (80).—A minor fraction of Shinki Khel, Babakki, Hassu Khel, Tor, Mallizad, Dawaris. Headman; Karar.

Char Khel.—A section of Alisher Khel, Gadaizai, Iliaszai, Bunerwals.

Char Khel (Miranzai and Mastura valleys).—A division of the Malla Khel (800) "Hamsayas" of the Orakzais. Samil.

Char Khel.—A minor fraction of Zakho Khel, Janakhori (800), Hassan Khel, Adam Khel, Afridis.

Charkhil (40).—A minor fraction of Charkhil, Land, Malakh, Mallizad, Dawaris. Headmen; Gul Rahman, Landai, Id Muhammad.

Charkhil (85).—A section of Land, Malakh, Mallizad, Dawaris. Headmen; Badani, Kakir Shah, Gul Rahman.

Chawar Khel.—A sub-division of Bazoti (500), Daulatzai, Orakzais. Samil. Headman; Ahmad Shah.

Chotialiwal.—See Dzam, Spin Tarin.

CHUAR KHEL (388).—A clan of Sheranis. Headmen; Sadula and Azim.

CHUARZAI (6).—A sub-division of Malezai, Rakanwal, Lunis. Headman; see Malezai.

CHUHARI KOR (Bar Yakhdand).—A division of Utmanzai, Mohmands. Headmen; Badshah Muhammad, Ali Khan, Shamsai, Muhammad Abbas, Amir Baz, Shah Zarin.

CHUND KHEL (30).—A minor fraction of the Khoidad Khel, Gidi Khel, Manazai, Alizai, Mahsuds. Headmen; Foujdar, Pazal.

CHUTTAN (48).—A section of Zira Khel, Amzoni, Malizad, Dawaris. Headmen; Gaimal Khan, Gholam.

D

DABAR.—A division of Mandal, Utman Khels.

DABARZAI.—A minor fraction of Dardoni, Wuzi Khel, (800), Mohmit Khel, Utmanzai, Darwesh Khel, Wazirs.

DACHI KHEL (430).—A section of the Palli Khel, Manazai, Alizai, Mahsuds.

DADA KHEL (50; Black Mountain).—A sub-division of Hasanzai, Isazai, Yusufzais. Headmen; Habibulla, Sayad Ajab, Ghazi Khan.

DADAKZAI (236).—A minor fraction of Khanozai, Panizai, Harun Khel, Sanatia, Kakars. Headman; Kaium.

DADAR KHEL.—A minor fraction of Kalla Khel (700), Ashu Khel, Hassan Khel, Adam Khel, Afridis.

DADAR KHEL.—One of the sections of the Mir Ahmad Khel (Mir Hussain Khel), Firoz Khel (1,000), Daulatzai, Orakzais. Samil. Headman; Nazir.

DADI KHEL (160).—A section of Taru Khel, Boba, Dana, Battannis.

DADI KHEL.—A minor fraction of Durar (300), Khusrogi, Nasruddin, Zakha Khel, Afridis. Samil. Headmen; see Bucha Khel.

DADU KHEL (40).—A minor fraction of Dreplara, Khusrogi, Nasruddin, Zakha Khel, Afridis, Samil. Headmen; Murtaza, Purdil, Taza Khan, Arman Shah, Zaidulla.

DADU KHEL (2,050).—A division of Tarakzai, Mohmands. Headmen; Sofi, Abdullah, Jang, Lalo, Nawab, Najai, Achuk.

DALAK KHEL (250).—A subdivision of the Akhel (600), Ismailzai, Orakzais, Gar. Headmen; Muhammad, Mowazi, Khairulla Khan, Rasul Khan.

DALAT KHEL (20).—A subdivision of Zarakki, Mallizad, Dawaris. Headmen; Saadulla Jan, Badrang.

DALEL.—A minor fraction of the Saiad Khan Nmasi, Ali Karan, Mamuzai (3,500), Lashkarzai, Orakzais. Gar. Headman; Sher Khan (?).

DALEL KHEL.—A minor fraction of Gadia Khel, Tatar Khel or Akhorwal, Hassan Khel, Adam Khel, Afridis.

DALIL KHEL.—A minor fraction of Hassan Khel, Pakhai (1,000), Budai, Zakha Khel, Afridis. Samil. Headman; Morad Ali, Orakzai.

DALIL KOR.—A minor fraction of the Umar Khan Khel, Ali Karan, Mamuzai, Lashkarzai, Orakzais. Gar. Headman; Hussein Shah.

DALKHA KOR (750).—A subdivision of Dadu Khel, Tarakzai, Mohmands. Headmen; Jang, Abdullah, Lalo, Nawab, Najai, Achuk.

DALLA KHEL.—A minor fraction of Torsam Khel, Nazar Khel, Star Ali Khan Khel, Sarki Khel, Madda Khel, 1,600), Ibrahim Khel, Utmanzai, Darwesh Khel, Wazirs.

DALLU KHEL.—A minor fraction of Jalal Khel, Mali (or Muli) Khel, Salarzai, Iliaszai, Bunerwals.

DANA (2,080).—A clan of Battannis. Headmen; Dilasa Khan, Razza Khan, Jabari, Batur, Gula Khan, Morad Khan.

DANGAR KHEL (150).—A minor fraction of Piran Dangar Khel, Muhammad Khel, Malakh, Mallizad, Dawaris. Headman; see Piran Dangar Khel.

DANGZARI (9).—A sub-division of Banda, Tappizad, Dawaris. Headman; Sur Kamand.

DANI KHEL.—A minor fraction of Matkai, Malik Shahi (400), Wali Khel, Utmanzai, Darwesh Khel Wazirs. Headmen; Marota, Pirwal, Umar Khel, Achegul.

DANIS (Tirin and Derawat on the Helmand).—A tribe who claim to be Kakars.

DAORI KHEL.—A sub-division of Samozai, Khwazazai, Akozai—Yusufzai Swatis.

DAOZAI (West of Dera Ghazi Khan District).—A sub-division of Mangizai, Laharzai, Musa Khels. Headman; Mian Khan.

DARAK KHEL.—A minor fraction of Mandi Khel, Wuzi Khel (800), Mohmit Khel, Utmanzai, Darwesh Khel Wazirs.

DARDONI.—A section of Wuzi Khel (800), Mohmit Khel, Utmanzai, Darwesh Khel Wazirs. Headmen; Bozi, Wazir Khan, Nakir Khan.

DARGAI (30).—A minor fraction of Dochi Khel, Palli Khel, Wanazai, Alizai, Mahsuds. Headmen; Barkhudar, Tor.

DARIA KHEL (20; Dera Ismail Khan District).—Nomadic, a minor fraction of Umrzai, Sein Khel, Mian Khel, Lohana, Pawindahs. Headman; see Mian Khel.

DARIAAI (26).—A sub-division of Malezai, Rakanwal, Lanis.

DARI KHEL.—A section of Chapla, Muia, Waraspun, Battannis.

DARMAI KHEL.—A minor fraction of Tashi Khel, Sharaki (200), Galai, Adam Khel, Afridis.

DARMAL KHEL.—A minor fraction of Shadi Khel, Balal Khel, Hassan Khel (400), Mohmit Khel, Utmanzai, Darwesh Khel Wazirs. Headman; Khan Ghayat.

DARPA KHEL (235).—A division of Mallizad, Dawaris. Headmen; Shahzada, Gulmurg, Gulpir, Najib, Sheik and Mira.

DARRE KHEL (500).*—One of the four clans of the Chamkannis. The Darre Khel and Mirza Khel are sometimes known collectively as the Khwaja Khel.

DARRI KHEL (30).—A section of the Kasim Khel, Badanzai. Shaman Khel, Mahsuds. Headmen; Shadi, Mir and Wali Khan.

DARRI KHEL.—A minor fraction of Madda Khel, Miamai, Kabul Khel (2,600) Utmanzai, Darwesh Khel Wazirs.

DARRI KHEL.—A section of Madda Khel, Sher Gulla, Aka Khel, (1,800), Afridis. Samil.

DARWESH KHEL WAZIRS (24,560.)—The name given to the Utmanzai and Ahmadzai clans of Wazirs. Headmen; see Ahmadzai and Utmanzai.

DARWESH KHEL.—A minor fraction of Mintar Khel, Muhammad Khel, Hassan Khel, (400), Mohmit Khel, Utmanzai, Darwesh Khel Wazirs. Headman; Fazal Shah.

DARWEZ KHEL—A minor fraction of Babur Khel, Keimal Khel, Urmuz Khel, Sipah (1,200), Afridis. Headman; Khanezaman.

DARWI KHEL (Mastura).—One of the four divisions of the Mishti (3,000), "Hamsayas" of the Orakzais. Samil.

DARYA KHAN KHEL.—A division of Haji Khel, Chamkannis.

DARYA KHEL (13).—A section of Alizai, Darpa Khel, Mallizad, Dawaris. Headmen; Shermon, Gul Azam.

DARYA KHEL (100).—A minor fraction of the Kotar Khel Abdul Khel, Langar Khel, Khoidad Khel, Gidi Khel, Manazai, Alizai, Mahsuds. Headmen; Bola, Kissar, Gulaim.

DARYA KHEL, DARWESH KHEL.—A minor fraction of Bizen Khel (700), Shadi Khel, Nasra Din, Kalu Khel, Ahmadzai, Darwesh Khel Wazirs. Headman; Sahib Khan.

---

*NOTE—This includes the men of the Mirza Khel.

DARYAZAI.—A sub-division of Wara, Mamund, Tarkanis.

DARZA KHEL (50; Black Mountain).—A section of Aziz Khel, Akazai, Isazai, Yusufzais.

DASTA KHEL (17).—A minor fraction of Alli Khel, Barim Khel, Amzoni, Mallizad, Dawaris. Headmen; Jumma Khan, Shirak, Halim Khan, Gulab Din.

DATAK KHEL (British territory).—A minor fraction of Painda Khel (200), Shadi Khel, Nasra Din, Kalu Khel, Ahmadzai, Darwesh Khel Wazirs.

DATTA KHEL.—A section of Bara Khel, who having lands among the Khaddar Khel, are regarded as a section thereof for purposes of administration. Headman; Pambal.

DATTA KHEL.—A minor fraction of Abdul Khel, Bara Khel (1,000), Mohmit Khel, Utmanzai, Darwesh Khel Wazirs.

DATTA KHEL.—A minor fraction of Drepillari, Tori Khel (2,670), Ibrahim Khel, Utmanzai, Darwesh Khel Wazirs. Headman; Amaldar.

DATTA KHEL (23).—A sub-division of Zerakki, Mallizad, Dawaris. Headmen; Ahmad and Khonar.

DATTI KHEL (516).—The chief sub-division of the Galeshahi, Shaman Khel, Mahsuds.

DATTU KHEL.—A section of Shadi Khel, Bobak, Dana Battannis.

DAUD (30).—A section of Barim Khel, Amzoni, Mallizad, Dawaris. Headman; Tahir Shah.

DAUDI KHEL (40).—A section of the Astanai, Shabi Khel, Alizai, Mahsuds. Headmen; Abas, Talak.

DAUDZAI (160).—A division of Mamuzai or Muhammadzai, Zaimukhts.

DAUDZAI (Peshawar District).—A tribe of the same origin as the Mohmands, who live along the left bank of the Kabul river to its junction with the Bara.

DAULAT KHEL.—A minor fraction of Sikandar Khel, Abdul Khel, Bara Khel (1,000), Mohmit Khel, Utmanzai, Darwesh Khel Wazirs.

DAULAT KHEL (Bannu District).—A minor fraction of Ali Khel, Musa Khel, Hathi Khel (2,000), Shin Khel, Ahmadzai, Darwesh Khel Wazirs.

DAULAT KHEL.—A section of the Amar Khan Khel, Alisherzai (3,000), Lashkarzai, Orakzais. Samil. Headman; Mirza Hassan.

DAULAT KHEL (40).—A minor fraction of the Bammi Khel, Khoidad Khel, Gidi Khel, Manazai, Alizai, Mahsuds. Headman; Shale Khan.

DAULAT KHEL.—A section of Ghalib Khan Khel, Malikdin Khel MalikdinKhel, (4,000), Afridis. Samil. Headmen; Alam Khan, Gholai, Kassim, Hamid, Said Ghulam, Majid Akhundzada, Miran, Mir Mir Azim, Mir Salim, Alam, Mir Ahmad, Nur Jan.

DAULAT KHEL.—A minor fraction of Bash Khel, Anna, (1,000), Budai, Zakha Khel, Afridis. Samil. Headmen; Pir Gul, Safar, Dost Hak, Khanezaman, Zeb Jan, Rahmatulla, Madakki.

DAULAT KHEL (65; Tartara). —A division of Mullagoris, a vassal clan of the Mohmands.

DAULATZAI (Zhob).—A minor fraction of Ibrahimzai, Shadozai, Ali Khel, Sanzar, Kakars.

DAULATZAI.—A division of Mansur, Gaduns.

DAULATZAI (2,400; Mastura valley and Landuki pass).—One of the four clans of the Orakzais. Samil. 100 of them are Shiahs.

DAULATZAIS (500; Ghazni and Kalat-i-Ghilzai).—One of the Pawindah trading clans.

DAULATZAI (50; Zarghun mountain, east of Quetta).—A division of Dumar, Kakars.

DAULAT KHAN KHEL.—A section of the Ibrahim Khel, Gadaizai, Iliaszai, Bunerwals.

DAULATAN KHEL.—A section of Manzar Khel, (360), Ibrahim Khel, Utmanzai Darwesh Khel Wazirs. Headman; Gul Muhammad Shah.

DAULATZAI (700; Zhob).—A section of Shadzai, Alizai, Sanzar, Kakars. Headman; Hamzai.

DAULATZAI. (1,500; Both banks of the Barandu river, part of Topdara valley and hills around).—A division of the Malizai, Bunerwals.

DAUR KHEL (45).—A minor fraction of the Nekzan Khel, Sher Khel, Haibat Khel, Nana Khel, Bahlolzai, Mahsuds. Headmen; Zamani, Makhmad.

DAUTANIS (700; Wana). One of the leading Pawindah trading tribes.

DAWAR KHEL.—A minor fraction of Ismail Khel, Bozi Khel, Madda Khel (1,600), Ibrahim Khel, Utmanzai, Darwesh Khel Wazirs.

DAWARAN KHEL.—A minor fraction of Jambai Khel, Waruka Ali Khan Khel, Sarki Khel, Madda Khel (1,600), Ibrahim Khel, Utmanzai, Darwesh Khel Wazirs.

DAWARIS (5,119; Tochi valley). —The Dawaris are divided into two main factions called Mallikad or Malia, and Tappizad. They are priest ridden and fanatical, and bear the reputation of being cowardly. Though speaking Pushtu, the Dawaris do not themselves claim the title of Pathan. They are industrious and skilful cultivators, and before our occupation their Waziri neighbours, who surround their country, looked on the riches of Dawar as their natural prey. Dawari villages are consequently strongly walled and flanked, while towers are found scattered among the fields to protect the cultivators and their crops.

DAWARZAI (West of Dera Ghazi Khan District).—A section of Dedazai, Nokuzai, Laharzai, Musa Khels. Headman; Bazi.

DAWAT or DAUD KHEL.—A section of Kadai Kor, Gandab, Halimzai, Mohmands. Headmen; Muhammad Habib, Mirak Suleiman.

DAWAT or DAUTA KHEL (Bohai Dag; a few at Goshta, Kabul river).—A division of Khwaezai, Mohmands. Headmen Bara Khan, Muhammad Sharif Khan, Said.

DAWEZAI (1,000).—One of the affiliated Mohmand clans. Headmen; Hazur Khan, Habib Jan; see note on page 46.

DAWIZAI (West of Dera Ghazi Khan District).—A sub-division of Nozai, Laharzai, Musa Khels. Headman; Shah Baz.

DEHGAN.—A minor fraction of Umar Khel, Ali Khel, Khaddar Khel (770), Mohmit Khel, Utmanzai, Darwesh Khel Wazirs.

DEHGAN.—A tribe inhabiting Kunar, Laghman and Ningrahar. A few Dehgans are also to be found in Zurmat and Bajaur. The Dehgans are said to be descendants of the Indian races originally inhabiting North-Eastern Afghanistan.

DERVEZI KHEL.—A minor fraction of Mohmand Khel, Kattia Khel, Hassan Khel, Mitha Khan Khel, Kuki Khel (4,500), Afridis. Gar.

DESHIWALS (720; Black Mountain).—A tribe of Swati origin.

DEWARZAI (40; Zarghun mountain, east of Quetta.)—A division of the Dumar, Kakars.

DHANNI KHEL (40).—A minor fraction of the Shumi Khel, Palli Khel, Manazai, Alizai, Mahsuds. Headmen; Bare Khan, Ahmad Khan.

DHANNI KHEL (35).—A minor fraction of the Gurri Khel, Dochi Khel, Palli Khel, Manazai, Alizai, Mahsuds. Headmen; Azam, Diwar.

DHUNI KHEL.—A minor fraction of Hilal Khel, Keimal Khel, Urmuz Khel, Sipah (1,200), Afridis. Samil. Headmen; Gul, Salim.

DIDAOBI.—A sub-division of Waruke, Dana, Battannis. Headman; Adam Khan.

DIGAN KHEL.—A minor fraction of Datta Khel, Abdul Khel, Bora Khel (1,000) Mohmit Khel, Utmanzai, Darwesh Khel Wazirs.

DIGAR KHEL.—A minor fraction of Morib Khel, Utman Khel, Takhti Khel, Bakka Khel, Wali Khel, Utmanzai, Darwesh Khel Wazirs. Headman; Islam Khan.

DIHGAN (15).—A minor fraction of Idal Khel, Muhammad Khel, Malakh, Mallizad, Dawaris. Headman; Zarbadshah.

DILAZAKS.—A people Scythic origin who inhabited the Peshawar valley before the Pathan invasion. Scattered families of them are still to be found along the left bank of the Indus in the Hazara and Rawal Pindi districts.

DILDAR KHEL.—A minor, fraction of Mohmand Khel Khattia Khel, Hassan Khel, Mitha Khan Khel, Kuki Khel (4,500), Afridis. Gar. Headmen; Baghi, Saidal, Ghanni, Torbaz.

DIL PIYARI (14).—A minor fraction of Boya, Tappizad, Dawaris. Headman; Sheikh Nabi.

DINAR.—A minor fraction of Umar Khel, Ali Khel, Khaddar Khel (770), Mohmit Khel, Utmanzai, Darwesh Khel Wazirs. Headman; Zarak.

DINAR.—A minor fraction of Ali Khel, Shugai, Tori Khel (2,670), Ibrahim Khel, Utmanzai, Darwesh Khel Wazirs. Headman; Gulli.

DINAR (40).—A sub-division of Arghund, Mallizad, Dawaris. Headman; Miamai.

DINJAN KHEL.—A minor fraction of Shpalkai Khel, Zargun Khel (300), Galai, Adam Khel, Afridis.

DOD KHEL.—A minor fraction of Mir Hasani, Macha, Madda Khel (1,600), Ibrahim Khel, Utmanzai, Darwesh Khel Wazirs.

DODAZAI (West of Dera Ghazi Khan District).—A section of Malizai, Ahmadzai, Balil Khel, Musa Khels. Headman; Lawangai.

DUPARZAI (1,600; Kuram).—A division of Chardai, Turis.

DODI KHEL.—A minor fraction of Titar Khel, Khan Khel, Takhti Khel, Bakka Khel (1,000), Wali Khel, Utmanzai, Darwesh Khel Wazirs. Headman; Gulazamir.

DODI KHEL (Bannu District) —A minor fraction of Khandar Khan Khel, Hathi Khel, Shin Khel, Ahmadzai, Darwesh Khel Wazirs. Headmen; Nizam Khan.

DODI KHEL (50).—A sub-division of Khaddi, Malliaad, Dawaris. Headman; Shahmaddi.

DODI KHEL.—See Laghar (or Dodi) Khel.

Dosalli.—A section of Wuzi Khel (800), Mohmit Khel, Utmanzai, Darwesh Khel Wazirs. Headman; Niyaz Gul.

Dosalli.—Said to be a section of Khaddar Khel (770). They are really, however, a section of Wuzi Khel, Mohmit Khel (see above), owning land among the Khaddar Khel.

Dodal (Nandihar).—A division of the Nandihari Swatis.

Dodam Khel.—(Bannu District). A minor fraction of Ali Khel, Musa Khel, Hathi Khel (2,000), Shin Khel, Ahmadzai, Darwesh Khel Wazirs.

Dodazai (150; West of Dera Ghazi Khan District).—A sub-division of Nokuzai, Laharzai, Musa Khel. Headmen; Panzai, Balak, Dawarzai, Bazi, Mandizais Khan Daoran.

Dost Mali Khel.—A section of the Bazar Khan Khel, Utman Khel (400), Daulatzai, Orakzais. Samil.

Dotannis.—See Dautanis.

Dotial (1,695).—A clan of the Allaiwals.

Dre Dariz.—A minor fraction of Ali Khel, Shugai, Tori, Khel (2,670), Ibrahim Khel, Utmanzai, Darwesh Khel Wazirs. Headman; Gul Baid.

Dre Khel.—A section of Wuzi Khel (800), Mohmit Khel, Utmanzai, Darwesh Khel Wazirs.

Drema.—See Kattagarm.

Dre Nami.—A minor fraction of Musakki, Wuzi Khel (800), Mohmit Khel, Utmanzai, Darwesh Khel Wazirs.

Dre Nami.—A minor fraction of Balal Khel, Hasan Khel (400), Mohmit Khel, Utmanzai, Darwesh Khel Wazirs. Headmen; Malakdin Khan, Niyaz Muhammad.

Drepilara.—A sub-division of Shakhi, Waraspun, Battannis. Headmen; Husen (Ghurburu), Ashak (Miani), Saidal (Ismailak).

Dre Pillari.—A minor fraction of Asat Khel, Wuzi Khel (800), Mohmit Khel, Utmanzai, Darwesh Khel Wazirs.

Dre Pillari.—A minor fraction of Muhammad Khel, Hassan Khel (400), Mohmit Khel, Utmanzai, Darwesh Khel Wazirs. Headman; Sippar.

Dre Pillari.—A section of Tori Khel (2,670), Ibrahim Khel, Utmanzai, Darwesh Khel Wazirs. Headmen; Miandin Khan, Khari, Shahzadin, Amaldar, Keili.

Drepillari—A minor fraction of Sarki Khel, Madda Khel (1,600), Ibrahim Khel, Utmanzai, Darwesh Khel Wazirs. Headmen; Modai, Pyall, Aki Khan, Umar Khan and Biyan.

Dreplara (260).—A section of Khusrogi, Nasr-uddin, Zakha Khel Afridis. Samil. Headmen; see Mir Kalan Khel, Dadu Khel, and Burhan Khel sub-sections.

Dreplara.—A section of Paindai (940), Nasr-uddin, Zakha Khel Afridis. Samil. Headmen; Chikkun, Tamas, Anwar, Nazr Din.

Drigzai (374; Thal Choti ali).—A clan of the Lunis.

Dulha Khel (Dir).—A section of Sultan Khel, Sesada, Malizai, Yusafzais.

Dumars (340; Zarghun Mountain, east of Quetta).—A Kakar clan. Headmen; Azmal, Umar, and Kwadad (Nokarzai), Rahimdad, Lalhan, Bahawal (Burzai); Lalbeg (Dewarzai), Sabur (Daulatzai), Husen (Faizai).

Dumars (1,885).—A division of Sanzar, Kakars.

Dur, see Madi Khel and Dur.

Duranis.—(100,000) The dominant race of Afghans; and the one to which the present ruling family of Kabul belongs. The Duranis have two branches, the Zirak and the Panjpai. To the former belong the Popalzai, Alikozai, Barakzai and Achakzai, to the latter the Nurzai, Alizai, Isakzai, Khokani and Maku tribes. See also Sadozais and Bar Duranis.

Durar (300).—A section of Khusrogi, Nasruddin, Zakha Khel Afridis. Samil. Headmen; see Bucha Khel.

DURBA KHEL.—A section of Hamza Khel, Gandab Halimzai, Mohmands. Headmen; Rogh Muhammad, Dauran, Saraf, Sahibroz, Yar Gul Akbar, Gul Ali, Izzat Khan, Amir Khan.

DURBA KHEL.—A section of Hamza Khel, Kamali, Halimzai, Mohmands. Headman; Jamal Khan.

DURBI KHEL.—A sub-division of Kambar, Kambar Khel (4,500), Afridis. Gar. Headmen; Muhammad Sher Khwaja Ali, Yaro, Nurai Sher Khan, Hamid.

DURDAN KHEL.—A section of Musa Khel, Kuz-Sulizai, Baizai, Akozai—Yusufzai Swatis.

DURJI KHEL.—A sub-division of Karna Khel, Malikdin Khel (4,000), Afridis. Samil. Headmen; see Yar Muhammad Khel.

DUR KHEL (105).—A minor fraction of Babakki, Hassu Khel, Tor, Mallizad, Dawaris. Headmen; Badar, Mir Kazam, Diwana Khan, Niazgai.

DURMA KOR (500; Lalpura, Loi Shilman).—A section of Shah Mansur Khel, Dadu Khel, Tarakzai, Mohmands. Headman; Akbar Khan, Khan of Lalpura.

DURMUR KHEL (65).—A section of Umar Khel, Nana Khel, Bahlolzai, Mahsuds. Headman; Zawakal.

DUTANNIS.—See Dautanis.

DZAM OR CHOTIALIWAL.—(28). —A division of Spin, Tarins. Headman; Shahbaz Khan.

E

EMANI KHEL.—A minor fraction of Baghdad Khel, Keimal Khel, Urmuz Khel, Sipah (1,200), Afridis. Samil. Headmen; Khanezaman, Lal Muhammad, Sher Jan.

F

Faizai (30; east of Quetta).—A division of Dumar, Kakars.

Faizulla Kor.—A minor fraction of Banra Khel, Shati Khel, Wali Beg Kor. Gandab, Halimzai, Mohmands. Headman; Mushki.

Fakiran.—A section of Barim Khel, Amzoni, Mallizad, Dawaris. Headman; Gul Khan.

Fakiran (12).—A minor fraction of Khuttay, Taib Khel, Amzoni, Mallizad, Dawaris. Headmen; Arsalaband, Juma Akbar.

Fakir Khel.—A minor fraction of Ashrab Khel, Ismail Khel, Bozi Khel, Madda Khel (1,600), Ibrahim Khel, Utmanzai, Darwesh Khel Wazirs.

"**Fakirnama.**"—A term which covers Gujars, gardeners, ploughmen, tanners, musicians, artizans, menial servants, carriers, pedlars, etc, who live amongst the Yusufzais and are taxed by them.

Fakirzai (Zhob).—A section of Mirzai, Alizai, Sanzar, Kakars.

Faridai (80).—A minor fraction of Khamar Khel, Gidi Khel, Manazai, Alizai, Mahsuds.

Farid Khel (Khanki valley).—A sub-division of Sada Khel (80), Ismailzai, Orakzais. Samil.

Farid Khel.—A minor fraction of Feroz Khel, Mashi Khel, Mannia Khel, Hassan Khel, Mitha Khan Khel, Kuki Khel (4,500), Afridis. Gar. Headmen; Mulla Nazir, Mirwal, Said Gul.

Farigh Shah Kor (South of Kharmana river).—A section of Alizai (50), Masuzai, Lashkarzai, Orakzais. Samil. Headman; Nur Khan.

Farigh Shah Nmasi (Samana, and Khanki valley).—A sub-division of

Rabia Khel (700), Ismailzai, Orakzais. Samil. Headmen; Tahir Shah, Kamar, Azadi, Muhammad Zaman, Mir Afzal, Ghulam Muhiuddin, Wali, Wazir.

FATEH KHAN KHEL.—A subdivision of Utman Khel (400), Daulatzai, Orakzais. Samil. Headman; Khanak.

FATEH KHAN KHEL.–A minor fraction of Maruf Khel, Basi Khel, Kamal Khel, Sahib Jan, Aka Khel, (1,800), Afridis. Samil.

FATEH KHEL.—A minor fraction of Sab Khel, Shekhai, Annai (1,000), Budai, Zakha Khel, Afridis. Samil. Headmen; Khalu, Alimast, Khanmast, Aligul.

FATEH KHEL.—A minor fraction of Sultan Khel, Suran Khel, Babakri, Sipah 1,200), Afridis. Samil. Headmen; Naz Karim, Iran, Gul Muhammad.

FATEH KHEL.—A sub-division of Abdul Khel, Kuki Khel (4,500), Afridis. Gar. Headmen; Mulla Anwar Shah, Gulnur, Said Ali.

FATEH KHEL.—A minor fraction of Hati Khel, Mali (or Muli) Khel, Salarzai, Iliaszai, Bunerwals.

FATEHMIR KHEL.—A minor fraction of Ahmadbeg Khel, Mohib Khel, Shekhai, Annai (1,000), Budai, Zakha Khel Afridis. Samil. Headmen; Shahzada, Arsala, Aligul.

FATIMA KOR.—A minor fraction of Sharagh Khel, Kaddam Khel, Feroz Khel, Mashi Khel, Mannia Khel, Hassan Khel, Mitha Khan Khel, Kuki Khel (4,500), Afridis. Gar. Headmen; see Farid Khel Section.

FATOZAI.—A section of Mirzai, Alizai, Sanzar, Kakars.

FATTEH KHEL.—A minor fraction of Miri Khel, Pakhai (1,000), Budai, Zakha Khel, Afridis. Samil. Headmen; see Shahbeg and Wallibeg Khel.

FATTEH KHEL.—A section of Tari Khel, Shakhi, Waraspun, Battannis.

FATTEH KHEL.—A sub-division of Abazai, Khwazazai, Akozai—Yusufzai, Swatis.

FATTEH KHEL.—A sub-division of Ali Khel, Bar-Ranizai, Akozai—Yusufzai Swatis.

Fatteh Khel (8).—A section of Barim Khel, Amzoni, Mallizad, Dawaris. Headman; Bahawal Khan.

Fatteh Kor.—A minor fraction of Rami Khel, Kadai Kor Gandab, Halimzai, Mohmands. Headman; Sarkai.

Fatwa Khel.—A minor fraction of Muhammad Khel (700), Isperka, Kalu Khel, Ahmadzai, Darwesh Khel Waziris. Headman; Habib Gul.

Fazil Khel.—A minor fraction of Ya Khel, Babu Khel, Adinzai, Khwazazai, Akozai —Yusufzai Swatis.

Fazli Kor.—A minor fraction of Rasul Kor, Wali Beg Kor Gandab, Halimzai Mohmands. Headmen; Bahadur, Zulkadar, Nazro.

Feroz Khel.—A section of Tor Sapar (350), Galai, Adam Khel, Afridis.

Feroz Khel.—A minor fraction of Mashi Khel, Mannia Khel, Hassan Khel, Mitha Khan Khel, Kuki Khel (4,500), Afridis. Headman; see Mashi Khel.

Firoz Khan Kor.—A minor fraction of Ali Khan Khel, Ali Karan, Mamuzai (3,500), Lashkarzai, Orakzais. Headman; Firoz Khan.

Firozai (1,000, extreme north-east of Buner).—A sub-division of Chagarzai, Malizai, Bunerwals.

Firoz Khel (20; Dera Ismail Khan District).—Nomadic, a minor fraction of Baloch Khel, Isot Khel, Mian Khel, Lohana, Pawindahs. Headman; see Mian Khel.

Firoz Khel (30; Dera Ismail Khan District).—Nomadic, a minor fraction of Pasani, Isot Khel, Mian Khel, Lohana, Pawindahs. Headman; see Mian Khel.

Firoz Khel.—A sub-division of Niamat Khel, Tatta, Battannis. Headman; Dinak.

Firoz Khel (1,000; Maulrghar, and Mastura valley).—A division of the Daulatzai, Orakzais. Samil.

Futteh Khel.—A minor fraction of Kattia Khel, Hassan Khel, Mitha Khan Khel, Kuki Khel (4,500), Afridis. Gar. Headmen; Gul Hassan and Asad Khan.

G

GADAI KHEL.—A section of Kambar Khel, Bazoti (500). Daulatzai, Orakzais. Samil.

GADAIZAI (900; Southern slopes of the Ilam and Dosirri mountains).—A division of Iliaszai, Bunerwals.

GADAZAI (West of Dera Ghazi Khan District).—A section of Inzai, Hasan Khel, Balil Khel, Musa Khels. Headman; Ali Muhammad.

GADGI KHEL (50; Dera Ismail Khan District).—Nomadic, a minor fraction of Umrzai, Sein Khel, Mian Khel, Lohana, Pawindahs. Headman; see Mian Khel.

GADIA KHEL.—A section of Tatar Khel or Akhorwal (300), Hassan Khel, Adam Khel, Afridis.

GADO.—A division of Mandal, Utman Khels.

GADOZAI (30).—A section of Land, Amand, Ahmad Khel, Oba Khel, Sheranis.

GADUNS (2,800; Mahaban). A tribe of Pathans, some of whom also live in British territory.

GAGALZAIS (450).—A clan of the Ushtaranas. The divisions, etc., of the Gagelzais are not separately indexed in this Dictionary.

GAJJI KHEL (30).—A minor fraction of Salimi Khel, Dachi Khel, Palli Khel, Manazai, Alizai, Mahsuds. Headman; Ayaz Shah.

GAJRAI (4).—A sub division of Shamezai, Rakanwal Lunis. Headman; see Shamezai.

GAZER KOR.—A section of the Umar Khan Khel, Alisherzai (3,000) Lashkarzai, Orakzais. Samil. Headman; Ali Sheikh.

GALAI (1,400).—A division of Adam Khel, Afridis.

GALESHAHI (696).—A division of Shaman Khel, Alizai Mahsuds.

GALI KHEL.—A minor fraction of Kasim Khel (256), Kimat Khel, Jawaki, Adam Khel, Afridis.

GALLA KHEL (7).—A sub-division of Boya, Tappizad, Dawaris. Headman; Shahnawaz.

GALL PAO (Bajaur).—A section of Kalut Khel, Nur Khel, Samilzai, Tarkanis.

GALZADA KHEL.—A minor fraction of Aib Kor, Shaikh Khel, Aib Khel, Salarzai, Iliaszai, Bunerwals.

GANDAPURS (1,300; Dera Ismail Khan District).—A small tribe, of Pawindah origin. Headmen; Guldad Khan, Naurang Khan. The clans, etc., of the Gandapurs are not separately indexed in this dictionary.

GANGI KHEL (400, Wana; 400, Gumatti).—A minor fraction of Bomi Khel, Nasradin, Kalu Khel, Ahmadzai, Darwesh Khel, Wazirs.

GARA KHEL.—A minor fraction of Kundai, Tor Khel, Umarzai (600), Shin Khel, Ahmadzai, Darwesh Khel, Wazirs, Headman; Fazal.

GARFRAI (170).—A minor fraction of the Shumi Khel, Palli Khel, Manazai, Alizai Mahsuds.

GARWIS (3,000).—A tribe inhabiting the head of the Swat valley. They are probably allied to the Kohistanis.

GAUHAR KHEL.—A minor fraction of Torsam Khel, Nazar Khel, Star Ali Khan Khel, Sarki Khel, Madda Khel (1,600), Ibrahim Khel, Utmanzai, Darwesh Khel, Wazirs.

GAZNI.—A section of Khakizai, Ashazai, Iliaszai, Bunerwals.

GEGA KHEL (140).—A minor fraction of Sher Khel, Haibat Khel, Nana Khel, Bahlolzai, Mahsuds.

GHAIBI KHEL.—A sub-division of Babakri, Sipah (1,200), Afridis. Samil. Headman; Darya Khan.

GHAIBI KHEL.—A sub-division of Bahram-ka-Khel, Bar Ranizai, Akozai—Yusufzai Swatis.

GHAIM KOR.—A minor fraction of Sroh, Busha Khel,

Kamali, Halimzai, Mohmands. Headman; Khanizaman.

GHAIBAT KHEL.—A minor fraction of Bakar Khel, Idal Khel, Hathi Khel (2,000), Shin Khel, Ahmadzai, Darwesh Khel Wazirs.

GHAL.—A minor fraction of Karim Khel, Jamal Khel, Malik Shahi (400), Wali Khel, Utmanzai, Darwesh Khel, Wazirs. Headman; Pirjao.

GHALAP KHEL.—A minor fraction of Dosalli, Wuzi Khel (800), Mohmit Khel, Utmanzai, Darwesh Khel Wazirs.

GHALAT KHEL (Bannu District).—A minor fraction of Kundi, Pirba Khel, Hathi Khel (2,000), Shin Khel, Ahmadzai, Darwesh Khel Wazirs.

GHALIB KHAN KHEL.—A sub-division of Malikdin Khel, Malikdin Khel (4,000), Afridis.. Samil. Headmen; Bazmir, Gholai Jan, Huzrat Gul, Kolkai, Miran Mir, Zaman, Mulla Mansur Payao, Rasul, Salim, Sardar, Akbar, Dostai, Sher Gul, Zarif, Shamsuddin.

GHALIB KHAN KHEL.—A section of the Mir Ahmad Khel, Alisherzai (3,000), Lashkarzai, Orakzais. Samil. Headman; Ibrahim Khan.

GHALIB KHAN KOR.—A minor fraction of Ali Khan Khel, Ali Karan, Mamuzai (3,500). Lashkarzai, Orakzais, Gar. Headman; Arsala.

GHALIB KHEL (151).—A subdivision of the Badanzai, Shaman Khel, Mahsuds.

GHALIBZAI (13).—A division of Drigzai, Lunis. Headmen; Khudar (Jafarzai), Surat (Shambozai), Ghani (Gaganzai).

GHANI KHEL.—A minor fraction of Mir Hasani, Macha, Madda Khel (1,600), Ibrahim Khel, Utmanzai, Darwesh Khel Wazirs.

GHARU KHEL.—A minor fraction of Ashraf Khel, Kamal Khel, Sahib Jan, Aka Khel, (1,800), Afridis. Samil.

GHAZALMAI KILLA (35).—A minor fraction of Dangar Khel, Piran Dangar Khel, Muhammad Khel, Malakh, Mallizad, Dawaris. Headmen; Ghazo Shah, Sarwar.

GHAZI BEG KOR (100).—A section of Ibrahim Khel, Kamali, Halimzai, Mohmands. Headmen ; 'Abbas, Mudasir, Muhammad Gul, Badshah, Gul Said.

GHAZI KHAN (50 ; Black Mountain).—A section of Tasan Khel, Akazai, Isazai, Yusufzais.

GHAZI KHEL.—A minor fraction of Baghdad Khel, Keimal Khel, Urmuz Khel, Sipah (1,200), Afridis. Samil. Headman ; Ahmad Shah.

GHAZI KHEL.—A sub-division of Dawat Khel, Khwaezai, Mohmands. Headman ; Said, who is the Khan of Lalpura's "Kazi."

GHAZI KHEL.—A minor fraction of Mannia Khel, Hassan Khel, Mitha Khan Khel, Kuki Khel, (4,500), Afridis. Gar. Headmen ; see Mashi Khel.

GHAZI KHEL.—A minor fraction of Mamun Kor, Kandai, Isa Khel, Pandiali, Mohmands. Headmen ; see Isa Khel.

GHAZI KOR.—A minor fraction of Durba Khel, Hamza Khel, Gandab, Halimzai, Mohmands. Headman ; see Durba Khel.

GHAZI KOR.—A minor fraction of Yardil Kor, Kadaikor, Gandab, Halimzai, Mohmands. Headmen ; see Yardi Kor.

GHAZIZAI (300).—A section of Mehtarzai, Harun Khel, Sanatia, Kakars. Headman ; Alif.

GHAZIZAI (15).—A sub-division of Shamezai, Rakanwal, Lunis. Headman ; see Shamezai.

GHAZNI KHEL.—A minor fraction of Ismail Khel, Makhozai, Nasuzai, Iliaszai, Bunerwals.

GHILZAI KOR.—A sub-division of Masaud, Safis, a vassal clan of the Mohmands.

GHILZAIS (25,000).—A large and widespread Afghan tribe, who extend[illegible] from Khelat-i-Ghilzai on the south to the Kabul river on the north, and from the Gul Koh range on the west to the Indian Border on the east, in many places overflowing these boundaries. The main branches of the

Ghilzais are the Hotaks, Tokhis, Nasirs, Kharotis, Hezabs, Andars, Tarakis and Sahaks. The Ghilzais all execrate the Duranis, whom they regard as usurpers.

GHOLAM KHEL (50).—A minor fraction of Khuttay, Taib Khel, Amzoni, Mallizad, Dawaris. Headmen; Hathi Khel, Mehtar Shah.

GHOLAM KHEL (7).—A section of Alizai, Darpa Khel, Mallizad, Dawaris. Headman; Sheikh Muhammad Din.

GHORANAI (10).—A division of Drigzai, Lunis.

GHORIZAI (500).—A sub-division of Alizai, Sanzar, Kakars.

GHOZIKAI (40).—A minor fraction of the Panj Pilara, Abdullai, Aimal Khel, Bahlolzai, Mahsuds.

GHOZI KHEL (60).—A minor fraction of the Shah Alam Khel, Kasim Khel, Chahar Khel, Shaman Khel, Mahsuds. Headmen; Nasir Khan, Amin, Shahboz.

GHULAM ALI KHEL.—A minor fraction of Ghuli Khel, Ambar Khel, Mat Khan Khel, Kambar Khel (4,500), Afridis Gar Headmen; Sher Khan, Hamid, and Nurai.

GHULI KHEL.—A section of Amber Khol, Mat Khan Khel, Kambar Khel (4,500), Afridis. Gar. Headmen; Sher Khan. Hamid, Nurai.

GHULAM KHEL.—A minor fraction of Balli Khel. Shadi Khel, Bora Khel (1,000), Utmanzai. Darwesh Khel Wazirs.

GHULAM KHEL (00).—A section of Haibat Khel, Jawaki, Adam Khel, Afridis.

GHULAM KHEL (15; Dera Ismail Khan District).—Nomadic, a minor fraction of Saiad Khel, Isot Khel, Mian Khel. Lohana, Pawindahs. Headman; see Mian Khel.

GHUNDA KHEL.—A minor fraction of Ranra Khel, Shati Khel, Wali Beg Kor, Gandah, Halimzai, Mohmands. This fraction goes with the Buch Khel. Headman; Hazrat Shah.

GHUNDI (15).—A section of Barim Khel, Amzoni,

Mallizad, Dawaris. Headman; Jalat.

GHURBUN.—A section of Dreplara, Shakhi, Waraspun, Battannis.

GHUT KARRA.—A minor fraction of Karra Khel, Ghaibi Khel, Babakri, Sipah (1,200), Afridis. Samil. Headmen, see Korra Khel.

GHWARAZAIS (110; Gomal). A clan of Kakars, living separately from the bulk of the tribe.

GIDI KHEL (1,077).—A sub division of the Manazai, Alizai, Mahsuds.

GIGIANI.—A small clan attached to Ranra Khel, Shati Khel, Wali Beg Kor, Gandab, Halimzai, Mohmands. Headman; Mir Bajan.

GILAL (600).—A clan of Allaiwals.

GIGIANIS.—See Gugianis.

GIRANI KHEL.—A minor fraction of Muhammad Khel (700), Isperka, Kalu Khel, Ahmadzai, Darwesh Khel Wazirs.

GITA KHEL (75.)—A section of Muhammad Khel, Malakh, Mallizad, Dawaris. Headmen; Muhammad Azam, Sawan, Watanai.

GOGAI.—A minor fraction of Mandi Khel, Wuzi Khel (800), Mohmit Khel, Utmanzai, Darwesh Khel Wazirs.

GOHURA KOR.—A minor fraction of Behram Kor, Dildar Khel, Mohmand Khel, Kattia Khel, Hassan Khel, Mitha Khan Khel, Kuki Khel (4,500), Afridis. Gar. Headmen; Ghanni and Torbaz.

GORAI (600; Scattered on confines of Bajaur).—One of the eight clans of the Utman Khels.

GORI KHEL.—A minor fraction of Khoji Khel, Bozi Khel, Madda Khel (1,600), Ibrahim Khel, Utmanzai, Darwesh Khel Wazirs.

GOWHAR KHEL.—A section of Durbi Khel, Kambar Khel, Kambar Khel (4,500), Afridis. Gar. Headmen; Muhammad Sher, Khwaja Ali, Yaro, Nurai.

GUJARS.—A stalwart Mussalman pastoral tribe of Aryan or Tartar origin, scattered in large numbers amongst the Pathan tribes, from the Black Mountain to the Kunar river. They own separate villages in or near the lower hills, and in summer migrate with their flocks to the mountains. Gujars are numerous in north-western India and Kashmir. They speak the language of their winter homes, but have a few words peculiar to themselves.

GUGIANI.—(Peshawar District). A tribe who inhabit the *Doaba* or plain in the angle between the Kabul and Swát rivers.

GUL AHMAD KOR.—A section of Khalil Khel, Kasim Khel, Tarakzai, Mohmands. Headman; Saifal.

GULA KHEL.—A minor fraction of Pira Khel, Mir Hasani, Macha, Madda Khel (1,600), Ibrahim Khel, Utmanzai, Darwesh Khel Wazirs.

GULA KHEL (70).—A minor fraction of Walidad Khel, Ladi Khel, Abdullai, Aimal Khel, Bahlolzai, Mahsuds. Headman; Aligai.

GULANZAI (West of Dera Ghazi Khan District).—A section of Inzai, Hasan Khel, Balil Khel, Musa Khels. Headman; Haru.

GULAPIR (10).—A section of Barim Khel, Amzoni, Mallizad. Dawaris. Headman; Gulapir.

GULDIN KHEL.—A minor fraction of Dawar Khel, Ismail Khel, Bozi Khel, Madda Khel (1,600), Ibrahim Khel, Utmanzai, Darwesh Khel Wazirs.

GULI KHEL.—A section of Adizai, Bobak, Dana, Battannis.

GUL KHEL.—A section of Ali Khel, Bobak, Dana, Battannis.

GULLA KHEL (Wana).—A minor fraction of Zalli Khel (3,000), Bomi Khel, Nasradin, Kalu Khel, Ahmadzai, Darwesh Khel Wazirs.

GULLI KHEL (Bannu District).—A minor fraction of Waligai, Musa Khel, Hathi Khel (2,000), Shin Khel, Ahmadzai, Darwesh Khel Wazirs. Headman; Adam Khan.

GULNAM KHEL (15).—A minor fraction of Poi Khel,

Muhammad Khel, Malakh, Mallizad, Dawaris. Headman; Gulnam.

GULO KHEL (Yakhdand).—A division of Utmanzai, Mohmands. Headmen; see Utmanzai.

GUMARZAI (West of Dera Ghazi Khan District).—A section of Kabalzai Nokuzai, Laharzai, Musa Khels. Headman; Khatol.

GUNDA KHEL (Mahaban).—A section of Hasanbaz Khel, Mada Khel, Isazai, Yusufzais. Headmen; see Hasanbaz Khel.

GUNDI KHEL (1,000; Kuram).—A sub-division of Landizai, Chardai, Turis.

GUNNA KHEL (60).—A minor fraction of the Shamak Khel, Abdullai, Aimal Khel, Bahlolzai, Mahsuds. Headman; Mamak.

GURBAZ (1,000; southern border of Khost).—Originally a clan of Wazir origin who have since lost all connection with the parent tribe. A few families still reside in Shawal, (Headmen; Khan Sahib and Paidil) in the Tochi, (Headman; Massan Shah) at Spin Nimal Khel in Mahsud country, and at Miriam, in Bannu District.

GURBUZ.—A minor fraction of Khan Khel, Takhto Khel, Bakka Khel (1,000), Wali Khel, Utmanzai, Darwesh Khel Wazirs. Headman; Rahmat Shah.

GURBUZ.—One of the four divisions of the Safis, who are a vassal clan of the Mohmands.

GURBUZAI (35).—A sub-division of Darpa Khel, Mallizad, Dawaris. Headmen; Shahzada, Shadi Khel, Manzar Khel, Shahdarra.

GURRI KHEL (120).—A minor fraction of the Dachi Khel, Palli Khel, Manazai, Alizai, Mahsuds.

GURRI KHEL (60).—A section of the Shamerai, Manazai, Alizai, Mahsuds. Headmen; Zale Khan, Karim Khan, Loku.

H

Habib.—A sub-division of Nasruddin (1,200 to 1,500), Zakha Khel, Afridis. Samil. Headmen; Chikkun, Tamas, Anwar, Nazr Din.

Habibian.—A minor fraction of Dreplara, Paindai (940), Nasruddin, Zakha Khel, Afridis. Samil. Headmen; see Habib.

Habibzai (30).—A sub-division of Manuzai, Oba Khel, Sheranis.

Hafiz Kor.—A section of Kani Khel, Kasim Khel. Tarakzai, Mohmands. Headman; Abdullah.

Haiat Khel.—A minor fraction of Musa Khel, Makhozai Nasuzai, Iliaszai, Bunerwals.

Haiazi.—A division of the Mahmud Khel, Zmarais. Headman; Sardar Hakim Khan.

Haibat Khel.—A minor fraction of Dardoni, Wuzi Khel, (8(0), Mohmit Khel, Utmanzai. Darwesh Khel Wazirs.

Haibat Khel (1,100).—A sub-division of Jawaki, Adam Khel, Afridis.

Haibat Khel (1,118).—The most important sub-division of the Nana Khel, Bahlolzai, Mahsuds.

Haibat Khel.—A minor fraction of Aka Khel, Ismailzai, Daulatzai, Malizai, Bunerwals.

Haibtanai.—A section of Tori Khel (2,670), Ibrahim Khel, Utmanzai, Darwesh Khel Wazirs. Headmen; Gulzamir Khan, Miandad, and Lal Khan.

Haidar Ali Khel.—A section of the Fateh Khan Khel, Utman Khel (400), Daulatzai, Orakzais. Samil.

Haidar Khel (Mastura valley).—One of the four divisions of the Mishtis (3,000), "Hamsayas" of the; Orakzais. Samil. Headman Mehrban.

Haidar Khel.—A section of the Ali Karan, Mamuzai,

Lashkarzai, Orakzais. Gar. Headman; Lal Khan.

HAIDAR KHEL.—A section of the Mir Ahmad Khel, (Mir Hussain Khel), Firoz Khel (1,000), Daulatzai, Orakzais. Samil. Headman; Shirin.

HAIDAR KHEL (852).—A sub-division of the Tor, Tappizad, Dawaris. Headmen; Mad Alam, Alif Khan, Gul Khan, Lal Khan, Nazar Khan.

HAIDAR KOR.—A sub-division of Asaf Khel, Tarakzai, Mohmands. Headmen; see Asaf Khel.

HAIDRAI (123).—A sub-division of Chahar Khel, Shaman Khel, Mahsuds.

HAJAI KOR.—A sub-division of Babazai Kor, Dawezai, Mohmands. Headmen; Hazur Khan, Khalik Jan.

HAIDARZAI (100).—A sub-division of Alizai, Sanzar, Kakars.

HAIDARZAI (280).—A section of Natozai, Dumar, Sanzar, Kakars. Headman; Khani.

HAJI KHEL (20).—A minor fraction of Poi Khel, Muhammad Khel, Malakh, Mallizad, Dawaris. Headman; Juma Khan.

HAJI KHEL (400).—A clan of Chamkannis.

HAJI KOR.—A division of Utmanzai Mohmands. Headman; see Utmanzais.

HAJIZAI.—A sub-division of Ladu, Rakanwal, Lunis. Headman; see Ladu.

HAKIM KHEL.—A minor fraction of Machi Khel, Abdul Khel, Bara Khel (1,000), Mohmit Khel, Utmanzai, Darwesh Khel Wazirs.

HAKIM KHEL.—A minor fraction of Pira Khel, Jamal Khel, Malik Shahi (400), Wali Khel, Utmanzai, Darwesh Khel Wazirs. Headman; Zariban.

HAKIM KHEL.—A minor fraction of Sani Khel, Zargun Khel (300), Galai, Adam Khel, Afridis.

HAKIM KHEL.—A minor fraction of Sharagh Khel, Kadam Khel, Firoz Khel, Mashi Khel, Mannia Khel, Hassan Khel, Mitha Khan Khel, Kuki Khel (4,500), Afridis. Gar. Headmen; Abbas, Hakim and Nazir.

Hakim Khel (99).—A subdivision of Mubarak Shahi, Mallizad, Dawaris. Headmen; Shandai, Ahmad Shah, Mir Alam, and Sakhadin.

Hakimzai (30).—A section of Sah, Yahia Khel, Sen Khel, Sheranis.

Halal Tabar.—A minor fraction of Sikandar Khel, Kandai, Isa Khel Pandiali, Mohmands. For Headmen; see Isa Khel.

Halim Kor.—A minor fraction of Bucha Khel, Durar (300), Khusrogi, Nasruddin, Zakha Khel Afridis. Samil. Headmen; see Bucha Khel.

Halimzai (130).—A section of Bazai, Harun Khel, Sanatia, Kakars. Headmen; Taj Muhammad and Zargar.

Halimzais of Gandab (1,650).—A sub-division (according to location) of the Halimzai Gandab Mohmands. For headmen; see Sultan Khel, Durba Khel Babi Khel, Baru Khel, Yardil Kor, Rahmatal Kor, Tatasar, Dawat Khel, Rami Khel, Shati Khel, Rasul Khel. See note on page 46.

Halimzais of Kamali (800).—A division (according to location) of Halimzai Kamali Mohmands. For headmen; see Lakai Kor, Khwaju Kuhai Kor, Ghazi Beg Kor, Nahaki or Yusuf Kor, Hamza Khel (Kamali), Ato Khel, Sroh. See note on page 46.

Halkamar Kor.—A minor fraction of Rasul Kor, Wali Beg Kor, Gandab, Halimzai, Mohmands. Headmen; Abdulla Khan, Yakub, Kokai.

Hamsayagan (20).—A section of Hakim Khel, Mubarak Shahi, Mallizad, Dawaris. Headmen; Mir Alam, Sakhadin, Jamadar.

Hamsayajan (13).—A section of Nawar Khel, Miram Shah, Tappizad, Dawaris. Headmen; Mir Hassan, Gulistan, Pir Khan.

Hamza Khel (1,000; Kuram).—A division of Sargalli, Turis.

Hamza Khel (450).—A subdivision of Gandab, Halimzai, Mohmands. For headmen; see Sultan Khel, Durba Khel, Babi Khel, Baru Khel.

HAMZA KHEL of KAMALI (150).—A sub-division of Kamali, Halimzai, Mohmands. Headmen; Jamal Khan (Durba Khel), Jabbar, Raza Khan, Faiz Talab, Ghani, Jamal, Muhabbat, Zarghun, Ghansai, Jangia, Baz Khan, Zainulla Khan, Sarfaraz Khan, Morcha, Dara Shah, Ajmer.

HAMZA KHEL.—A section of Barkazai, Daulatzai, Malizai, Bunerwals.

HAMZAZAI (1,000; West of Dera Ghazi Khan District).—A division of Balil Khel, Musa Khels.

HAMZAZAIS (2,000; Mekhtar). A division of Sanzar, Kakars. Headmen; Gano (Pakehzai), Anwar Khan (Barozai), Wazir Khan (Mahozai), Shama Khan (Mandozai), Yasin (Sofarzai).

HANGU KHEL (Bannu District).—A minor fraction of Dodi Khel, Khandar Khan Khel, Hathi Khel, Shin Khel, Ahmadzai, Darwesh Khel Wazirs.

HANI.—A sub-division of Panezun, Sanzar, Kakars.

HARAMZAI (60).—A division of Mathel, Sheranis.

HARIF KOR (Part in Mohmand, part in British territory).—A section of Kani Khel, Kasim Khel, Tarakzai, Mohmands. Headmen; Khad Gul, Khadi Gul, Jallal, Zehr Gul.

HARIPAL (800).—A clan of Sheranis. Headman; Mulla Abdul Hak.

HARUN KHEL (6,108).—One of the two divisions of Samatia, Kakars. Headmen; Guldad (Shamozai), Sirdar Habo Khan (Mehtarzai), Sirdar Bai Khan (Sarangzai), Baidula (Bazai), Sirdar Ibrahim Khan (Panizai).

HARUN KHEL (100; Dera Ismail Khan District).—Nomadic, a minor fraction of Baloch Khel, Isot Khel, Mian Khel, Lohana, Pawindahs. Headman; see Mian Khel.

HASAN BEG KHEL.—A minor fraction of Kandao Khel (400), Ashu Khel, Hassan Khel, Adam Khel, Afridis.

HASAN KHEL (450; Mahaban). A sub-division of Mada Khel, Isazai, Yusufzais.

HASAN KHEL.—A minor fraction of Jalal Khel, Mali (or

Muli)Khel, Salarzai, Iliaszai, Bunerwals.

HASAN KHEL.—A sub-division of Gadaizai, Iliaszai, Bunerwals.

HASAN KHEL.—A sub-division of Shamezai, Khwazazai, Akozai—Yusufzai Swatis.

HASAN KHEL (296).—A division of Khoidad Khel, Zaimukhts.

HASAN KHEL.—A minor fraction of Mawal Khel (760), Haibat Khel, Jawaki, Adam Khel, Afridis.

HASAN KHEL (1,500; West of Dera Ghazi Khan District).—A division of Balil Khel, Musa Khels.

HASANBAZ KHEL (450; Mahaban).—A sub-division of Mada Khel, Isazai, Yusufzais.

ASAN ZAI (50).—A section of Barakzai, Taraghari, Sanzar, Kakars. Headman; Guli.

HASANZAIS (2,300; Black Mountain and both sides of Indus). A division of Isazai, Yusufzais. Headmen; Hashim Ali Khan, (Khan Khel, and Khan of the Hasanzais), Hamid Khan (Kotwal), Sherdad (Mir Ahmad Khel), Najim Khan, (Zakaria Khel), Tora Khan, (Lughman Khel), Aladad (Kaka Khel), Saiad Azim Shah.

HASHAM KOR (Utmanzai); (Yakhdand).—A division of Utmanzai, one of the affiliated Mohmand clans. Headmen; see Utmanzai.

HASHAM KOR (Khwaezai).—A sub-division of Khadi Khel, Khwaezai, Mohmands.

HASHMI KHEL.—A section of of the Bazar Khan Khel, Utman Khel (400), Daulatzai, Orakzais. Samil.

HASN.—A sub-division of Panezun, Sanzar, Kakars.

HASSANI KOR.—A sub-division of Muhammad Khan Kor, Burhan Khel, Mohmands. Headmen; Said Gul, Shahlai, Badshah, Narai, Malik.

HASSAN KHANZAI (2).—A sub-division of Salezai, Rakanwal, Lunis. Headman; see Salezai.

HASSÁN KHEL.—A sub-division of Abba Khel, Tatta, Battannis.

HASSAN KHEL (Ningrahar and Upper Helmand).—Nomadic, A sub-division of Dawezai, Kuchis. Headmen ; Haji Islam, Abdul Karim, Abdul Wahab, Ghulam, Lalagai.

HASSAN KHEL.—A sub-division of Alisherzai (3,000), Lashkarzai, Orakzais. Samil. Headman ; Shalabaz.

HASSAN KHEL (30).—A section of Shamerai, Manazai, Alizai, Mahsuds. Headmen ; Khudari, Zardast.

HASSAN KHEL (40).—A minor fraction of the Kharmach Khel, Nazar Khel, Aimal Khel, Bahlolzai, Mahsuds. Headmen ; Aitwar, Ashik, Shawar Din.

HASSAN KHEL.—A division of Dawezai, Mohmands. Headman ; Habib Jan.

HASSAN KHEL (400 ; Kaitu and Laram).—A sub-division of Mohmit Khel, Utmanzai, Darwesh Khel Wazirs. Headmen ; see Muhammad Khel and Balal Khel.

HASSAN KHEL.—A sub-division of Khabi Khel, Malikdin Khel (4,000), Afridis. Samil. Headmen ; Darya Khan, Dauran, Yar Khan.

HASSAN KHEL.—A section of Pakkai (1,000), Budai, Zakha Khel, Afridis. Samil. Headmen ; Zarin, Sharabat, Saidai, Mirdin, Madrai, Nadir, Golab Shah.

HASSAN KHEL. (1,900 ; Kohat pass).—A division of Adam Khel, Afridis.

HASSAN KHEL.—A sub-division of Mitha Khan Khel, Kuki Khel (4,500), Afridis. Gar. Headmen ; Zaman Khan is the chief ; see also Makki Khel, Futteh Khel and Mohmand Khel.

HASSAN KHEL.—A sub-division of Shekh Ali Khel, Kamrai Khel (600), Afridis. Samil. Headmen ; Mulla Amir Shah, Mulla Akhundzada, and Sher Walli.

HASSAN KHEL (70).—A section of Urmuz, Tor, Mallizad, Dawaris. Headmen ; Nezam Din, Sheikhdan.

HASSAN KOR (Loi Shilman).—A section of Shah Mansur Khel, Dadu Khel, Tarakzai, Mohmands. Headmen ; Khaista Khan, Gulistan.

HASSANZAI (Mastura valley).—One of the four divisions of the Mishtis (3,000), "Hamsayas" of the Orakzais. Samil.

HASSEN KHEL (340).—A sub-division of Mada Khel, Isazai, Yusufzais.

HASSU KHEL (808).—A sub-division of Tor, Mallizad, Dawaris. Headmen; Bedil, Dini, Painda Khan, Madda Khel, Gul Hassan, Mir Kazam, Faujdar, Mad Afzal, Badar, Mir Kazam.

HATAI KOR.—A sub-division of Muhammad Khan Kor, Burhan Khel, Mohmands. Headmen; Mahar Khan, Azam, Razo, Saiddal, Muhammad Shere.

HATHI KHEL (2,000; Bannu District, Thal, Shakai, Birmal and Wana). A sub-division of Shin or Sani Khel, Ahmadzai, Darwesh Khel Wazirs. Headmen; see Khandar Khan Khel, Idal Khel, Pirba Khel and Musa Khel.

HATI KHEL.—A section of Mali (or Muli) Khel, Salarzai, Iliaszai, Bunerwals.

HATU KHEL (5; Dera Ismail Khan District).—Nomadic, a minor fraction of Shadi Khel, Isot Khel, Mian Khel, Lohana, Pawindahs. Headman; see Mian Khel.

HAZAR BUZ.—Nomadic, a sub-division of Dawezai, Kuchi, Mohmands. Headmen; Sher Muhammad, Fazl, Fazli Ahmad.

HEZAI (West of the Dera Ghazi Khan District).—A sub-division of Hamzazai, Balil Khel, Musa Khels. Headman; Saidal.

HEZAI (115).—See Yahia Ahmad Khel, Oba Khel, Sheranis.

HIDARZAI (100).—A section of Barakzai, Yahia Khel, Sen Khel, Sheranis.

HIDER KHEL (97).—A division of Chuar Khel, Sheranis.

HILAL KHEL.—A section of Keimal Khel, Urmuz Khel, Sipah (1,200), Afridis. Samil. Headman; Gul Salim.

HIMMAT KOR.—A minor fraction of Ghazi Khel, Mannia Khel, Hassan Khel, Mitha Khan Khel, Kuki Khel (4,500), Afridis. Headmen; see Mashi Khel.

HINDI KHEL.—A minor fraction of Tor, Jani Khel (1,000), Wali Khel, Utmanzai, Darwesh Khel Wazirs. Headmen; Malkun, Pir Makhmad.

HINDKI.—The name given to the Hindus who inhabit Afghanistan. They are of the Khatri class, and are found all over the country, even among the wildest tribes. Bellew estimates their number at about 300,000 souls. The name Hindki is also loosely used on the Upper Indus, in Dir, Bajaur &c. to denote the speakers of Punjabi or any of its dialects; and it is further sometimes applied, in a historical sense, to the Buddhist inhabitants of the Peshawar valley north of the Kabul river, who were driven thence about the 5th or 6th century, and settled in the neighbourhood of Kandahar.

HINDKI KOR.—A minor fraction of Rasul Kor, Wali Beg Kor, Gandab, Halimzai, Mohmands. Headmen; Malikdad, Hussain, Gulab Khan.

HINDUSTANI FANATICS.—A band of fanatics recruited from Hindustan, who have inhabited various portions of the Chagharzai, Amazai, Chamla, and Buner hills. They are now said to be residing in Chagharzai territory, and to number some 900 men under their aged leader, Maulvi Saiad Abdulla. Latest information points to their desire to return to Amazai limits.

HOSENZAI (250).—A minor fraction of Barakzai, Targhari, Sanzar, Kakars.

HOTIZAI (8).—A sub-division of Malezai, Rakanwal, Lunis.

HOZI KHEL (23).—A section of Gurbuzai, Darpa Khel, Mallizad, Dawaris. Headmen; Damai, Zerakki, Madi Shah, Zanpir Shah.

HURAMZAI (300; Zhob).—A division of (Northern) Sanzar, Kakars.

HURUM SHAZAI (150).—A minor fraction of Mulazai, Panizai, Harun Khel, Sanatia, Kakars. Headman; Mulla Nur Muhammad.

HUSAIN KHEL (Sen Khel).—A sub-division of Utmanzai, Bar Ranizai, Akozai—Yusufzai Swatis.

HUSENZAI (West of Dera Ghazi Khan District).—A sub-division of Ahmadzai, Balil Khel, Musa Khels.

HUSENZAI.—A division of Mahmud Khel, Zmarais.

Headmen; Kaki Khan Landai.

HUSSAIN KHEL.—A sub-division of Khabi Khel, Malikdin Khel (4,000), Afridis. Samil. Headmen; Darya Khan, Dauran, Yar Khan.

HUSSAIN KHEL.—A division of Haji Khel, Chamkannis.

HUSSAIN KHEL (10).—A sub-division of Khaddi, Mallizad, Dawaris. Headmen; Janai, Sheikh Majid.

HUSSEIN KHEL.—A division of Salarzai, Tarkanis.

HYATAI KOR (400).—A section of Shah Mansur Khel, Dadu Khel, Tarakzai, Mohmands. Headmen; Abdullah, Babujan, Sayad Rasul, Dawezai, Sofi, Multan.

HYDER KHEL.—A minor fraction of Khizar Khel, Mintar Khel, Muhammad Khel, Hassan Khel (400), Mohmit Khel, Utmanzai. Darwesh Khel Wazirs. Headman; Misrai.

I

IBA KHEL (12).—A section, of Tarota, Idak, Tappizad, Dawaris. Headman; Faqir.

IBRAHIM KHEL.—A minor fraction of Kasim Khel (250), Timal Khel, Jawaki, Adam Khel, Afridis.

IBRAHIM KHEL.—A minor fraction of Daulat Khel, Ghalib Khan Khel, Malikdin Khel, Malikdin Khel (4,000), Afridis. Samil. Headmen; see Daulat Khel.

IBRAHIM KHEL.—A sub-division of Landi Khel, Sipah (1,200), Afridis. Samil. Haedmen; Amir, Walli.

IBRAHIM KHEL.—A minor fraction of Tarkial Khel, Mughal Khel, Barmi Khel, Kamrai Khel (600), Afridis. Samil. Headmen; Amar, Bahadur Shah, Sifat Shah, Sheradin, Zardad Mir Ali.

IBRAHIM KHEL (4,630).—One of the three great divisions of the Utmanzai branch of the Darwesh Khel Wazirs, viz., Mohmit Khel, Wali Khel) and Ibrahim Khel, The Ibrahim Khel includes the Manzar, Madda and Tori Khels. Headmen; see the above sub-divisions.

IBRAHIM KHEL.—A sub-division of Utmanzai, Bar Kanizai, Akozai—Yusufzai Swatis. Headmen; Alam Khan, Aslam Khan.

IBRAHIM KHEL.—A minor fraction of Musa Khel, Makozai, Nasuzai, Iliaszai, Bunerwals.

IBRAHIM KHEL.—A sub-division of Gadaizai, Iliaszai, Bunerwals.

IBRAHIM KHEL (Bajaur).—A division of Salarzai, Tarkanis. This is the "Khan" Khel of the elan.

IBRAHIM KHEL (Kharmana river).—A minor fraction of the Abdul Mirzi (410), Landaizai, Masuzai, Lashkarzai, Orakzais. Gar. Headmen; Azghar, Hazrat Nur, Hussain.

IBRAHIM KHEL (400).—A sub-division of Kamali, Halimzai, Mohmands. Headmen; Antar, Arsalla Khan, Redai, Nurai, Umar Din, Dauran Shah. (Lakai Kor and Khwazu Kuhai Kor.)—Abbas, Mudassir, Muhammad Gul Badshah, Gul Said. (Ghazi Beg Kor).—Saimal Gul Shah, Zai Khan, Post Khan, Gul Hamesh. (Nahaki or Yusaf Kor).

IBRAHIM KOR.—A minor fraction of Dildar Khel, Mohmand Khel, Kathia Khel, Hasan Khel, Mitha Khan Khel, Kuki Khel (4,500), Afridis. Gar. Headmen; Baghi, Saidal.

IBRAHIM KOR. (Loi Shilman).—A minor fraction of Durma Kor, Shah Mansur Khel, Dadu Khel, Tarakzai Mohmands.

IBRAHIM TABAR.—A minor fraction of Rajai Khel, Yusuf Khel, Isa Khel, Pandiali, Mohmands. Headmen; see Isa Khel.

IBRAHIM ZAI (40).—A division of Marhel, Sheranis.

IBRAHIMZAIS (Zhob).—A section of Shadozai, Ali Khel, Sanzar, Kakars.

IDAK (615).—A division of the Tappizad, Dawaris. Some authorities however, say they are a separate clan belonging neither to Tappizad, nor Mallizad. Headmen; Mazaiband, Daisab.

IDAL KHEL (Bannu, Shakai' Birmal and Wana).—A section of Hathi Khel (2,000), Shin Khel, Ahmadzai, Darwesh Khel Wazirs. Headmen; Bandar Khan, Sheikh Piyao, Landai, Rasim Shah.

IDAL KHEL.— A sub-division of Ali Khel, Bar Ranizai, Akozai—Yusafzai Swatis.

IDAL KHEL (72).—A section of Muhammad Khel, Malakh, Mallizad Dawaris. Headmen; Kazi, Shahid Khan.

IDAR KHEL.—A minor fraction of Ali Khel, Khaddar Khel (770), Mohmit Khel, Utmanzai, Darwesh Khel Wazirs. Headmen; Nur Muhammad, Ahmad Din, Makach, Ziarai, Sakhe Man, Akhmad, Nambuti.

IDIA KHEL.—A section of Jani Khel (1,000), Wali Khel, Utmanzai. Darwesh Khel Wazirs. Headmen; Nazam Khan, Mir Birjan, Zarghun Shah, Gul Ghafar, Akaldin, Zargai, Sheikh Majid.

IDU KHEL.—A section of Ali Khel, Bobak, Dana, Battannis.

IKHTAYAR KHEL.—A minor fraction of Badi Khel, Dardoni, Wuzi Khel (800), Mohmit Khel, Utmanzai, Darwesh Khel Wazirs.

IKHTIYAR KHEL.—A minor fraction of Mohib Khel, Shekhai, Annai (1,000), Budal, Zakha Khel, Afridis. Samil. Headmen; Mir Khan, Kadir.

IKHTIYAR KHEL.—A sub-division of Yar Ali Khel, Kamrai Khel (600), Afridis. Samil.

IKHTIYAR KOR (Kharmana river).—A minor fraction of Ash Khel (580), Khwaja Khel, Masuzai, Lashkarzai, Orakzais. Samil. Headman; Said Ali.

IKHTIYAR KOR (Loi Shilman).—A minor fraction of Durma Kor, Shah Mansur Khel, Dadu Khel, Tarakzai, Mohmands.

ILAL KHEL.—A division of Salarzai, Tarkanis.

ILIASZAI (6,000; Buner valley. Slopes of Dosirri range): One of the two clans of Bunerwals. Headman; Hastam Khan of Bampokha, (Salarzai).

IMAR KHEL.—A minor fraction of Torsam Khel, Nazar Khel, Star Ali Khan Khel, Sarki Khel, Madda Khel (1,600), Ibrahim Khel, Utmanzai, Darwesh Khel Wazirs.

INAM KHOR.—A sub-division of Wara, Mamund, Tarkanis.

INDAS KHEL.—A minor fraction of Bizen Khel (700), Shadi Khel, Nasra Din, Kalu Khel, Ahmadzai, Darwesh Khel Wazirs. Headman ; Nazir Khan.

INDUS KHEL.—A minor fraction of Indus Khel, Drepillari, Sarki Khel, Madda Khel (1,600), Ibrahim Khel, Utmanzai, Darwesh Khel Wazirs.

INDUS KHEL.—A minor fraction of Drepillari, Sarki Khel, Madda Khel (1,600), Ibrahim Khel, Utmanzai, Darwesh Khel Wazirs.

INUS KHEL.—A minor fraction of Painda Khel, Manak Khel, Pakhshi Khel, Madda Khel (1,600), Ibrahim Khel, Utmanzai, Darwesh Khel Wazirs.

INZAI (West of Dera Ghazi Khan District).—A sub-division of Hasan Khel, Balil Khel, Musa Khels.

IPI (186).—A section of Haidar Khel, Tor, Tappizad Dawaris. Headmen ; Andaram Khan, Fatteh Khan, Kashmir, Ibrahim Gul.

IRABZAI.—A section of Ahmad Khel, Targhari, Sanzar, Kakars (Hamsayas).

ISAB KHEL (40).—A section of Tappi Khel, Badanzai, Shaman Khel, Mahsuds. Headman ; Adil Din.

ISAB KHEL.—A minor fraction of Shadi Khel, Bara Khel (1000), Mohmit Khel, Utmanzai, Darwesh Khel Wazirs.

ISAB KHEL (20).—A minor fraction of Nasr Khel, Haidar Khel, Tor, Tappizad, Dawaris. Headmen ; Shujo, Ghazo.

ISA KHEL (Jarobi).—A sub-division of Usman Khel, Baezai, Mohmands. Headmen ; Payo, Tola, Gul Muhammad, Mazid.

ISA KHEL (21).—A section of the Birri Khel, Galeshahi, Shaman Khel, Mahsuds. Headmen ; Piyao Shah and Kasab.

ISA KHEL.—A section of the Umar Khan Khel Alisherzai (3,000), Lashkarzai, Orakzais. Samil. Headman ; Ahmad.

ISA KHEL (250 ; Samana with Mishtis and Ali Khels) A

divisions of the Ismailzai, Orakzais. A religious sect. Samil.

Isa Khel.—A minor fraction of Bakar Khel, Idal Khel, Hathi Khel, Shin Khel, Ahmedzai, Darwesh Khel Wazirs. Headman; Sheikh Piyao.

Isa Khel.—A minor fraction of Dosalli, Wuzi Khel (800), Mohmit Khel, Utmanzai, Darwesh Khel Wazirs.

Isa Khel.—A minor fraction of Saifali, Kabul Khel (4,600), Wali Khel, Utmanzai, Darwesh Khel Wazirs.

Isa Khel (398).—A sub-division of the Ahmad Khel, Oba Khel, Sheranis.

Isa Khel (1,265).—One of the two divisions of Sanatia, Kakars.

Isa Khel (500).—A division of Pandiali, Mohmands. Headmen; Ghulam Khan Pai-ud-din, Hakim, Shah Dad, Guldost, Rahmgul-Kachkol, Chat, Said Khan, Sohbat, Zaidullah.—See note on page 46.

Isa Khel.—A minor fraction of Mandi Khel, Wuzi Khel (800), Mohmit Khel, Utmanzai, Darwesh Khel, Wazirs.

Isazai (West of Dera Ghazi Khan District).—A sub-division of Hozai, Laharzai, Musa Khels. Headman; Gulsher.

Isazai (44).—A division of Drigzai, Lunis.

Isazais (Bajaur).—One of the four clans of Tarkanis occupying the Jandol valley. Headman; Saiad Ahmad Khan.

Isazais.*—(On the Indus between the Black Mountain and Mahaban). A clan of Yusufzais.

Isuzai.—A division of Alizai, Utman Khels.

Ismail.—A section of Khadin Khel, Ashazai, Iliaszai, Bunerwals.

Ismail Khel. (3,000; Shamil valley, Khost).—A clan of Khostwals.

Ismail Khel.—A section of Makhozai, Nasuzai, Iliaszai, Bunerwals.

Ismail Khel.—A sub-division of Sultan-ka-khel, Bar Ranizai, Akozai—Yusufzai Swatis.

* This term is not much used.

ISMAIL KHEL.—A sub-division of the Khoja Hawas Khel, Ali Khel (3,000), "Hamsayas" of the Orakzais. Gar. ⅓ Shiah.

ISMAIL KHEL.—A section of the Sturi Khel (400), Alizai (Sturi Khel), Daulatzai, Orakzais. Samil. Headman; Madak.

ISMAIL KHEL.—A minor fraction of Bozi Khel, Madda Khel (1,600), Ibrahim Khel, Utmanzai, Darwesh Khel Wazirs. Headmen; Rahman Shah, Nazar Khan.

ISMAIL KHEL (150).—A section of Kimat Khel, Jawaki, Adam Khel, Afridis.

ISMAIL KHEL.—A minor fraction of Warrukai, Idia Khel, Jani Khel (1,000), Wali Khel, Utmanzai, Darwesh Khel Wazirs. Headman; Zargai.

ISMAIL KHEL.—A minor fraction of Dildar Khel, Mohmand Khel, Kattia Khel, Hassan Khel, Mitha Khan Khel, Kuki Khel (4,500), Afridis. Gar. Headmen; Kamlar, Boner, Kaddam Khan.

ISMAIL KOR.—A section of Hatai Kor, Muhammad Khan Kor, or 'Bar' Burhan Khel, Pandiali, Mohmands. Headman; Muhammad Shere.

ISMAILAK.—A section of Dreplara, Sakhi, Waraspun, Battannis.

ISMAILALAGH (361).—A division of Spin, Tarins. Headmen; Sher Khan, Panid Khan, Mobin and others.

ISMAILZAI (Gomal).—A division of Miani, Sheranis.

ISMAILZAI.—A sub-division of Daulatzai, Malizai, Bunerwals.

ISMAILZAI (8,100).—The most powerful of the eight clans of the Utman Khels.

ISMAILZAI (70).—A sub-division of Manuzai, Aba Khel, Sheranis.

ISMAILZAI (Zhob).—A sub-division of the Alizai, Sanzar, Kakars.

ISMAILZAI (2,030; Samana and the Khanki valley).—One of the four clans of the Orakzais; 600 Gar, remainder Samil. Headman; Ramzan.

ISMAILZAI (7).—A section of Barim Khel, Amzoni, Mallizad, Dawaris. Headman; Haji Muhammad.

ISOT KHEL (600; Dera Ismail Khan District).—Nomadic, a sub-division of Mian Khel, Lohana, Pawindahs. Headman; Azim Khan, (Mian Khel).

ISOTS or SOTS (480).—A small tribe of nomads, who live in the caves of hills west of the Dera Ismail Khan frontier. Headman; Bhagu Khan, Nohzai.

ISPERKA (1,350; Bannu District, Shakai and Birmal).—A sub-division of Kalu Khel, Ahmadzai, Darwesh Khel Wazirs. Headmen; Mani Khan is the leading man; for others, see Muhammad Khel, Sudan Khel, Sadda Khel.

ISPIN KHEL (8).—A section of Shujawal, Mubarak Shahi, Mallizad, Dawaris. Headmen; Idak, Mir Kazam.

ISSUBI (135).—A sub-division of Tor, Tappizad, Dawaris. Headmen; Samand Khan, Muni Shah, Khwaja Muhammad Khan.

J

JABALZAI (100).—A section of Brahimzai, Yahia Khel, Sen Khel, Sheranis.

JABAR KHEL.—A minor fraction of Manak Khel, Bakhshi Khel, Madda Khel (1,600), Ibrahim Khel, Utmanzai, Darwesh Khel Wazirs.

J[illegible]AR KHEL.—A section of Musa Khel, Sepah, Baezai, Mohmands. Headmen; Khairat, Ahmad Nur, Rahmat, Sarfaraz.

JABI KHEL (Bajaur).—A division of Samilzai, Tarkanis.

JABI KOR.—A minor fraction of Sangar Khel, Yusuf Khel, Isa Khel, Pandiali, Mohmands. Headmen; see Yusuf Khel.

JADOR (180; Black Mountain).—A division of Deshiwal, Swatis. Headmen; Ambul Shahi, Izzatullah.

JADRANS; see ZADRANS.

Jadrans.—A small tribe, occupying the east slopes of the Suliman range, east of Zurmat.

Jaduns.; see Gaduns.

Jafar Khel.—A minor fraction of Daulat Khel, Ghalib Khan Khel, Malikdin Khel, Malikdin Khel (4,000), Afridis. Samil. Headmen; see Daulat Khel.

Jafars (630).—A small tribe living on the spurs of the Suliman range. Headman; Kalu Khan.

Jajis.—(1,590; Khost, in the valley of the Hariab, an affluent of the Kuram river beyond the British border).—A tribe of Khost.

Jalal Khel.—A minor fraction of Khoji Khel, Bozi, Khel, Madda Khel (1,600) Ibrahim Khel, Utmanzai, Darwesh Khel Wazirs.

Jalal Khel.—A section of Mali (or Muli) Khel, Salarzai, Iliaszai, Bunerwals.

Jalal Khel (250).—A section of the Sher Khel, Haibat Khel, Nana Khel, Bahlolzai, Mahsuds.

Jalal Khel.—A sub-division of Sarsa, Tatta, Battannis. Headman; Sher Khan.

Jalal Khel (Dir).—A section of Painda Khel, Sesada, Malizai, Yusufzais.

Jalalzai (West of Dera Ghazi Khan District).—A sub-division of Nozai, Laharzai, Musa Khels. Headman; Mendak.

Jalalzai (40).—A section of Mehtarzai, Harun Khel, Sanatia, Kakars. Headman; Saudagar.

Jalalzai (Zhob).—A section of Shadozai, Ali Khel, Sanzar, Kakars.

Jalalzai (West of the Dera Ghazi Khan District).—A sub-division of Hasan Khel, Balil Khel, Musa Khels, Headmen; K h o i d a d, (Salem Khanzai,) Mian (Sadozai), Lawang. (Mirdadzai.)

Jalalzai (3,300).—A sub-division of Alizai, Sanzar, Kakars. Headmen; Sirdar Shah Jehan, Dost Muhammad, and Saifula.

Jalandarzai (57).—A section of Bazai, Harun Khel,

Sanatia, Kakars. Headman; Mir Afzal.

Jalangial Kamoi Badeshi (400).—A clan of Allaiwals.

Jalanzai (40).—A "Hamsaya", section of Natozai, Dumar, Sanzar, Kakars Headman; Haidar.

Jalezai (10).—A sub-division of Ladu, Rakanwal, Lunis. Headman; see Ladu.

Jalil Khel.—A section of Durbi Khel, Kambar Khel, Kambar Khel (4,500), Afridis. Gar. Headmen; Muhammad Sher, Khwaja Ali, Yuno, Nurai.

Jallal Khel.—A minor fraction of Shadi Khel, Bora Khel (1,000), Mohmit Khel, Utmanzai, Darwesh Khel Wazirs.

Jallal Khel.—A minor fraction of Khan Khel, Takht Khel, Bakka Khel, Wali Khel, Utmanzai, Darwesh Khel Wazirs. Headman; Mirza.

Jallal Kor (Kung).—A subdivision of Maimana Khel, Khwaezai, Mohmands. Headmen; Khalil, Tawar.

Jamal Khel (27).—A minor fraction of Ali Khel, Barim Khel, Amzoni, Mallizad, Dawaris. Headmen; Shahbadin, Namballi Khan, Patila Khan.

Jamal Khel.—A minor fraction of Kaddam Khel, Feroz Khel, Mashi Khel, Mannia Khel, Hassan Khel, Mitha Khan Khel, Kuki Khel (4,500), Afridis. Gar. Headmen; Amir Sher, Zaman.

Jamal Khel.—A minor fraction of Mir Husani, Macha, Madda Khel (1,600), Ibrahim Khel, Utmanzai, Darwesh Khel Wazirs.

Jamal Khel.—A minor fraction of Durar (300), Khusrogi, Nasruddin, Zakha Khel, Afridis. Samil. Headman; see Bucha Khel.

Jamal Khel (Bannu District).—A minor fraction of Ali Khel, Musa Khel, Hathi Khel (2,000), Shin Khel, Ahmadzai, Darwesh Khel Wazirs.

Jamal Khel.—A minor fraction of Badi Khel, Dardoni, Wuzi Khel (800), Mohmit Khel, Utmanzai, Darwesh Khel Wazirs.

JAMAL KHEL (Dir).—A section of Painda Khel, Sesada, Malizai, Yusufzais.

JAMAL KHEL.—A section of Malik Shahi (400), Wali Khel, Utmanzai, Darwesh Khel Wazirs. Headmen; Jumazan Khan, Muhammad, Pirjao, Sarjamal, Taghar, Urmur, Hussaini, Zariband, Gulla Khan, Pirzai, Sulemani.

JAMAL KHEL (30).—A section of the Ghalib Khel, Badanzai, Shaman Khel, Mahsuds. Headman; Fatteh Roz.

JAMAL KHEL.—A section of the Haidrai, Chahar Khel, Shaman Khel, Mahsuds.

JAMAL KHEL (20).—A minor fraction of Shadi Khel, Lar Larai, Land, Malakh, Mallizad, Dawaris. Headmen; Nazar Din, Gul Azam.

JAMALDIN KHEL.—A minor fraction of Wadin Khel, Khazzar Khel, Star Ali Khan Khel, Sarki Khel, Madda Khel (1,600), Ibrahim Khel, Utmanzai, Darwesh Khel Wazirs.

JAMALI KHEL (Right bank of Mastura river).—A sub-division of the Mani Khel (1,000), Muhammad Khel, Orakzais. Gar. Shiah.

JAMALZAI (West of Dera Ghazi Khan District).—A division of Umrzai, Musa Khels. Headman; Sadak.

JAMALZAI (200).—A section of Arozai, Ahmad Khel, Sen Khel, Sheranis.

JAMALZAI (12).—A sub-division of Ladu, Rakanwal, Lunis, Headman; see Ladu.

JAMALZAI (8).—A sub-division of Shamezai, Rakanwal, Lunis. Headman; see Shamezai.

JAMALZAI (100).—A section of Sarangzai, Harun Khel, Sanatia, Kakars. Headman; Galun.

JAMALZAI (60).—A section of Barangzai, Kebzai, Sanzar, Kakars. Headman; Gulzar.

JAMBAI KHEL.—A minor fraction of Waruka Ali Khan Khel, Sarki Khel, Madda Khel (1,600), Ibrahim Khel, Utmanzai, Darwesh Khel Wazirs.

JAMDURAI.—A minor fraction of Painda Khel, Manak Khel, Bakhshi Khel, Madda Khel, (1,600), Ibrahim Khel Utmanzai, Darwesh Khel Wazirs.

JAMI KOR.—A minor fraction of Sultan Khel, Hamza Khel, Gandab, Halimzai, Mohmands. Headman; Ghulam Murad.

JAM SHER KOR.—A minor fraction of Abdur Rahman Khel (200), Musa Khel, Mamuzai, Lashkarzai, Orakzais. Gar. Headman; Kammir.

JANAI KHEL.—A minor fraction of Usman Khel, Takhti Khel, Bakka Khel (1,000), Wali Khel, Utmanzai, Darwesh Khel Wazirs. Headman; Akmad Din.

JANAKHORI (800).—A subdivision of Hassan Khel, Adam Khel, Afridis.

JANAL KHEL.—A minor fraction of Feroz Khel, Tor Sapar (350), Galai, Adam Khel, Afridis.

JANBEG KHEL.—A sub-division of Pabbi Khel, Kambar Khel (4,500), Afridis. Gar. Headmen; Muhammad Sher, Khwaja Ali, Yaro, Nurai.

JAN BEG KOR.—A minor fraction of Sangar Khel, Yusuf Khel, Isa Khel, Pandiali, Mohmands. Headmen; see Isa Khel.

JAN BEG KOR (Part in Mohmand, part in British territory).—A section of Kani Khel, Kasim Khel, Tarakzai, Mohmands. Headman; Sheraz.

JANGAR KHEL.—A minor fraction of Said Khel, Umarzai (600), Shin Khel, Ahmadzai, Darwesh Khel Wazirs.

JANGI KHEL.—A minor fraction of Machi Khel, Abdul Khel, Bora Khel (1,000), Mohmit Khel, Utmanzai, Darwesh Khel, Wazirs.

JANGI TABAR.—A minor fraction of Mamun Kor, Kandai, Isa Khel, Pandiali, Mohmands. Headmen; see Isa Khel.

JANI KHEL.—A minor fraction of Khadi Khel, Mannia Khel, Hassan Khel, Mitha Khan Khel, Kuki Khel (4,500), Afridis. Gar. Headmen; Kashmir, Abdulla Khan, Bazai.

JANI KHEL (Kharmana river).—A minor fraction of the

Abdul Mirzi (410), Landaizai, Masuzai, Lashkarzai, Orakzais. Gar. Headman; Hussain.

JANI KHEL (1,000; Khasora and Wana).—A sub-division of Wali Khel, Utmanzai, Darwesh Khel Wazirs. Headmen; see Idia Khel, Tor, and Malik Shahi.

JANI KHEL (7).—A minor fraction of Ali Khel, Barim Khel, Amzoni, Mallizad, Dawaris. Headman; Gubzir.

JAN KHAN KHEL (35).—A minor fraction of Sogi Khel, Muhammad Khel, Malakh, Mallizad, Dawaris. Headman; Ghonsamir.

JAN KHAN KHEL (6).—A sub-division of Boya, Tappizad, Dawaris.

JAN MUHAMMAD KOR (Kharmana river).—A section of the Alizai (50), Masuzai, Lashkarzai, Orakzais. Samil. Headman; Muhammad Gul.

JASRAT KHEL.—A sub-division of the Khoja Hawas Khel, Ali Khel (3,000), "Hamsayas" of the Orakzais. Gar. ½ Shiah. Headman; Yaru.

JAWAKAI.—A sub-division of Babakri, Sipah (1,200), Afridis. Samil. Headman; Ahmad.

JAWAKAIS (1,200).—A division of Adam Khel, Afridis.

JAWAL KHEL.—A sub-division of Abba Khel, Tatta, Battannis. Headman; Mehrban.

JEWAN KOR.—A sub-division of Dawat or Dauta Khel, Khawaezai, Mohmands. Headman; Bara Khan.

JHANDA KHEL.—A section of Ghalib Khan Khel, Malikdin Khel, Malikdin Khel (4,000), Afridis. Samil. Headmen; see Nathu Khel.

JILAKZAI (30).—A section of Shabazai, Dumar, Sanzar. Kakars. Headman; Mulla Hasan.

JILAN KHEL.—A minor fraction of Kambir (or Kambo) Khel, Aib Khel, Salarzai, Iliaszai, Bunerwals.

JINIZAI (West of Dera Ghazi Khan District).—A section of Maghduzai, Ahmadzai, Balil Khel, Musa Khels. Headman; Lat.

JIMKI KHEL. (1,200*).—A sub-division of Bar Sulizai, Baizai, Akozai—Yusufzai Swatis.

JIRAKI (Bannu District).—A minor fraction of Pirba Khel, Hathi Khel (2,000), Shin Khel, Ahmadzai, Darwesh Khel Wazirs. Headmen; Musharrab Khan, Gulbagh.

JOGA.—A section of Khakizai, Ashazai, Iliaszai, Bunerwals.

JOGIZAI (2,000).—A section of Jalalzai, Alizai, Sanzar, Kakars. Headman; Sirdar Shah Jehan.

JOJI KHEL (40; Black Mountain).—A section of Painda Khel, Akazai, Isazai, Yusufzais.

JUGGI KHEL.—A section of Kemal Khel, Abazai, Khwazazai, Akozai—Yusufzai Swatis.

JULA KHEL.—A section of Aka Maruf, Babuzai, Baizai, Akozai—Yusufzai Swatis.

JUMALAI.—A minor fraction of Datta Khel, Abdul Khel, Bara Khel (1,000), Mohmit Khel, Utmanzai, Darwesh Khel Wazirs.

JUMA KHEL (45; Dera Ismail Khan District).—Nomadic, a sub-section of Warrki, Sein Khel, Mian Khel, Lohana, Pawindahs. Headmen; see Mian Khel.

JUNA KHEL.—A section of Firozai, Chagarzai, Malizai, Bunerwals.

K

KABALZAI (300; West of Dera Ghazi Khan District).—A sub-division of Nokuzai, Laharzai, Musa Khels. Headmen; Khatol (Gumarzai), Momin (Barakzai), Mula Nadar (Brahimzai), Hasan (Bilalzai), Momin (Sandurzai).

KABALZAI (Bori, Zhob).—A sub-division of Kibzai, Saran, Kakars.

KABIL KHEL (7[illegible]).—A section of the Teri (or Tori) Khel, Tapiai, Tappizad, Dawaris. Headmen; Said Shah, Zakor Shah, Salik Din, Awarzai, Shaikhtan.

* These numbers include 3,000 men living beyond Swati limits.

Kasir Khel (Khanki valley).—A sub-division of the Sada Khel (80), Ismailzai, Orakzais. Samil. Headman; Fakir.

Kabul Khel (2,600; Kurram, Shawal, and Birmal).—A sub-division of Wali Khel, Utmanzai, Darwesh Khel, Wazirs. Headmen; see Saifali, Paipali, and Miamai. Mezhaik and Gulba Khan, of the Miamai section, are the chief men.

Kachu Khel.—A section of Azi Khel, Ali Khel, Bar Ranizai, Akozai—Yusufzai Swatis.

Kadai Kor (400).—A sub-division of Gandab, Halimzai, Mohmands. Headmen; see Yardil Kor, Rahmatal Kor, Katasar, Daud Khel, Rami Khel.

Kadam Khel (Mastura river).—A sub-division of Abdul. Aziz Khel (80), Muhammad Khel, Orakzais. Gar. Shiah.

Kadam Khel (60).—A minor fraction of the Ali Khel, Haidar Khel. Tor, Tappizad, Dawaris. Headmen; Mad Alam, Saifal Salandar.

Kadar Khel (5).—A minor fraction of Alli Khel, Barim Khel, Amzoni, Mallizad, Dawaris. Headman; Piyavi.

Kaddam Khel.—A minor fraction of Feroz Khel, Mashi Khel, Mannia Khel, Hassan Khel, Mitha Khan Khel, Kuki Khel (4,500), Afridis. Gar. Headmen; Abbas, Hakim, Nazir, Mulla Wali, Khaza Khan, Amir Sher, Zaman.

Kadrai Khel.—A minor fraction of Khairak Khel, Wadin Khel, Khazzar Khel, Star Ali Khan Khel, Sarki Khel, Madda Khel (1,600), Ibrahim Khel, Utmanzai, Darwesh Khel Wazirs.

Kaduzai (600).—A section of Bazai, Harun Khel, Sanatia, Kakars. Headmen; Mulla Baidula, and Mulla Majib.

Kafshi Khel (12).—A minor fraction of the Nasi Khel, Haidar Khel, Tor, Tappizad, Dawaris. Headmen; Mir Lazam, Mir Ali.

Kahi Khel (120).—A minor fraction of the Khoidad Khel, Gidi Khel, Manazai, Alizai, Mahsuds. Headman; At Muhammad.

Kahman Kor.—A division of Gorai, Utman Khels.

Kaim Khel.—A section of Suran Khel, Babakri, Sipah (1,200), Afridis, Samil. Headmen; Niaz Karim, Iran, Gul Muhammad.

Kaim Khel.—A section of Sheikhmal, Kambar Khel, Kambar Khel (4,500), Afridis, Gar. Headman; Zaman.

Kaim Khel.—A minor fraction of Ismail Khel, Bazi Khel, Madda Khel (1,600), Ibrahim Khel, Utmanzai, Darwesh Khel Wazirs.

Kaim Khel (5).—A minor fraction of Alli Khel, Barim Khel, Amzoni, Mallizad, Dawaris. Headman; Chorgand.

Kainzai (5).—A sub-division of Shamezai, Rakanwal, Lunis.

Kajji Khel.—A minor fraction of Paipali, Kabul Khel, (2,600), Wali Khel, Utmanzai, Darwesh Khel, Wazirs.

Kakai Kor.—A section of Ziauddin (200), Budai, Zakha Khel, Afridis, Samil. Headmen; see Surat Kor.

Kaka Khel.—A minor fraction of Idar Khel, Ali Khel, Khaddar Khel, (70), Mohmit Khel, Utmanzai, Darwesh Khel Wazirs. Headman; Akhmad.

Kaka Khel.—A section of Tari Khel, Shakhi, Waraspun, Battannis.

Kaka Khel (300; Black Mountain).—A sub-division of Hasanzai, Isazai, Yusufzais. Headman; Aladad.

Kaka Khel.—A sub-division of Niamat Khel, Tatta, Battannis. Headman; Khushal Khan.

Kaka Khel (110).—A section of the Datti Khel, Galeshahi, Shaman Khel, Mahsuds. Headmen; Khwaja Muhammad, Karim, Muhammad Yar.

Kaka Khel (10).—A minor fraction of Khare, Taib Khel, Amzoni, Mallizad, Dawaris. Headmen; Mina Khan, Ghulam Rasul.

Kaka Khel.—A clan of the Khattaks, descended from Shekh Rahim Kar; they are considered Mians, and are much venerated by other Pathans. They reside near Nowshera, and are great trans-frontier traders. Headman; Rahim Shah.

KAKARS (40,432 ; Quetta to the Gomal Pass).—A large tribe of Pathans.

KAKARZAI (3,000 ; Bajaur).—A division of Mamund, Tarkanis.

KALA KHEL (50 ; Black Mountain).—A section of Aziz Khel, Akazai, Isazai, Yusufzais.

KALAL KOR—A minor fraction of Shroh, Bussa Khel, Kamali, Halimzai, Mohmands. Headman ; Taza Gul.

KALAL KOR.—A minor fraction of Ranra Khel, Shati Khel, Wali Beg Kor, Gandab, Halimzai, Mohmands. Headman ; Jamdar.

KALANDAR KHEL.—A minor fraction of Ali Khel, Manzar Khel (360), Ibrahim Khel, Utmanzai, Darwesh Khel Wazirs. Headmen ; Mihrab Khan, Kabal, Nawaz Khan.

KALANDAR KHEL (Bannu District).—A minor fraction of Taos Khel, Pirba Khel, Hathi Khel (2,002), Shin Khel, Ahmadzai, Darwesh Khel Wazirs.

KALANDAR KHEL.—A section of Sadin, Ilal Khel, Salarzai, Tarkanis.

KALAT KHEL.—A minor fraction of Muhammad Khel (700), Isperka, Kalu Khel, Ahmadzai, Darwesh Khel Wazirs. Headman ; Muhammad Jan.

KALI KHEL.—A minor fraction of Morib Khel, Usman Khel, Takhti, Khel, Bakka Khel (1,000), Wali Khel, Utmanzai, Darwesh Khel Wazirs. Headman ; Khojamir.

KALI KHEL (300 ; Trans-frontier).—A division of Ali Sher Khel, Shinwaris.

KALLA KHEL (700) ; A section of Ashu Khel, Hassan Khel, Adam Khel, Afridis.

KALLANDAR KHEL.—A section of the Badzai, Kattagarm, Tatta, Battannis. Headman ; Nawaz.

KALLI KHEL.—A minor fraction of Bachagai, Tor, Jani Khel (1,000), Wali Khel, Utmanzai, Darwesh Khel Wazirs. Headman ; Kaimal.

KALU KHEL.—A minor fraction of Sikandar Khel, Abdul Khel, Bora Khel (1,000), Mohmit Khel, Utmanzai, Darwesh Khel Wazirs.

KALU KHEL (8,500).—A division of Ahmadzai, Darwesh Khel Wazirs. Mani Khan, Isperka, is the leading man; for other Headmen; see Isperka and Nasradin.

KALU KHEL.—A minor fraction of Musa Khel, Makhozai, Nasuzai, Iliaszai. Bunerwals.

KALUT KHEL (Bajaur).—A division of Samilzai, Tarkanis.

KALUZAI (60).—A section of Barakzai, Yahia Khel, Sen Khel, Sheranis.

KAMAL KHEL.—A sub-division of Sahib Jan, Aka Khel (1,800), Afridis. Samil.

KAMAL KHEL.—A minor fraction of Maddu Khel, Assad Khel, Mitha Khan Khel, Kuki Khel (4,500), Afridis. Gar. Headmen; Muhammad Amin, Gul Jan, Budai, Langar.

KAMAL KHEL.—A minor fraction of Bakar Khel, Idal Khel, Hathi Khel (2,000), Shin Khel, Ahmadzai, Darwesh Khel Wazirs. Headman; Landai.

KAMAL KHEL.—A sub-diivsion of the Kandahari Safis, who are a vassal clan of the Mohmands.

KAMAL KHEL (8).—A section of Ozbakai, Shingi, Bahlolzai, Mahsuds. Headman; Nizam.

KAMALZAI (9).—A sub-division of Shamezai, Rakanwal, Lunis. Headman; see Shamezai.

KAMALZAI (West of the Dera Ghazi Khan District).—A sub-division of Hamzazai, Balil Khel, Musa Khels. Headman; Hasan.

KAMALZAI (West of the Dera Ghazi Khan District). A section of Husenzai, Ahmadzai, Balil Khel, Musa Khels. Headman; Gulan.

KAMALZAI (25).—A division of Marhel, Sheranis.

KAMALZAI (100).—A section of Shabozai, Dumar, Sanzar, Kakars. Headman; Mazdar.

KAMAR KHEL; see KAMZAI.

KAMAR KHEL (35).—A minor fraction of the Karmach Khel, Malai, Shingi, Bahlolzai, Mahsuds. Headmen; Kajir Khan, Bakhtamir.

KAMAZAI (150).—A sub-division of Utmanzai, Mandan, Yusufzais.

KAMBAR KHEL (4,500 ; Shilobar, Bazar valley, and Kajurai).—One of the six Khyber Afridi clans. Gar. Headmen, Muhammad Amir, Saleh Muhammad, Jan Muhammad, Mehrban, Khair Muhammad.

KAMBAR KHEL.—A division of the Kambar Khel clan, (4,500) of Afridis. Gar. Headmen ; Jan Muhammad, Muhammad Amir.

KAMBAR KHEL.—One of the two sections of the Umarzai Sheikhan (3,000), "Hamsayas" of the Orakzais. Samil. Headman ; Misridad.

KAMBAR KHEL.—A sub-division of the Bazoti (500), Daulatzai, Orakzais. Samil. Headman ; Amir Shah.

KAMBAR KHEL.—A minor fraction of Warkam Khel, Aib Khel, Salarzai, Iliaszai, Bunerwals.

KAMBAR KOR.—A minor fraction of Sultan Khel, Hamza Khel, Gandab, Halimzai, Mohmands. Headman ; Mir Aghajan.

KAMBAR KOR.—A minor fraction of Asaf Khel, Dalkha Kor, Dadu Khel, Tarakzai, Mohmands.

KAMBIR (or KAMBO) KHEL.—A section of Aib Khel, Salarzai, Iliaszai, Bunerwals.

KAMR KHEL.—A minor fraction of Gadia Khel, Tatar Khel or Akhorwal (300), Hassan Khel, Adam Khel, Afridis.

KAMRAI or KAMAR KHEL.—(600 ; Extreme west of Bara valley, next the Sipah and Zakha Khels).—One of the six Khyber-Afridi clans. Samil. Headmen ; Hafiz Samandar and Azam Khan.

KANDAHARIS.—A division of the Safis, who are a vassal clan of the Mohmands.

KANDAI.—A sub-division of Isa Khel, Pandiali, Mohmands. Headmen ; Ghulam Khan, Paiuddin.

KANDAO KHEL (400).—A section of Ashu Khel, Hassan Khel, Adam Khel, Afridis.

KANEZAI.—A sub-division of Kattagarm, Tatta, Battannis. Headmen ; Miani (Alam), Khojak and Haan

(Senzai), Tor Khan (Pira), Daotan Khan (Tar).

KANI KHEL (600; Part in Mohmand, part in British territory).—A sub-division of Kasim Khel, Tarakzai, Mohmands.

KANJRAI (40).—A minor fraction of the Dachi Khel, Palli Khel, Manazai, Alizai, Mahsuds. Headman; Khan, Mirzai.

KANOZAI (400).—A "Hamsaya" section of Natozai, Dumar, Sanzar, Kakars Headman; Sher, Muhammad.

KANU KHEL (37).—A sub-division of Ahmed Khel, Oba Khel, Sheranis.

KANUZAI (West of Dera Ghazi Khan District).—A section of Malizai, Ahmadzai, Balil Khel, Musa Khels. Headman; Jala.

KANZAL KHEL.—A minor fraction of Alisher Khel, Musa Khel, Nurizai, Malizai, Bunerwals.

KAPIP (100).—A clan of Sheranis.

KAR KHEL (18).—A minor fraction of Ahmad Khel, Zira Khel, Amzoni, Mallizad, Dawaris. Headman; Channi.

KARAM KOR.—A section of Hassani Kor, Muhammad Khan Kor, or 'Bar' Burhan Khel, Pandiali, Mohmands. Headmen; Badshah, Baz, Malik.

KARE KHEL.—A section of Shadi Khel, Bobak, Dana, Battannis.

KARI KHEL.—A sub-division of Sultan-ka-Khel, Bar Ranizai, Akozai—Yusufzai Swatis.

KARIMDAD KHEL (48).—A minor fraction of Abdul Rahman Khel, Sher Khel, Haibat Khel, Nana Khel, Bahlolzai, Mahsuds.

KARIMDAD KHEL.—A minor fraction of Must Ali, Shaikh Khel, Aib Khel, Salarzai, Iliaszai, Bunerwals.

KARIM KHEL.—A minor fraction of Karim Khel, Jamal Khel, Malik Shahi (400), Wali Khel, Utmanzai, Darwesh Khel Wazirs. Headman; Khan Muhammad.

KARIM KHEL.—A minor fraction of Jamal Khel, Malik Shahi (400), Wali Khel,

Utmanzai, Darwesh Khel Wazirs. Headmen; Jumazan, Khan Muhammad Pirjas, Sarjamal, Taghar, Urmur.

KARIM KHEL.—A section of Fatteh Khel, Abazai, Khwazazai, Akozai—Yusufzai Swatis.

KARIM KOR.—A minor fraction of the Umar Khan Khel, Ali Karan, Mamuzai, Lashkarzai, Orakzais. Gar.

KARIMZAI (60).—A section of Mehtarzai, Harun Khel, Sanatia, Kakars. Headman; Paio.

KARM KHEL (50; Dera Ismail Khan District).—Nomadic, a minor fraction of Zakori, Sein Khel, Mian Khel, Lohana, Pawin-dahs. Headman; see Mian Khel.

KARMANDI KHAN.—A minor fraction of Madda Khel, Miamai, Kabul Khel (2,600), Utmanzai, Darwesh Khel Wazirs. Headman; Mehr Ali.

KARMANZ KHEL.—A minor fraction of Marchi Khel, Abdul Khel, Bara Khel (1,000), Mohmit Khel, Utmanzai, Darwesh Khel Wazirs.

KARMI KHEL (50).—A minor fraction of the Garri Khel, Dachi Khel, Sani Khel, Manazai, Alizai, Mahsuds. Headmen; Tar Khan, Liwand, Bandar Shah.

KARMO KHEL (Dir territory).—A section of Painda Khel, Sesada, Malizai, Yusufzais.

KARMOZAI (250).—A subdivision of Ahmad Khel, Sen Khel, Sheranis.

KARMUZAI (60).—A section of Mehtarzai, Harun Khel, Sanatia, Kakars. Headman; Mulla Kamal Ali.

KARNA KHEL.—A division of Malikdin Khel (4,000), Afridis. Samil. Headmen; Azim Din, Samand, Sharif Din.

KARRA KHEL (140).—A section of the Mamdai, Shingi, Bahlolzai, Mahsuds. Headmen; Kandhar, Baghdad, Mirza.

KARRA KHEL.—A section of Ghaibi Khel, Babakri, Sipah (1,200), Afridis. Samil. Headmen; Gul Mast, Jan Gul, Shah Murad, Malik Sher Muhammad.

KARRAM KHEL.—A minor fraction of Bar Khozhai,

Khaddar Khel (770), Mohmit Khel, Utmanzai, Darwesh Khel Wazirs. Headman ; Sadirai.

KABBI KHEL (180).—A section of the Manderi, Idak, Tappizad, Dawaris. Headmen ; Nazaiband, Kaim Shah, Khwaja Muhammad, Badda Khan, Mirab Khan.

KABBI KHEL (40).—A section of Mullagan, Tor, Mallizad Dawaris. Headman ; Fazali.

KABBI KHEL (60).—A section of Urmuz, Tor, Mallizad, Dawaris. Headmen ; Kalim Khidder Khan, Suhbat, Muhammad Amin, Gul Rahman.

KARU KHEL.—A section of Mali (or Muli) Khel, Salarzai, Iliaszai, Bunerwals.

KABUN KHEL.—A section of Asad Khel, Mitha Khan Khel, Kuki Khel (4,500), Afridis. Gar. Headmen ; see Shekhan and Mishak Khel.

KASAM.—A section of Khakizai, Ashazai, Iliaszai, Bunerwals.

KASAM KHEL (10).—A minor fraction of the Ali Khel, Haidar Khel, Tor, Tappizad, Dawaris. Headman ; Sardar.

KASAM KHEL (70).—A minor fraction of Dur Khel, Babakki, Hassu Khel, Tor, Mallizad, Dawaris. Headmen ; Diwana Khan, Niazgai.

KASIM KHEL (250).—A section of Kimat Khel, Jawaki, Adam Khel, Afridis.

KASIM KHEL.—A minor fraction of Aib Kor, Shaikh Khel, Aib Khel, Salarzai, Iliaszai, Bunerwals.

KASIM KHEL.—A section of Suran Khel, Babakri, Sipah (1,200), Afridis. Samil. Headmen ; Ghafar, Hassan, Shekh Khan Muhammad, Muhammad Asgar, Nawaz, Niaz Muhammad, Shekh Nur Alam, Syad Alam, Shekh Gul.

KASIM KHEL (80).—A subdivision of Badanzai, Shaman Khel, Mahsuds.

KASIM KHEL (60).—A section of Umar Khel, Nana Khel, Bahlolzai, Mahsuds.

KASIM KHEL (800 ; hills north of Michni, part in British territory).—A division of Tarakzai, Mohmands. Headmen; see Kani Khel and Khalil Khel.

Kasim Khel (Yakhdand).—A division of Utmanzai, Mohmands. Headmen; see Utmanzais.

Kasim Khel (228).—A subdivision of Chahar Khel, Shaman Khel, Mahsuds.

Kasim Kor.—A minor fraction of Rahmatal Kor, Kadai Kor, Gandab, Halimzai, Mohmands. Headmen; see Rahmatal Kor.

Kasu Khel.—A minor fraction of Pridai (150), Ashu Khel, Hassan Khel, Adam Khel, Afridis.

Katagaram (18).—A minor fraction of Umarzai, Zira Khel, Amzoni, Mallizad, Dawaris. Headmen; Jumazan, Khanbadshah.

Kata Gran.—A minor fraction of Shugai, Tori Khel (2,670), Ibrahim Khel, Utmanzai, Darwesh Khel Wazirs. Headmen; Khonamir, Pirai, Dalai, Makam, Muhammad Gul.

Kata Khel.—A section of Aka Maruf, Babuzai, Baizai, Akozai—Yusufzai Swatis.

Kata Khel (60).—A section of Manderi, Idak, Tappizad, Dawaris. Headmen; Sahib Khan, Zama Khan, Mughal Shah, Nizam Shah.

Kata Khel (77).—A division of Drigzai, Lunis.

Katal Khel (50).—A minor fraction of Walidad Khel, Lodi Khel, Abdullai, Aimal Khel, Bahlolzai, Mahsuds. Headman; Khoidad.

Katasar.—A section of Kadal Kor, Gandab, Halmzai, Mohmands. Headmen; Jamdad Abdul Wahid, Jamal, Shamozai, Ranjak, Charogai, Shah Munir, Bahadur, Samodin, Makaiz, Jallal, Khan Muhammad, Faizullah Rashatullah, Ghatol, Pir Muhammad, Wahab.

Kati Khel (15; Dera Ismail Khan District).—Nomadic, a minor fraction of Umrzai, Sein Khel, Mian Khel, Lohana, Pawindahs. Headman; see Mian Khel.

Katkai Khel.—A division of Salarzai, Tarkanis.

Katorzai (Bajaur) A division of Samilzai, Tarkanis.

Kattagarm (260).—A division of Tatta, Battannis, Headmen ; Nawaz (Kallandar); Saiad Khan, and Baram (Bazid).

Katta Khel.—A section of Sen Khel, Gadaizai, Iliaszai, Bunerwals.

Kattia Khel.—A section of Hassan Khel, Mitha Khan Khel. Kuki Khel (4500), Afridis. Gar. Headmen ; Miro, Mir Afzal, Shomsuddin, Zarin, Mazulla, Marai, Haidar, Ghulam Hamid.

Kattia Mir Khel.—A minor fraction of Sab Khel, Shekhai, Annai (1,000), Budai, Zakha Khel, Afridis. Samil. Headmen; Bukhan. Hukmat, Sattura Khan.

Katti Khel (10).—A minor fraction of Khoidadai, Malikshai, Aimal Khel, Bahlolzai, Mahsuds. Headman ; Arsala.

Kazian Kor.—A minor fraction of Nekki Khel, Hassan Khel, Pakhai (1,000), Budai, Zakha Khel, Afridis. Samil. Headmen; Said Rasul, Nur Habib.

Kazi Khel.—A minor fraction of Muhammad Khel (700), Isperka, Kalu Khel, Ahmadzai, Darwesh Khel Wazirs. Headman ; Pir Muhammad.

Keimal Khel.—A sub-division of Urmuz Khel, Sipah (1,200), Afridis. Samil. Headmen ; see Hilal Khel, Baghdad Khel and Babur Khel.

Kemal Khel.—A sub-division of Abazai, Khwazazai, Akozai—Yusufzai Swatis.

Kemal Khel.—A section of Babu Khel, Adinzai, Khwazazai, Akozai—Yusufzai Swatis.

Kemal Khel (12).—A section of the Ali Khel, Khadi Khel, Shaman Khel, Mahsuds. Headman ; Mir Alam.

Kemal Khel (50).—A minor fraction of the Panj Pilara, Abdullai, Aimal Khel, Bahlolzai, Mahsuds. Headman ; Zafar.

Kesama Kor.—A minor fraction of Mamun Kor, Kandai, Isa Khel, Pandiali, Mohmands. Headman ; Ghulam Khan.

Kesu.—A sub-division of Waruke, Dana, Battannis.

KHABI KHEL.—A division of Malikdin Khel (4,000), Afridis. Samil. Headmen; Darya Khan, Dauran, Yar Khan.

KHADAK KHEL.—A sub-division of Abdul Khel, Kuki Khel (4,500), Afridis. Gar.

KHADAKZAI (2,000).—A division of Khwazazai, Akozai—Yusafzai Swatis.

NOTE.—The number given includes the Dosha Khel division, which is now dependent on the Khan of Dir.

KHADAKZAI (40).—A section of Sarangzai, Harun Khel, Sanatia, Kakars. Headman; Mulla Abdulla.

KHADDAR KHEL (110; Tochi valley).—A sub-division of Mohmit Khel, Utmanzai, Darwesh Khel Wazirs. Headmen; see Ali Khel, Mad Khozhai, and Bar Khozhai.

KHADARZAI.—A division of Mansur, Gaduns.

KHADI (217).—A division of Mallizad, Dawaris. Headmen; Ketai and Rakhim Shah, Gulazam, Pilawar Khan, Aghar, Yanai, Sheikh Majid, Shah Madi, Fateh Khan, Wati, Mazid Khan, Madazan, Shah Zaman, Didar, Gul Rashid, Khoja Azam, Ajam, Tawan, Zarogha Din, Gulmir, Madazam, Khoja Muhammad Khan, Atalas.

KHADI KHEL (Bohai Dag).—A division of Khwaezai Mohmands. Headmen; Painda Khan, Gudai, Muhammad, Akram, Aziz Khan.

KHADI KHEL (North of Khanki valley).—A sub-division of Mamuzai (200), Ismailzai, Orakzais. Samil Headman; Halim Khan.

KHADI KHEL.—A minor fraction of Mannia Khel, Hassan Khel, Mitha Khan Khel, Kuki Khel (4,500), Afridis. Gar. Headmen; Kalandar, Tor, Mulla Usman, Abdulla.

KHADIN KHEL.—A sub-division of Ashazai, Iliaszai, Bunerwals.

KHADISH KHEL.—A minor fraction of Mir Asan Khel, Babu Khel, Adinzai, Khwazazai, Akozai—Yusufzai Swatis.

KHADIZAI (West of Dera Ghazi Khan District).—A sub-division of Mangizai Laharzai, Musa Khels. Headman; Alihan.

KHADIZAI (200; Khanki river).—A division of Ismailzai, Orakzais. Samil.

KHADU KHEL (520).—A division of Khoidad Khel, Zaimukhts.

KHADU KHEL (35; Dera Ismail Khan District).—Nomadic, a minor fraction of Saiad Khel, Isot Khel, Mian Khel, Lohana, Pawindahs. Headman; see Mian Khel.

KHAI.—A minor fraction of Kui Khel, Tor Sapar (350) Galai, Adam Khel Afridis.,

KHAIRAK KHEL.—A minor fraction of Wadin Khel, Khazzar Khel, Star Ali Khan Khel, Sarki Khel, Madda Khel (1,600), Ibrahim Khel, Utmanzai, Darwesh Khel, Wazirs.

KHAIRAT KHEL.—A minor fraction of Pira Khel, Mir Hasani, Macha, Madda Khel (1,600), Ibrahim Khel, Utmanzai, Darwesh Khel, Wazirs.

KHAIRGAN (6).—A section of Nana Khel, Tapiai, Tappizad Dawaris. Headman; Gulshahdad.

KHAIRULLA KOR.—A minor fraction of Ranra Khel, Shati Khel, Wali Beg Kor Gandab, Halimzai, Mohmands. Headman; Shere Muhammad.

KHAISTA KOR (Yakhdand).—A division of Utmanzai, Mohmands. Headmen; see Utmanzai.

KHAKIZAI.—A sub-division of Ashazai, Iliaszai, Bunerwals.

KHALAN KHEL (310).—A minor fraction of Sipah (Azad Khel), Ali Karan, Mamuzai, 3,500 Lashkarzai, Orakzais. Gar. Headman; Walidad.

KHALIDAD KOR.—A minor fraction of the Saiad Khan Nmasi, Ali Karan, Mamuzai (3,500), Lashkarzai, Orakzais. Gar. Headman; Sarandaz.

KHALIF KHEL.—A minor fraction of Usman Khel, Takhti Khel, Bakka Khel (1,000), Wali Khel, Utmanzai, Darwesh Khel Wazirs. Headman; Sakam.

KHALIL KHEL (200; Hills north of Michni, part in British territory).—A subdivision of Kasim Khel, Tarakzai, Mohmands. Headmen; Janai, Saifal, Shahzada, Gulfaraz.

Khalil Khel.—A minor fraction of Idar Khel, Ali Khel, Khaddar Khel (770), Mohmit Khel, Utmanzai, Darwesh Khel Wazirs. Headman ; Makhach.

Khabils (3,600 ; Peshawar District).—A tribe of the same origin as the Mohmands, who live east of the Khyber pass and along the left bank of lower Bara.

Khalilzai (120).—A sub-division of Yahia Khel, Sen Khel, Sheranis.

Khal Khel.—A section of Ghaibi Khel, Babakri, Sipah (1,200), Afridis. Samil. Headmen ; Akbar Hussain, Nur Shah, Amanat, Rahmat.

Khalli Khel (337).—A division of Shaman Khel, Mahsuds.

Khalozai.—A sub-division of Kakazai, Mamund, Tarkanis.

Khaluzai (West of Dera Ghazi Khan District).—A sub-division of Land Palai Laharzai, Musa Khels. Headman ; Soba Khan.

Khamar Khel (240).—A section of Gidi Khel, Manazai, Alizai, Mahsuds.

Khamba Khel.—A division of Haji Khel, Chamkannis.

Khamis (86).—A division of Spin, Tarins.

Khanakai Khel.—A minor fraction of Ali Khel (100), Ashu Khel, Hassan Khel, Adam Khel, Afridis.

Khana Khel (6 ; Dera Ismail Khan District).—Nomadic, a minor fraction of Musazai, Sein Khel, Mian Khel, Lohana, Pawindahs. Headman ; see Mian Khel.

Khanbeg Khel (Bannu District).—A minor fraction of Tori Khel, Musa Khel, Hathi Khel (2,000), Shin Khel, Ahmadzai, Darwesh Khel Wazirs.

Khan Bibi Khel.—A minor fraction of Khairak Khel, Wadin Khel, Khazzar Khel, Star Ali Khan Khel, Sarki Khel, Madda Khel (1,600), Ibrahim Khel, Utmanzai, Darwesh Khel Wazirs.

Khanda Khel.—A section of Khan Khel, Kuz—Sulizai, Baizai, Akozai—Yusufzai Swatis.

Khandar Khan Khel (Bannu District).—A section of Hathi Khel (2,000), Shin Khel, Ahmadzai, Darwesh

Khel Wazirs. Headmen ; Nizam Khan, Landai, Shah Tamoz.

KHANDAR KHEL.—A minor fraction of Paipali, Kabul Khel (2,600), Wali Khel, Utmanzai, Darwesh Khel Wazirs.

KHANI KHEL (600).—One of the four clans of Chamkannis.

KHAN KHEL (70 ; Black Mountain).—A section of Barat Khel, Akazai, Isazai, Yusufzais.

KHAN KHEL (3,000).—A minor fraction of Kuz Sulizai, Baizai, Akozai—Yusufzai Swatis.

KHAN KHEL (180 ; Daggar).—The family of the Khans of Daggar, distinct and very influential in Buner, and not belonging to any clan. Headman ; Hukmat Khan of Daggar.

KHAN KHEL (120 ; Black Mountain).—A division of Deshiwal, Swatis. Headmen ; Azad Khan, Kamal.

KHAN KHEL (Nandihar).—A division of Nandihari Swatis.

KHAN KHEL (300 ; The Black Mountain).—A sub-division of Hasanzai, Isazai, Yusufzais. Headman ; Hashim Ali Khan (Khan of the Hasanzais).

KHAN KHEL.—A minor fraction of Matkai, Malik Shahi (400), Wali Khel, Utmanzai, Darwesh Khel Wazirs. Headman ; Torabaz.

KHAN KHEL (25).—A section of Khan Khel, Shabi Khel, Alizai, Mahsuds, Headman ; Khar.

KHAN KHEL (75).—A sub-division of Shabi Khel, Alizai, Mahsuds.

KHAN KHEL.—A minor fraction of Takhti Khel, Bakka Khel (1,000), Wali Khel, Utmanzai, Darwesh Khel Wazirs. Headmen ; Khan Badshah, Khazan Khan, Miyan Khel, Gulazamir, Zamma Mir, Mirza, Gul Khatni, Rahmat Shah.

KHAN MAI TABAR.—A minor fraction of the Mamun Kor, Kandai, Isa Khel, Pandiali, Mohmands. Headman ; Paiuddin.

KHAN MUHAMMADZAI (West of Dera Ghazi Khan District).—A section of Muhammadzai, Ahmadzai, Balil Khel, Musa Khels. Headman; Khan Muhammad.

KHARE (80).—A minor fraction of Khare, Taib Khel, Amzoni, Mallizad, Dawaris. Headmen; Wazirgai, Bazid, Khalim Shah, Mir Ghazam.

KHARE (90).—A section of Taib Khel, Amzoni, Mallizad, Dawaris. Headmen; Wazirgai, Mina Khan.

KHARE KHEL.—A minor fraction of Mandi Khel, Mad Khozhai, Khaddar Khel (770), Mohmit Khel, Utmanzai, Darwesh Khel Wazirs. Headman; Kakar.

KHARI KHEL.—A minor fraction of Kata Gran, Shugai, Tori Khel (2,670), Ibrahim Khel, Utmanzai, Darwesh Khel Wazirs. Headman; Pirai.

KHARI KHEL.—A minor fraction of Ismail Khel (150), Kimat Khel, Jawaki, Adam Khel, Afridis.

KHARMACH KHEL (205).—A section of Nazar Khel, Aimal Khel, Bahlolzai, Mahsuds.

KHARMACH KHEL (51).—A section of Malai, Shingi, Bahlolzai, Mahsuds.

KHARMANJ KHEL.—A minor fraction of Madda Khel, Miamai, Kabul Khel (2,600), Utmanzai, Darwesh Khel Wazirs Headmen; Surkam and Gulbat Khan.

KHAROTIS (1,710; between Khorasan and India).—One of the Pawindah trading tribes.

KHARRI KHEL (70).—A section of the Kikarai, Nana Khel, Bahlolzai, Mahsuds. Headmen; Fatteh, Mamindar.

KHARSIN (200; Upper Tochi valley).—A small tribe, claiming to be Saiads from Abyssinia, settled amongst the Madda Khel Wazirs. Headmen; Sargwal, Khalikdad, Wodam, Natchak, Alimak. A larger branch of the same tribe resides in Sabarai, a district of Khost, east of Matun.

KHASTAI.—A small tribe living beyond the Dera Ghazi border. Headman; Jehan Khan.

KHATA KHEL (60—Dera Ismail Khan district).—Nomadic, a minor fraction of Pasani, Isot Khel, Mian Khel, Lohana, Pawindahs. Headman; see Mian Khel.

KHATALZAI (West of Dera Ghazi Khan District).—A section of Inzar, Hasan Khel, Balil Khel, Musa Khels. Headman; Kalandar.

KHATTAKS (24,000; South-eastern portion of the Peshawar district, and the southern and eastern portions of the Kohat district).—A great tribe of Pathans, whose main genealogical divisions are as follows, *viz.*, Tari, Taraki and Bolak. Irrespective of the above, however, the tribe has a local division into two main branches, *viz.*, Akora or eastern Khattaks, and Teri or western Khattaks. There is a third inter-tribal division which separates the three classes below mentioned from the general body of the Khattaks, *viz.*, the Khan Khel, which includes the relatives of all the chiefs; the Fakir Khel, who have a great reputation for sanctity, and the Kaka Khel. The divisions, etc., of the Khattaks, with the exception of the Kaka Khel, are not indexed in this Dictionary.

KHAWAS KHEL (18).—A section of the Haibat Khel, Nana Khel, Bahlolzai, Mahsuds.

KHAWAS KHEL.—A minor fraction of Ismail Khel (150), Kimat Khel, Jawaki, Adam Khel, Afridis.

KHAYASTA KOR.—A minor fraction of Abdur Rahman Khel (200), Musa Khel, Mamuzai, Lashkarzai, Orakzais. Gar. Headman; Musaki.

KHAZZAR KHEL.—A minor fraction of Star Ali Khan Khel, Sarki Khel, Madda Khel (1,600), Ibrahim Khel, Utmanzai, Darwesh Khel Wazirs. Headmen; Sadda Khan, Alambe Khan, Shadam Khan (Ger Madda Khels,) Sabir (Inzar Kach), Nur Shah (Sanzalai), Umar Khan (Inzar Kach).

KHECHE.—A sub-division of Shan Khel, Tatta, Battannis.

KHEPZAI (9).—A sub-division of Salezai, Rakanwal, Lunis. Headman; see Salezai.

KHESR KHEL.—A section of the Yarkuki Khel, Bazoti, (500) Daulatzai, Orakzais. Samil.

KHIDDAR KHEL (110).—A section of Astanai, Shabi Khel,

Alizai, Mahsuds. Headman ; Mawal.

KHIDDI KHEL (25).—A section of Baromai, Shabi Khel, Alizai, Mahsuds. Headman ; Muhammad Ayaz.

KHIDRANI (350).—A clan of the Jafar tribe.

KHIDRANI.—A sub-division of Mekhiani, Spin, Tarins. Headman ; Mauladad.

KHIDR KHEL.—A section of Sen Khel, Gadaizai, Iliaszai, Bunerwals.

KHIDR KHEL (40).—A Ham sayas section of Shabozai, Dumar, Sanzar, Kakars. Headman ; Hotan.

KHIDRI (100).—A section of Manderi, Idak, Tappizad, Dawaris. Headmen ; Alif Khan, Kaim Shah, Mir Abbas, Wali Hassan, Saleh Khan.

KHIDRIZAI.—A sub-division of Arbu Khel, Sanzar, Kakars.

KHIDRZAI (415).—A sub-division of Ahmad Khel, Oba Khel, Sheranis.

KHIRZAI (200).—A section of Natozai, Dumar, Sanzar, Kakars. Headman ; Karm Khan.

KHIZAR KHEL.—A minor fraction of Mintar Khel, Muhammad Khel, Hassan Khel (400), Mohmit Khel, Utmanzai, Darwesh Khel Wazirs. Headmen ; Misrai, Kabul, Khugalgai, Saadat Beg.

KHOA KHEL.—A minor fraction of Ali Khel, Manzar Khel (360), Ibrahim Khel, Utmanzai, Darwesh Khel Wazirs.

KHODADAD KHEL.—A minor fraction of Ismail, Khadin Khel Ashazai, Iliaszai, Bunerwals.

KHOIDADAI (74).—A section of Malikshai, Aimal Khel, Bahlolzai, Mahsuds.

KHOIDAD KHEL (777).—A section of the Gidi Khel, Manazai, Alizai, Mahsuds.

KHOIDAD KHEL ; see Bayuks.

KHOIDAD KHEL.—A sub-division of the Mamuzai, Mishtis (3,000), "Hamsayas" of the Orakzais. Samil. Headman ; Sultan.

KHOIDAD KOR or KHUDADAD KOR.—A sub-division of Babazai Kor, Dawezai, Mohmands. Headman ; Jafar.

KHOIDAD KOR.—A minor fraction of Sultan Khel, Hamza, Khel, Gandab, Halimzai, Mohmands. Headman; Muhammad Akram.

KHOIDADZAI (2,000).—A section of Shadozai, Alizai, Sanzar, Kakars.

KHOIDADZAI (Zhob).—A minor fraction of Ibrahimzai, Shadozai, Ali Khel, Sanzar, Kakars.

KHOJA KAWAS KHEL (Upper Mastura river).—A division of the Ali Khels (3,000), "Hamsayas" of the Orakzais. Gar. ⅛ Shiah. Headman; Hawas Khan.

KHOJAK (300).—A small tribe, an off-shoot of the Kakars. Headman; Lashkar Khan.

KHOJA KHEL (Gumatti and Wana).—A minor fraction of Ali Khel (10), Bomi Khel (5,410), Nasra Din, Kalu Khel, Ahmadzai, Darwesh Khel Wazirs.

KHOJA KHEL.—A minor fraction of Marchi Khel, Abdul Khel, Bora Khel (1,000), Mohmit Khel, Utmanzai, Darwesh Khel Wazirs.

KHOJA KHEL (30).—A minor fraction of the Kaimdad Khel, Abdul Rahman Khel, Sher Khel, Haibat Khel, Nana Khel, Bahlolzai Mahsuds. Headmen; Jangin, Maizar.

KHOJAKZAI (40).—A (Hamsayas) section of Umrzai, Dumar, Sanzar, Kakars.

KHOJAKZAI (50).—A section of Yahia, Ahmad Khel, Oba Khel, Sheranis.

KHOJAL KHEL.—A sub-division of Mat Khan Khel, Khambar Khel (4,500), Afridis. Gar. Headmen; Mehrdin, Gattai, Matta, Mirshak, Shahbaz, Jumma, Rahmat, Miro.

KHOJAL KHEL (600; Wana).—A minor fraction of Shadi Khel, Nasra Din, Kalu Khel, Ahmedzai, Darwesh Khel Wazirs. Headmen; Sarwar Khan, Amir Khan.

KHOJAWAS KOR, or KHWAJAWAS KOR.—A minor fraction of Rasul Kor, Wali Beg Kor, Gandab, Halimzai, Mohmands. Headmen; Abdul Amir, Ghafar.

KHOJI KHEL.—A minor fraction of Bozi Khel, Madda Khel (1,600), Ibrahim Khel, Utmanzai, Darwesh Khel Wazirs. Headman; Namwar Khan.

KHOJI KHEL (Bannu District).—A minor fraction of Daulat Khel, Ali Khel, Musa Khel, Hathi Khel (2,000), Shin Khel, Ahmadzai, Darwesh Khel Wazirs.

KHOJKAI (50).—A section of Khan Khel, Shabi Khel, Alizai, Mahsuds. Headmen; Pir, Watna, Waryam.

KHOJRAI (20).—A section of Shamerai, Manazai, Alizai, Mahsuds. Headman; Akbar Shah.

KHOJRAI (60).—A sub-division of Darpa Khel, Mallizad, Dawaris. Headmen; Shah Hossein, Muhammad Yar, Mianwar and Makhmad.

KHONI KHEL. A minor fraction of Dad Khel, Mir Hasani, Macha, Madda Khel (1,600), Ibrahim Khel, Utmanzai, Darwesh Khel Wazirs.

KHOSTI SHEKHS (204).—"Hamsayas" of the (western) Sanzar, Kakars.

KHOSTWAL (5).—A minor fraction of Ali Khel, Barim Khel, Amzoni, Mallizad, Dawaris. Headman; Lar.

KHOSTWALS (12,500).—An Afghan tribe descended partly from the Khugianis, partly from the Ghilzais, inhabiting the Shamil valley in Khost, north of the Tochi border.

KHUDADAD KHEL.—A minor fraction of Talagh Khel, Kaddam Khel, Feroz Khel, Mashi Khel, Mannia Khel, Hassan Khel, Mitha Khan Khel, Kuki Khel (4,500), Afridis. Gar. Headman; see Talagh Khel.

KHUDU KHEL (1,800; south of Buner).—A section of Sadozai, Utmanzai, Mandan, Yusufzais.

KHUGA KHEL. A sub-division of Usman Khel, Baezai Mohmands. Headmen; Pirai, Shahnam, Izzat, Allahdad, Hadi Gul.

KHUJAL KHEL.—A section of Mughul Khel, Barmi Khel, Kamrai Khel (600), Afridis. Samil. Headmen; Hafiz Samundar, and Feroz Khan.

Khujram Khel (35).—A minor fraction of Shinki Khel, Babaki, Hassu Khel, Tor, Mallizad, Dawaris. Headmen; Faujdar, Mad Afzal.

Khumari.—A minor fraction of Kanzal Khel, Alisher Khel, Musa Khel, Nurizai, Malizai, Bunerwals.

Khumari Khel.—A section of Jawakai, Babakri. Sipah (1,200), Afridis, Samil. Headman; Ahmad.

Khunda Khel.—A minor fraction of Warrukai, Idia Khel, Jani Khel (1,000), Wali Khel, Utmanzai, Darwesh Khel Wazirs. Headman; Sheikh Majid.

Khuni Khel (20).—A minor fraction of the Kharmach Khel, Nazar Khel, Aimal Khel, Bahlolzai, Mahsuds.

Khuniya Khel (200; Gumatti, temporarily).—A minor fraction of Shadi Khel, Nasra Din, Kalu Khel, Ahmadzai, Darwesh Khel Wazirs.

Khun Khel (20).—A minor fraction of the Shumi Khel, Palli Khel, Manazai, Alizai, Mahsuds. Headman; Lale.

Khuramzai (180).—A section of Baranzai, Kebzai, Sanzar, Kakars. Headman; Madai.

Khurri Khel (8).—A minor fraction of Kiki Khel, Muhammad Khel, Malakh, Mallizad, Dawaris. Headman; Miyan Khel.

Khushalai.—A section of Tori Khel (2,670), Ibrahim Khel, Utmanzai, Darwesh Khel Wazirs. Headmen; Fatteh Mir and Shahmak.

Khushal Kor.—A division of Gorai, Utman Khel.

Khusrogi (560).—A sub-division of Nasruddin, Zakha Khel Afridis. Samil. Headmen; Madraza, Mangar Shah, Nur Dost, Mir Khan, Jamrez, Shah Mard, Gulrez, Mir Hassan, Amir Shah, Haji Lawar Khan, Tor, Sultan Muhammad, Sheno, Bazak.

Khuttay (87).—A section of Taib Khel, Amzoni, Mallizad, Dawaris. Headmen; Hathi Khel, Gul Habib, Arsalaband.

Khwad Khel.—A section of Tara Khel, Muia, Waraspun, Battannis.

KHWAEZAI (2,500 ; Bohai Dag, Goshta, Kabul River) — One of the Mohmand clans. For Headmen ; see Dawat Khel, Maimana Khel, Khadi Khel.

KHWAIDAD KHEL.—A section of the Chawar Khel, Bazoti (500) Daulatzai, Orakzais. Samil.

KHWAIDAD KHEL (Between Khanki and Mastura valleys).—A sub-division of the Bar Muhammad Khel (1,000), Muhammad Khel, Orakzais. Gar. Shiah.

KHWAIDAD KHEL.—A sub-division of Barmi Khel, Kamrai Khel (600), Afridis. Samil. Headmen ; Azam Khan, Ali Jan, Azad Khan, Fateh Mir, Gulzar, Jumma, Mirabat, Mir Zaman, Mir Pashak, Temu, Hamid, Rahmat Khan, Mir, Zardad, Mohabat.

KHWAIDAD KHEL.—A minor fraction of Zamia Khel, Masti Khel, Kambar Khel, Kambar Khel (4,500), Afridis. Gar. Headman ; Muhammad Yar.

KHWAJA AHMAD KHEL.—A minor fraction of Waruka Ali Khan Khel, Sarki Khel, Madda Khel (1,600), Ibrahim Khel, Utmanzai, Darwesh Khel Wazirs.

KHWAJA ALI KHEL.—A minor fraction of Daulat Khel, Ghalib Khan Khel, Malikdin Khel, Malikdin Khel (4000), Afridis. Samil. Headmen ; see Daulat Khel.

KHWAJA DEBE KHAN.—A minor fraction of Idia Khel, Jani Khel (1,000), Wali Khel, Utmanzai, Darwesh Khel Wazirs. Headmen ; Mir, Bir Birjan.

KHWAJA HAWAS KHEL.—A sub-division of the Zanka Khel, Ali Khels (3,000), "Hamsayas" of the Orakzais. Gar. ½ Shiah.

KHWAJA KHEL (1,500 ; Kharmana river).—A sub-division of Masuzai, Lashkarzai, Orakzais. ½ Gar, ½ Samil. Headman ; Husain Shah.

KHWAJA KHEL (800 ; Loargai).—A division of Alisher Khel, Shinwaris. Headmen ; Kamran, Saiad Ghulam, Nadir Khan.

KHWAJA KHEL.—A section of Fatteh Khel, Abazai, Khwazazai, Akozai—Yusufzai Swatis.

KHWAJA KHEL.—A name sometimes given collectively to the Darre Khel and Mirza Khel, clans of the Chamkannis.

KHWAJA KHEL.—An unimportant division of Bar-Ranizai, Akozai,—Yusufzai Swatis.

KHWAJA KHEL.—A minor fraction of Ismail Khel (150), Kimat Khel, Jawaki, Adam Khel, Afridis.

KHWAJA KHEL.—A minor fraction of Miamai, Kabul Khel (2,600), Wali Khel, Utmanzai, Darwesh Khel Wazirs. Headmen; Surkam, Gulbat Khan, Mehr Ali.

KHWAJA KHIDR KHEL.—A section of Mir Kudi Khel, Bazoti (500), Daulatzai, Orakzais. Samil.

KHWAJI KHEL (50; Dera Ismail Khan District).—Nomadic, a minor fraction of Baloch Khel, Isot Khel, Mian Khel, Lohana, Pawindahs. Headman; see Mian Khel.

KHWAJOKUHAI KOR.—A section of Ibrahim Khel, Kamali, Halimzai, Mohmands. Headmen (with those of Lakkai Kor); Antar, Arsalla Khan, Said Fakir, Redai, Nurai, Haidar Khan, Umar Din, Dauran Shah, Ghulam Jan.

KHWAS KHEL (150).—A section of Ali Karan, Mamuzai, Lashkarzai, Orakzais. Gar. Headman; Ibrahim.

KHWAS KHEL.—A minor fraction of Madda Khel. Miamai, Kabul Khel (2,600), Utmanzai, Darwesh Khel Wazirs.

KHWAZAZAI (18,000; right bank of the Swat river, from Kohistan to the Panjkora river).—One of the three clans of Akozai—Yusufzai, Swatis.

KHWAZOZAI (Bajaur).—A division of Isazai, Tarkanis.

KIBZAI, KEBZAI, or KEWAZAI (1,180; Zhob).—A division of Sanzar, Kakars. Headmen; Bangar Zakariazai, (Mareghutzai); Mian Khan (Baranzai).

KIKARAI (117).—A sub-division of Nana Khel, Bahlolzai, Mahsuds.

KIKHAI (105). A section of Dodi Khel, Galeshahi, Shaman Khel, Mahsuds. Headmen ; Id Akbar, Sawan, Amzun, Saifal.

KIKI KHEL (73).—A section of Muhammad Khel, Malakh, Mallizad, Dawaris. Headmen ; Niazmand, Tirob, Mian Khel.

KIMAT KHEL (330).—A subdivision of Jawaki, Adam Khel, Afridis.

KIMAT KHEL (140).—A section of Haidar Khel, Tor, Tappizad, Dawaris. Headmen ; Nasar Khan, Gul Badin, Mad Akbar.

KINI KHEL (12).—A subdivision of Khaddi, Mallizad, Dawaris. Headmen ; Gul Rashid, and Khoja Azam.

KIRCH KHEL (9).—A section of Hakim Khel, Mubarak Shahi, Mallizad, Dawaris. Headmen ; Ain Shah and Jafar.

KISSADIN KHEL (40).—A minor fraction of Salimi Khel, Dachi Khel, Palli Khel, Manazai, Alizai, Mahsuds. Headman ; Ajabnir.

KIZ KILLA (35).—A minor fraction of Dangar Khel, Piran Dangar Khel, Muhammad Khel, Malakh, Mallizad Dawaris. Headmen ; Sahibgai, Gulli, Pir Badshah.

KIZ PAREZ KHEL (12).—A section of Tapiai, Tappizad, Dawaris. Headmen ; Fatteh Khan, Kazim Khan.

KOB KHEL.—A section of Sultan Khel, Sher Gulla, Aka Khel (1,800), Afridis. Samil.

KODA KHEL.—A minor fraction of Muhammad Khel (700), Isperka, Kalu Khel, Ahmadzai, Darwesh Khel Wazirs. Headman ; Wasila Khel.

KODA KHEL (Bohai Dag).—A sub-division of Usman Khel, Baezai Mohmands. Headmen ; Yad Gul, Ghafar, Shad Nam, Gulistan, Almas.

KOI KHEL (15).—A section of Malla Khel, Chahar Khel, Shaman Khel, Mahsuds. Headman ; Momindar, Mirdad.

KOLI KHEL Dakka, Girdi, Peshawar, and Upper Helmand).—(Nomadic, a subdivision of Kuchi, Utmanzai, Mohmands.

KOTAR KHEL (160).—A minor fraction of the Abdul Khel, Langar Khel, Khoidad Khel, Gidi Khel, Manazai, Alizai, Mahsuds.

KOTWAL (440; Black Mountain).—A sub-division of Hasanzai, Isazai, Yusufzais Headmen; Hamid Khan, Bostan, Dawa Khan.

KOTWAL KHEL.—A section of Aya Khel, Ashazai, Iliaszai, Bunerwals.

KUCHELAI (90; Black Mountain).—A division of Deshiwal, Swatis. Headmen; Ahmad, Mir Husein.

KUCHIS (Utmanzai; Upper Helmand and Ningrahar).—Nomadic, as distinguished from the Udredunkai, are a division of Utmanzai, Mohmands. Headmen; Asim, Abdullah, Nur, Khandad, Musahibdin.

KUCHIS (Dawezai, Upper Helmand and Ningrahar).—Nomadic, as distinguished from the Udredunkai, are a division of Dawezai, Mohmands. In winter they leave their families in Ningrahar, and carry merchandize between Kabul and Peshawar. They are sub-divided into Hassan Khel, Mandozai, Hazarbuz, with an associated clan called Za Khel.

KUDA KHEL.—A sub-division of the Umarzai, Sheikhans, (3,000), "Hamsayas" of the Orakzais. Samil. Headman; Nurulla.

KUDEZAI (80).—A section of Baranzai, Kebzai, Sanzar, Kakars. Headmen; Mir Shah, Walidad.

KUDIZAI (West of Dera Ghazi Khan District).—A sub-division of Ahmadzai, Balil Khel, Musa Khels. Headmen; Lal Khan (Shamizai), Dost Muhammad (Ali Khanzai).

KUHADAR KHEL.—A minor fraction of Misri Khel, Bosti Khel (150), Galai, Adam Khel, Afridis.

KUI KHEL.—A section of Tor, Sapar (350), Galai, Adam Khel, Afridis.

KUI KHEL.—A minor fraction of Durar (300), Khusrogi, Nasruddin, Zakha Khel, Afridis. Samil. Headmen; see Bucha Khel.

KUKI KHEL (4,500 ; Bara Maidan, Rajgal, the Gudar and Lashora valleys).—One of the six Khyber Afridi clans. Gar. Headmen; Zaman Khan, Kambar Khan and Khaista Khan.

KUKI KHEL.—A minor fraction of Manak Khel, Bakhshi Khel, Madda Khel (1,600), Ibrahim Khel, Utmanzai, Darwesh Khel Wazirs.

KUKKOZAI (Right bank of Kabul river).—One of the affiliated Mohmand clans.

KULLA KHEL.—A sub-division of Malikdin Khel, Malikdin Khel (4,000), Afridis. Samil. Headmen; Akbar, Dostai, Sher Gul, Zarif, Shamsuddin.

KULLI KHEL.—A minor fraction of Dildar Khel, Mohmand Khel, Kattia Khel, Hassan Khel, Mitha Khan Khel, Kuki Khel, Afridis. Gar. Headman; Mirwal.

KULLI KHEL.—A sub-division of Shekh Ali Khel, Kamrai Khel (600), Afridis. Samil. Headmen; Mulla Amir Shah, Mulla Akhundzada and Sher Walli.

KUNAI.—A minor fraction of Sudan Khel (350), Isperka, Kalu Khel, Ahmadzai, Darwesh Khel Wazirs.

KUNDAI.—A minor fraction of Jambai Khel, Waruka Ali Khan Khel, Sarki Khel, Madda Khel (1,600), Ibrahim Khel, Utmanzai, Darwesh Khel Wazirs.

KUNDAI.—A minor fraction of Tor Khel, Umarzai (600), Shin Khel, Ahmadzai, Darwesh Khel Wazirs. Headmen; Niazzi, Fazal, Zaid Gul, Ghallai.

KUNDAI.—A minor fraction of Bizen Khel (700), Shadi Khel, Nasra Din, Kalu Khel, Ahmadzai, Darwesh Khel Wazirs. Headman; Jalal Khan.

KUNDI (Bannu District).—A minor fraction of Pirba Khel, Hathi Khel (2,000), Shin Khel, Ahmadzai, Darwesh Khel Wazirs. Headmen; Shakhai Khel, Wani Khel, Ghalat Khel, Mian Gul Khel.

KUNDIS (200 ; North-west of Dera Ismail Khan District). —One of the lesser Pawindah trading tribes.

KUNI KHEL (60; Kharmana river).—A minor fraction of the Abdul Mirzi, Landaizai, Masuzai, Lashkarzai, Orakzais. Gar. Headman; Mian Khan.

KURTO KHEL.—A minor fraction of Kui Khel, Tor, Sapar (350), Galai, Adam Khel, Afridis.

KURAMZAI (West of the Dera Ghazi Khan District).—A sub-division of Hamzazai, Balil Khel, Musa Khels. Headman; Gulan.

KURWAY (14).—A section of Taib Khel, Amzoni, Mallizad, Dawaris. Headman; Khalat Shah.

KUSHA KHEL.—A sub-division of the Zakka Khel, Ali Khels (3,000), "Hamsayas" of the Orakzais, ⅓ Shiah. Gar. Headman; Khan Muhammad.

KUSHAB.—A minor fraction of Kanzal Khel, Alisher Khel, Musa Khel, Nurizai, Malizai, Bunerwals.

KUSHI KOR (Kabul River, west of Michni, and part in British territory).—A minor fraction of Asaf Khel, Dalkha Kor, Dadu Khel, Tarakzai, Mohmands. For Headmen; see Asaf Khel.

KUTAB KHEL.—A section of the Badzai, Kattagarm, Tatta, Battannis.

KUTAB KHEL.—A minor fraction of Balli Khel Shadi Khel, Bara Khel (1,000), Mohmit Khel, Utmanzai, Darwesh Khel Wazirs.

KUTA KHEL.—A division of Sanizai, Cis-Swat Utman Khels. Headmen; Saiad Shah, Mir Alam.

KUTAB KHEL (Miranzai and Mastura valleys).—A division of Mada Khels (800), "Hamsayas" of the Orakzais. Samil.

KUTAR KHEL.—A minor fraction of Hindi Khel, Tor, Jani Khel (1,000), Wali Khel, Utmanzai, Darwesh Khel Wazirs. Headman; Pir Makhmad.

KUTTA KHEL.—A minor fraction of Mir Ali Khel, Idia Khel, Jani Khel (1,000), Wali Khel, Utmanzai, Darwesh Khel Wazirs. Headman; Gul Ghafar.

Kutti Khel.—A section of Umar Khan Khel, Malikdin Khel, Malikdin Khel (4,000), Afridis. Samil. Headmen; Bazmir, Gholai Jan, Hazrat Gul, Kolki, Miran, Mir Zaman, Mulla Mansur, Payao, Rasul, Salim, Sardar, Akbar, Dostai, Sher Gul, Zarif, Shams-ud-din.

Kutti Khel (40).—A section of Nawar Khel, Miran Shah, Tappizad, Dawaris. Headmen; Din Muhammad, Sheikha Din, Sharob.

Kuz (or Khrappawal) Burhan Khel.—A sub-division of Burhan Khel, Pandiali, Mohmands. Headmen.

Kuz Khel.—A minor fraction of Bolaki Khel, Tatar Khel or Akborwal (300), Hassan Khel, Adam Khel, Afridis.

Kuz Sulizai (6,500; left bank of Swat river, from Thana to Maniar).—A division of Baizai, Akozai—Yusufzai Swatis.

Kuzi Khel.—A sub-division of Shekh Ali Khel, Kamrai Khel (600), Afridis. Samil. Headmen; Mulla Amir Shah, Mulla Akhundzada, and Sher Walli.

Kwaja.—A section of Khadin Khel, Ashazai, Iliaszai, Bunerwals.

L

Ladday (30).—A section of Tarota, Idak, Tappizad, Dawaris. Headmen; Idar, Nambala.

Laddi Khel (30).—A minor fraction of the Nekzan Khel, Sher Khel, Haibat Khel, Nana Khel, Bahlolzai, Mahsuds. Headmen; Daraz, Aman Shah.

Ladi Khel (70).—A section of Musakki, Tor, Mallizad Dawaris. Headmen; Dilband, Pasta Khan, Muhammad Zamir, Mihrjan.

Ladi Khel.—A minor fraction of Khan Khel, Takhti Khel, Bakka Khel (1,000), Wali Khel, Utmanzai, Darwesh Khel Wazirs. Headmen; Zamma, Mir.

Ladi Khel.—A minor fraction of Tashi Khel, Sharaki (2 0), Galai, Adam Khel Afridis.

Ladu (60).—A division of Rakanwal, Lunis. Headmen; Rahmdil, Malikzai, Galdad, Hajizai, Lal Khan, Jamalzai, Khandai, Jalezai, Lal Gul, Malwanzai, Dasmal Boiazai, Fatehan, Sidzai.

Lag Khel.—A minor fraction of Mira Khel, Mad Khozbai, Khaddar Khel (770), Mohmit Khel, Utmanzai, Darwesh Khel Wazirs. Headman; Sanobar.

Laghar (3).—A sub-division of Shamezai, Rakanwal, Lunis.

Laghar Khel (or Dodi).—A minor fraction of Khazzar Khel, Star Ali Khan Khel, Sarki Khel, Madda Khel, (1,600), Ibrahim Khel, Utmanzai, Darwesh Khel Wazirs.

Laghar Khel.—A minor fraction of Ashrab Khel, Ismail Khel, Bozi Khel, Madda Khel (1,600), Ibrahim Khel, Utmanzai, Darwesh Khel Wazirs.

Laghman Khel.—A minor fraction of Karu Khel, Malia (or Muli) Khel, Salarzai, Iliaszai, Bunerwals.

Laharzai (1,050).—A division of Musa Khels. Headmen; see Nozai, Nokuzai, Land Palai, Mangizai.

Laili.—According to to tradition, a tribe of Wazirs residing on the north-western slopes of the Safed Koh; but they have never been identified.

Lakai Kor.—A section of Ibrahim Khel, Kamali, Halimzai, Mohmands.

Lakhari Khel (Close to Ublan Pass).—A sub-division of Sipah (400), Muhammad Khel, Orakzais. Gar. Shiah.

Lakhi Khel.—A minor fraction of Pridai (150), Ashu Khel, Hassan Khel, Adam Khel Afridis.

Lakkan (1,000; Kaitu valley, Khost).—A clan of the Khostwals.

Lalakzai (87).—A section of Shamozai, Harun Khel, Sanatia, Kakars. Headmen; Isaf Kach, Guldad (Headman of the Shamozai), Ghafur, Mian Khan.

LALAT KOR.—A minor fraction of Rami Khel, Kadai Kor, Gandab, Halimzai, Mohmands. Headman; Aman.

LALAY KHEL (8).—A subdivision of Khaddi, Mallizad, Dawaris. Headman; Atlas.

LALBA KHEL.—A section of the Sturi Khel (400), Alizai, Daulatzai, Orakzais. Samil. Headmen; Aziz Khan, Sheraz.

LALI; see LAILI.

LALI KHEL (25).—A minor fraction of Rahimdad Khel, Abdul Rahman Khel, Sher Khel, Haibat Khel, Nana Khel, Bahlolzai, Mahsuds. Headmen; Nazar, Mitha.

LALI KHEL.—A minor fraction of Tol Khel, Abdul Khel, Bora Khel (1,000), Mohmit Khel, Utmanzai, Darwesh Khel Wazirs. Headman; Pahlwan.

LALIZAI (West of Dera Ghazi Khan District).—A subdivision of Mangizai, Labarzai, Musa Khels. Headman; Jamal.

LAL KHAN KOR.—A minor fraction of Said Khan Nmasi, Ali Karan, Mamuzai (3,500), Lashkarzai, Orakzais. Gar.

LAL KHEL (60; Black Mountain).—A section of Painda Khel, Akazai, Isazai, Yusufzais.

LAL KHEL; A section of Abdul Khel, Urmuz Khel, Sipah (1,200), Afridis. Samil. Headman; Chimnai.

LAL KHEL.—A minor fraction of Nikki Khel, Hassan Khel, Pakhai (1,000), Budai, Zakha Khel, Afridis. Samil. Headmen; Niazgul, Mahbub, Mir Abbas, Hamid, Jumma, Zaman, Mir Azim.

LALLA KHEL. (British territory).—A minor fraction of Painda Khel (200), Shadi Khel, Nasra Din, Khalu Khel, Ahmadzai, Darwesh Khel, Wazirs. Headman; Gulbaz.

LALLA KHEL.—A minor fraction of Jamaldin Khel, Wadin Khel, Khazzar Khel, Star Ali Khan Khel, Sarki Khel, Madda Khel (1,600), Ibrahim Khel, Utmanzai, Darwesh Khel Wazirs.

Lalli Khel (408).—A section of Abdullai, Aimal Khel, Bahlolzai, Mahsuds.

Lalzai (West of Dera Ghazi Khan District).—A section of Inzai, Hasan Khel, Balil Khel, Musa Khels. Headman; Ghulam.

Lamar.—A section of Kesu, Waruke, Dana, Battannis.

Lamar (200).—A small Kakar clan. Headman; Ainudin.

Lamma Khel (50).—A section of Maryam Khel, Darpa Khel, Mallizad, Dawaris. Headmen; Mirai, Shamali, Niazi, Lagar Shah.

Land (20).—A section of Urmuz, Tor, Mallizad Dawaris. Headmen; Ghain Shah.

Land (300).—A sub-division of Malakh, Mallizad, Dawaris. Headmen; Muhammad Akbar Khan, Nazar Din.

Land Amand (217).—A sub-division of Ahmad Khel, Oba Khel, Sheranis.

Landai.—A minor fraction of Jambai Khel, Waruka Ali-Khan Khel, Sarki Khel, Madda Khel (1,600), Ibrahim Khel, Utmanzai, Darwesh Khel Wazirs.

Landaizai (2,800; Kharmana river).—The largest of the sub-divisions of Masuzai, Lashkarzai, Orakzais. ⅘ Gar. (north of the river), ⅕ Samil (south of the river).

Landi Baddar Khel.—A minor fraction of Saadat Khel, Drepillari, Sarki Khel, Madda Khel (1,600), Ibrahim Khel, Utmanzai, Darwesh Khel Wazirs.

Landi Khel.—A minor fraction of Gadia Khel, Tatar Khel or Akhorwal (300), Hassan Khel, Adam Khel, Afridis.

Landi Khel.—A division of Sipah (1,200) Afridis. Samil. Headmen; Sher Muhammad Khan, Gul Salim, Ali Shah, Amir, Walli.

Landi Khel.—A minor fraction of Said Khel, Umarzai (600), Shin Khel, Ahmadzai, Darwesh Khel Wazirs.

Landi Khel.—A minor fraction of Kata Gran, Shugai, Tori Khel (2,670), Ibrahim Khel, Utmanzai, Darwesh Khel Wazirs. Headman; Dalai.

Landi Khel (14).—A section of the Ali Khel, Khalli Khel, Shaman Khel, Mahsuds. Headman ; Masta Khan.

Landiwal Khel.—A minor fraction of Ghulam Khel (300), Haibat Khel, Jawaki, Adam Khel, Afridis.

Landizai (2,000 ; Kurram).—A division of Chardai, Turis.

Land Palai (11).—A sub-division of Salezai, Rakanwal, Lunis.

Land Palai (200).—A division of Laharzai, Musa Khels. Headmen ; Khan Dasrand, Soba Khan, Ali Khan.

Landun.—A minor fraction of Mir Husani, Macha, Madda Khel (1,600), Ibrahim Khel, Utmanzai, Darwesh Khel Wazirs.

Langar Khel.—A minor fraction of Aziz Khel, Shadi Khel, Bara Khel (1,000), Mohmit Khel, Utmanzai, Darwesh Khel Wazirs.

Langar Khel (165).—A minor fraction of the Khoidad Khel, Gidi Khel, Manazai, Alizai, Mahsuds.

Langar Kor.—A minor fraction of the Umar Khan Khel, Ali Karan, Mamuzai, Lashkarzai, Orakzais. Gar. Headman ; Madaki.

Lar Lorai (95).—A section of Land, Malakh, Mallizad, Dawaris. Headmen ; Nazir Din, Sanobar, Akub, Balyam.

Lashkari (29).—A section of Utman, Miram Shah, Tappizad, Dawaris. Headmen ; Nakkar, Said Akbar.

Lashkari Khel.—A minor fraction of Misri Khel, Bosti Khel (150), Galai, Adam Khel, Afridis.

Lashkari Khel.—A minor fraction of the Abrahim Khel (560), Ali Karan, Mamuzai, Lashkarzai, Orakzais. Gar. Headman ; Mulla Umra.

Lashkarzai (11,500 ; Khanki and Kharmana valleys).—The largest and most important of the four clans of the Orakzais. Gar. 6,000 ; Samil 5,500.

Lashkarzai (7.)—A sub-division of Mizrai, Rakanwal Lunis. Headman ; see Mizrai.

LATKI KHEL.—A minor fraction of Marchi Khel, Abdul Khel, Bora Khel (1,000), Mohmit Khel, Utmanzai, Darwesh Khel Wazirs.

LAUS KHEL (8).—A section of the Ozbakai, Shingi, Bahlolzai, Mahsuds. Headman; Mir Afzal.

LIASZAI (87).—A section of Shamozai, Harun Khel, Sanatia, Kakars. Headmen; Nur Muhammad, Asha, Mulla Abdulla, Paind, Aulia.

LIWANNI KHEL (25).—A minor fraction of Poi Khel, Muhammad Khel, Malakh, Mallizad, Dawaris. Headman; Pirnam.

LOCHI KHEL.—A minor fraction of Dosalli, Wuzi Khel (800), Mohmit Khel, Utmanzai, Darwesh Khel Wazirs. Headmen; Niaz Gul.

LOHANAS (Ghazni in winter, Derajat in summer).—A clan of the great trading tribe of Pawindahs.

LOLL KHEL.—A minor fraction of Idar Khel, Ali Khel, Khaddar Khel, (770), Mohmit Khel, Utmanzai, Darwesh Khel Wazirs. Headman; Nambuti.

LUDANA.—A minor fraction of Manzur Khel, Tor Khel, Umarzai (600), Shin Khel, Ahmadzai, Darwesh Khel Wazirs. Headman; Alam Khan.

LUKMAN KHEL.—A minor fraction of Karim Khel, Jamal Khel, Malik Shahi (400), Wali Khel, Utmanzai, Darwesh Khel Wazirs. Headman: Urmur.

LULL (8).—A section of Taib Khel, Amzoni, Mallizad, Dawaris. Headman; Mir Hamza.

LUNDA KHEL.—A sub-division of Usman Khel, Bar Ranizai, Akozai—Yusufzai Swatis.

LUNDI KHEL (16).—A subsection of the Khoidadai, Malikshai, Aimal Khel, Bahlolzai, Mahsuds. Headman; Khissani.

LUNIS (900; from the Bori and Thal plains to the foot of the main eastern branch of the Suleman hills).—A Pathan tribe, nomadic until recent years. They are Saraband Afghans by descent; their chief is Samandar Khan.

M

Macha.—A section of Madda Khel (1,600), Ibrahim Khel, Utmanzai, Darwesh Khel Wazirs. Headmen; Mirza Shah, Shah Badan, Ware Khan.

Macha Khel.—A sub-division of Bahram-ka-Khel, Bar-Ranizai, Akozai-Yusufzai Swatis.

Machi Khel.—A minor fraction of Abdul Khel, Bora Khel (1,000) Mohmit Khel, Utmanzai, Darwesh Khel Wazirs.

Machi Khel (580).—The largest and most important of the minor fractions of the Shumi Khel, Palli Khel, Manazai, Alizai, Mahsuds.

Machi Khel (Khanki valley.)—A sub-division of the Mamuzai, Ismailzai, Orakzais. Samil. Headman; Saidan Shah.

Madak (Babukarrah valley).—A division of Salarzai, Tarkanis.

Madak.—A section of Bada, Asil, Ismailzai, Utman Khels.

Mada Khel (2,085; Mahaban).—A division of Isazai, Yusufzais.

Mada Khel.—A minor fraction of Bai Khel, Firozai, Chagarzai, Malizai, Bunerwals.

Mada Khel (570).—A section of the Allaiwals.

Madarki Khel.—A minor fraction of Bash Khel, Annai (1,000), Budai, Zakha Khel Afridis. Samil. Headmen; Gulbaz, Mir Akbar, Nawaz Khan, Zardan, Zabar, Zarin, Rahman.

Mada Nama (950).—A sub-division of Mada Khel, Isazai, Yusufzais.

Madar Khel.—A sub-division of Abdul Khel, Kuki Khel (4,500), Afridis. Gar. Headmen; Mulla Amir, Gulsani, Sherulla, Budai.

Madda Khel (1,600; Tochi and Shawal valleys).—A subdivision of the Ibrahim Khel, Utmanzai, Darwesh Khel Wazirs. Headmen; Sadda Khan and Alambo are the foremost; see also Sarki Khel, Bakhshi Khel, Bozi Khel, Macha.

MADDA KHEL.—A minor fraction of Miamai, Kabul Khel (2,600), Walli Khel, Utmanzai, Darwesh Khel Wazirs. Headman; Mezhai.

MADDA KHEL (40).—A minor fraction of the Salimi Khel, Dachi Khel, Palli Khel, Manazai, Alizai, Mahsuds. Headmen; Badshah Khan, Lalgai.

MADDA KHEL.—A sub-division of Sher Gulla, Aka Khel, (1,800), Afridis. Samil.

MADDI KHEL.—A minor fraction of Haibatanai, Tori Khel (2,670), Ibrahim Khel, Utmanzai, Darwesh Khel Wazirs. Headman; Gulzamir Khan.

MADDI KHEL.—A minor fraction of Mir Husani, Macha, Madda Khel (1,600), Ibrahim Khel, Utmanzai, Darwesh Khel Wazirs.

MADDI KHEL (34).—A section of Zarri Khel, Chahar Khel, Shaman Khel, Mahsuds. Headmen; Zargul, Mir Akbar.

MADDI KHEL.—A sub-division of Utmanzai, Bar Ranizai, Akozai—Yusufzai, Swatis.

MADDU KHEL.—A section of Asad Khel, Mitha Khan Khel, Kuki Khel (4,500), Afridis. Gar. Headmen; Muhammad Amin, Gul Jan, Budai, Langar, Mir Khan, Gul Khan, Zalmai, Mulla Nazir, Mirwal, Said Gul.

MADI KHEL and DUR.—A minor fraction of Bizen Khel (700), Shadi Khel, Nasra Din, Kalu Khel, Ahmadzai, Darwesh Khel Wazirs. Headman; Gul Adam.

MADI KHEL.—A minor fraction of Aziz Khel, Shadi Khel, Bora Khel (1,000), Mohmit Khel, Utmanzai, Darwesh Khel Wazirs.

MADI KHEL (Bannu District).—A minor fraction of Jiraki, Pirba Khel, Hathi Khel (2,000), Shin Khel, Ahmadzai, Darwesh Khel Wazirs. Headman; Musharrab Khan.

MADI KHEL (12; Dera Ismail Khan District.) Nomadic, a minor fraction of Musazai, Sein Khel, Mian Khel, Lohana, Pawindahs. Headman; see Mian Khel.

MADI KHEL (10).—A subsection of Malik Khel, Miri

Khel, Land, Malakh, Mallizad, Dawaris. Headman; Manna Khan.

Mad Khozhai.—A section of Khaddar Khel (770), Mohmit Khel, Utmanzai, Darwesh Khel Wazirs. Headmen; Watanrai, Sanobar, Rakhm Shah, Pir Muhammad, Kakar, Magule, Amzalla.

Madur Kor.—A sub-division of Masand, Safis, who are a vassal clan of the Mohmands.

Maghduzai (West of Dera Ghazi Khan District).—A sub-division of Ahmadzai, Balil Khel, Musa Khels. Headmen; Halim, Patozai, Sardar Khan, Brahimzai Lat, Jinizai, Jamal, Tolazai.

Mahmud or Mahmmad, Khel.—A clan of the Zmarais. Headmen; Sadar Hakim Khan, Bara Khan, Khakai Khan, Landai.

Maghzai.—A section of Tara Khel, Muia, Waraspun, Battannis.

Mahbub Kor.—A minor fraction of Rasul Kor, Walibeg Kor, Gandab, Halimzai, Mohmands. Headmen; Jamdad, Illias Khan, Tilla.

Mahmadai.—A section of Ashu Khel (1,400), Hassan Khel, Adam Khel, Afridis.

Mahmaddi Kor (Kharmana river).—A section of the Alizai, Masuzai, Lashkarzai, Orakzais. Samil.

Mahmadzai (West of Dera Ghazi Khan District).—A sub-division of Ahmadzai, Balil Khel, Musa Khels. Headmen; Khan Muhammad Khan (Muhammadzai), Fateh Khan (Arabzai.)

Mahmud Khan Khel.—A division of Khani Khel, Chamkannis.

Mahmud Khel.—A minor fraction of Aib Kor, Shaikh Khel, Aib Khel, Salarzai, Illiaszai, Bunerwals.

Mahmud Khel.—A minor fraction of Karu Khel, Mali, (or Muli) Khel, Salarzai, Iliaszai, Bunerwals.

Mahmud or Muhammad Khel.—A clan of the Zmarais. Headmen; Sardar Hakim Khan, Bara Khan, Khakai Khan, Landai.

Mahozai.—A sub-division of Hamzazai, Sanzar, Kakars.

MAHSUD KHEL.—A sub-division of Kakazai, Mamund, Tarkanis.

MAHSUDS or MAHSUD WAZIRS (10,048)—An important tribe, whose country is situated roughly between 32° and 32°45′ N. Lat. and 69°30′ and 70°30′ E. Long.

MAIMANA KHEL (Bohai Dag). A main division of Khwaezai, Mohmands.

MAISSZAI.—A sub-division of Woruke, Dana, Battannis.

MAIZAI.—A sub-division of Nas Khel, Sanzar, Kakars.

MAKH KOR (Hills north west of Michni, Halki Gandao).—A minor fraction of Asaf Khel, Dalkha Kor, Dadu Khel, Tarakzai, Mohmands.

MAKHAL (40).—A minor fraction of the Kimat Khel, Haidar Khel, Tor, Tappizad, Dawaris. Headmen; Gul Badin, Gul Salam, Shahzada.

MAKHAL KHEL.—A section of Shadi Khel, Bobak, Dana, Battannis.

MAKHALZAI (40).—A section of Sarangzai, Harun Khel, Sanatia, Kakars. Headmen; Galun and Juma.

MAKHAN KHEL.—A minor fraction of Dad Khel, Mir Hasani, Macha, Madda Khel (1,600), Ibrahim Khel, Utmanzai, Darwesh Khel Wazirs.

MAKHBALS or MUKHBALS.—A tribe of Khost, bordering Upper Kurram; they lie to the west of the Chakmanis.

MAKHI (40).—A minor fraction of Ipi, Haidar Khel, Tor, Tappizad, Dawaris. Headmen; Ibrahim Gul, Dalle.

MAKHI KHEL (80).—A minor fraction of the Wazirgai, Khamar Khel, Gidi Khel, Manazai, Alizai, Mahsuds. Headmen; Nizam, Amar Din, Mani, Banrai.

MAKHMAD KHEL.—A minor fraction of Shpalkai Khel, Zargun Khel (300), Galai, Adam Khel, Afridis.

MAKHOZAI (Part of Puran valley, and east slopes of Dosirri mountain).—A sub-division of Nasuzai, Iliaszai, Bunerwals.

MAKI KHEL.—A section of Firozai, Chagarzai, Malizai, Bunerwals.

Makki Khel.—A minor fraction of Kattia Khel, Hassan Khel, Mitha Khan Khel, Kuki Khel (4,500). Afridis. Gar. Headmen; Mero, Mir Afzal, Shams-uddin, Zarin.

Malai (100).—A sub-section of the Dachi Khel, Palli Khel, Manazai, Alizai, Mahsuds.

Malai (294).—A sub-division of Shingi, Bahlolzai, Mahsuds.

Mala Khel (40).—A small colony of "Hamsayas" of the Battannis living near the Larzan Pass.

Mala Khel (10; Dera Ismail Khan District.)—Nomadic, a minor fraction of Aba Khel, Isot Khel, Mian Khel, Lohana, Pawindahs. Headman; see Mian Khel.

Malak Kail (70)—A minor fraction of Taos Khel, Sogi Khel, Muhammad Khel, Malakh, Mallizad, Dawaris. Headmen; Khan Muhammad Khan, Gulat, Muhammad Khan, Said Muhammad Tarkai.

Malak Khel (40; Dera Ismail Khan District).—Nomadic, a minor fraction of Saiad Khel, Isot Khel, Mian Khel, Lohana, Pawindahs. Headman; Azim Khan.

Malak Khel.—A minor fraction of Sikandar Khel, Abdul Khel, Bora Khel (1,000), Mohmit Khel, Utmanzai, Darwesh Khel Wazirs.

Malam Khor (Khanki valley).—A sub-division of Khadizai (200), Ismailzai, Orakzais. Samil. Headman; Mian Din.

Marang Khel (80).—A minor fraction of Torang Khel, Lalli Khel, Abdullai, Aimal Khel, Bahlolzai, Mahsuds.

Malazai.—A sub-division of Arbu Khel, Sanzar, Kakars.

Malezai (91).—A division of Bakanwal, Lunis. Headmen; Pail (Chuarzai), Bilanda Khairat, Baze (Dariazai), Dilwash, Bangi (Marufzai), Madat (Ahmedzai) Nura Khan (Sadazai), Juma, Baloch Khan (Hotizai).

Maldabanai (66).—A sub-division of Ismailalagh, Spin, Tarins. Headman; Dumar.

Malikdad Khel (20).—A minor fraction of the Pirdad Khel, Abdul Rahman Khel, Sher Khel, Haibat Khel, Nana Khel, Bahlolzai, Mahsuds. Headmen; Guldad, Talib.

Malik Dinai (230).—A subdivision of Manazai, Alizai, Mahsuds.

Malikdin Khel (4,000; Maidan, Tirah, Chora and Kajurai).—One of the 6 Khyber Afridi clans. Headmen; Sultan Muhammad, Feroz, Darya Khan, and Gul Hassan.

Malikdin Khel.—A division of Malikdin Khel (4,000), Afridis. Samil. Headmen; Sultan Muhammad Khan, Feroz Khan, Yar Muhammad Khan.

Malikdin Khel.—A section of Panjpai, Nasuzai, Iliaszai, Bunerwals.

Mali Khel.—A minor fraction of Kasim Khel (250), Kimat Khel, Jawaki Adam Khel, Afridis.

Mali (or Muli) Khel (Western Buner).—A sub-division of Salarzai, Iliaszai, Bunerwals.

Mali Khel.—A sub-division of Ali Khel, Bar Ranizai, Akozai—Yusufzai Swatis.

Malik Khel.—A section of Musa Khel, Kuz Sulizai, Baizai, Akozai—Yusufzai Swatis.

Malik Khel (30).—A minor fraction of Miri Khel, Land, Malakh, Mallizad, Dawaris. Headmen; Pir Shah Alam, Mama Khan, Sheikband.

Malikshai (155).—A sub-division of Aimal Khel, Bahlolzai, Mahsuds.

Malik Shahi (400; Siah Koh and Kurram).—Nomadic, a small sub-division of Walli Khel, Utmanzai, Darwesh Khel Wazirs. Headmen; see Jamal Khel and Matkai.

Malik Shahi.—A section of Jani Khel (1,000), Wali Khel, Utmanzai, Darwesh Khel, Wazirs. Headmen; Pawindah Khan, Piyao Khan, Sahib Gul.

Malikzai (West of Dera Ghazi Khan District).—A sub-division of Mangizai, Laharzai, Musakhels. Headman; Gul Khan.

Malikzai (50).—A section of Yahia, Ahmad Khel, Oba Khel, Sheranis.

Malikzai (20).—A sub-division of Ladu, Rakanwal Lunis. Headmen; see Ladu.

Malizai.—(W. of Dera Ghazi Khan District).—A sub-division of Ahmadzai, Balil Khel, Musa Khels. Headmen; Jala (Kanuzai), Rahman (Mursenzai), Lawangai (Dodazai), Wadan (Marizai).

Malizai (3,700; Buner and northern Chamla).—One of the two clans of the Bunerwals.

Malizai (200).—A section of Baranzai, Kebzai, Sanzar, Kakars. Headman; Mian Khan.

Malizai.—A division of the Mahmud Khel, Zmarais. Headman; Bara Khan.

Malkals (150; North of Agror).—One of the leading sections of the Tikriwals.

Malla Khel (800; Miranzai and Mastura valleys).—One of the four "Hamsaya" clans of the Orakzais. Samil.

Malla Khel.—A section of Sturi Khel (400), Alizai, Daulatzai, Orakzais. Samil.

Malla Khel (31).—A sub-division of Chahar Khel, Shaman Khel, Mahsuds.

Mallakh (1,000).—One of the eight divisions of Mallizad, Dawaris. Headmen; see Charkhel, Miri Khel, Lar Lorai, Abdul Rahman Khel, Gita Khel, Kiki Khel, Sogi Khel, Idal Khel, Poi Khel, Piran, Dangar Khel, Oji Khel.

Malli (2,000; Samil valley, Khost).—A clan of the Khostwals.

Malli Khel (18).—A minor fraction of Pir Muhammad Khel, Haidrai, Chahar Khel, Shaman Khel, Mahsuds. Headman; Zole Khan.

Malli Khel (155).—A sub-division of Idak, Tappizad, Dawaris. Headmen; Nazar Shah, Walli Hassan, Mokhsein, Mirsak, Said Shah.

Malli Khel (Wana).—A minor fraction of Tojiya Khel (1,600), Bomi Khel, Nasra Din Khel, Kalu Khel, Ahmadzai, Darwesh Khel Wazirs.

Mallizad (4,008).—One of the two clans (*viz.*, Tappizad and Mallizad) of Dawaris. Headmen ; see Tor, Mallakh, Amzoni, Darpa Khel, Mubarak Shahi, Khaddi, Zerrakki and Argund Khel.

Malwanzai (10).—A sub-division of Ladu, Rakanwal, Lunis. Headman : see Ladu.

Mamadzai.—A section of Hasn, Panezun, Sanzar, Kakars.

Mama Khel.—A minor fraction of Machi Khel, Abdul Khel, Bora Khel (1,000), Mohmit Khel, Utmanzai, Darwesh Khel Wazirs. Headman ; Khoja Mir.

Mama Khel.—A sub-division of Shamozai, Khwazazai, Akozai—Yusufzai Swatis.

Mama Khel.—A minor fraction of Adam Khel, Nazar Khel, Star Ali Khan Khel, Sarki Khel, Madda Khel (1,600), Ibrahim Khel, Utmanzai, Darwesh Khel Wazirs.

Mama Khel (60).—A section of Malli Khel, Idak, Tappizad, Dawaris. Headmen ; Mirsak, Ghanamrang, Zardad.

Mama Khel (20).—A section of Tarota, Idak, Tappizad, Dawaris. Headman ; Bamali.

Mamal Khel (40).—A minor fraction of Wujji Khel, Haidrai, Chahar Khel, Shaman Khel, Mahsuds. Headmen ; Muhammad Yar, Nazi, Azmat.

Mamandzai (80).—A section of Isa Khel, Ahmad Khel, Oba Khel, Sheranis.

Mamanzai (16 ; Dera Ismail Khan District).—Nomadic, a minor fraction of Musazai, Sein Khel, Mian Khel, Lohana, Pawindahs. Headman ; Azim Khan.

Mamaras Khel (17).—A section of the Kikarai, Nana Khel, Bahlolzai, Mahsuds Headmen ; Khost and Didari.

Mamdai (250).—A sub-division of Shingi, Bahlolzai, Mahsuds.

Mami Khel (53).—A section of the Malai, Shingi, Bahlolzai, Mahsuds. Headmen ; Ambri, Rahimdad, Gulpir, Zardak, Muhammad Ali, Guldad, Rahman.

Mami Khel (320).—A minor fraction of Kharmach Khel, Nazar Khel, Aimal Khel, Bahlolzai, Mahsuds. Headman; Amir Shadai.

Mamil Khel.—A section of Suran Khel, Babakri, Sipah (1,200), Afridis. Samil. Headmen; Amir Shah, Faizu, Kadir Shah, Mir.

Mamit Khel (60).—A minor fraction of Mashi Khel, Shumi Khel, Palli Khel, Manazai, Alizai, Mahsuds. Headmen; Tawakal, Tirsam, Jim.

Mamizai (West of Dera Ghazi Khan District).—A sub-division of Land Talai, Laharzai, Musa Khels. Headman; Ali Khan.

Mamli Khel.—A sub-division of Umar Khel, Tatta Battannis.

Mamozai (Foot of Sampagha pass).—One of the four divisions of the Mishtis (3,000), "Hamsayas" of the Orakzais. They are the black sheep of the Mishti clan. Samil. Headman; Neku.

Mamrez Khel.—A minor fraction of Badi Khel, Dardoni, Wuzi Khel (800), Mohmit Khel, Utmanzai, Darwesh Khel Wazirs.

Mamrez Khel (Bannu District).—A minor fraction of Barimi Khel, Khandar Khan Khel, Hathi Khel (2,000), Shin Khel, Ahmadzai, Darwesh Khel Wazirs.

Mamu Khel.—A minor fraction of Malik Shahi, Jani Khel (1,000), Wali Khel, Utmanzai, Darwesh Khel Wazirs. Headman; Powindah Khan.

Mamun.—A sub-division of Nas Khel, Sanzar, Kakars.

Mamunds (6,000; Bajaur, principally in Watelai valley, but they own villages on both sides of the Durand line).—One of the four clans of Tarkanis. Headmen; Muhammad Amin Khan of Inayat Kila, Momin Khan.

Mamun Kor.—A section of Kandai, Isa Khel, Pandiali, Mohmands. Headmen; Ghulam Khan, Paiuddin.

Mamunzai.—A division of Alizai, Utman Khels.

Mamuzai or Muhammadzai (Western) Zaimukhts (1,830).—One of the two clans of Zaimukhts.

Mamuzai (3,500; sources of Khanki river).—One of the three divisions of the Lashkarzai, Orakzais. Gar.

Mamuzai (Yusufzai Plain).—A division of Razar, Yusufzais.

Mamuzai (80; Black Mountain).—A section of Tasan Khel, Akazai, Isazai, Yusufzais.

Manak Khel.—A minor fraction of Bakhshi Khel, Madda Khel (1,600), Ibrahim Khel, Utmanzai, Darwesh Khel Wazirs. Headmen; Gulli of Stara, and Alam Shah.

Manatuwal (900).—A division of Mamuzai or Muhammadzai, Zaimukhts.

Manazai (2,772).—The larger of two divisions of Alizai, Mahsuds.

Manazai (200; Daradar, Khanki valley).—One of the six divisions of the Ismailzai, Orakzais. Samil.

Mandal (1,000).—One of the eight clans of the Utman Khels.

Mandan or Mandanr(25,000—30,000; Peshawar District).—A great clan of the Yusufzais, who hold that portion of the Peshawar district not occupied by Khalils, Daudzais, Gugianis, Baizais, or Muhammudzais.

Mandani (260).—A division of Mamuzai or Muhammadzai, Zaimukhts.

Mandar (Laman).—A division of Ismailzai, Utman Khels.

Mandar Khel(8; Dera Ismail Khan District).—Nomadic, a minor fraction of Said Khel, Isot Khel, Mian Khel, Lohana, Pawindahs.

Mandazai.—A sub-division of Daolatzai, Malizai, Bunerwals.

Manderi (460).—A sub-division of the Idak, Tappizad, Dawaris. Headmen; Zarmak, Sahib Khan, Nazarband, Tanai Khan, Alif Khan.

Mandezai (Bajaur).—A division of Isazai, Tarkanis.

Mandezai.—A sub-division of Husenzai, Mahmud Khel, Zmarais. Headman; Landai.

Mandi Khel.—A minor fraction of Sadda Khel (300), Isperka, Kalu Khel, Ahmadzai, Darwesh Khel Wazirs.

Mandi Khel.—A section of Wuzi Khel (800), Mohmit Khel, Utmanzai, Darwesh Khel Wazirs.

Mandi Khel.—A minor fraction of Mad Khozhai, Khaddar Khel, (770) Mohmit, Khel, Utmanzai, Darwesh Khel Wazirs. Headmen; Kakar, Maguli and Amzalla.

Mandi Khel.—A section of Chapla, Muia, Waraspun, Battannis.

Mandi Khel (24).—A section of Nana Khel, Tapiai, Tappizad, Dawaris. Headmen; Azim Khan, Shaiz Khan.

Mandizai (West of Dera Ghazi Khan District).—A sub-division of the Land Palai, Laharzai, Musa Khels. Headman; Khan Dasrand.

Mandizai (West of Dera Ghazi Khan District).—A section of Dodazai, Nokuzai, Laharzai, Musa Khels. Headman; Khan Daoran.

Mando Khel (500; Zhob).—A division of (Northern) Sanzar, Kakars.

Mandozai (1,000—Shamil valley, Khost).—A clan of Khostwals.

Mandozai.—A sub-division of Hamzazai, Sanzar, Kakars.

Mandozai (Chardeh, Kabul river, Peshawar valley and Upper Helmand).—Nomadic, a sub-division of Dawezai, Kuchi, Mohmands.

Mandra Khel.—A minor fraction of Ali Khel (100), Ashu Khel, Hassan Khel, Adam Khel, Afridis.

Mandra Khel.—A minor fraction of Dildar Khel, Mohmand Khel, Kattia Khel, Hasan Khel, Mitha Khan Khel, Kuki Khel (4,500) Afridis. Gar. Headmen; Kambar, Boner. Kaddam Khan.

Mandrak Khel.—A sub-division of Firoz Khel (1,000), Daulatzai, Orkzais. Samil. Headman; Abid Khan.

Mandrashi Kor.—A minor fraction of Sroh Busha Khel, Kamali, Halimzai, Mohmands. Headmen; see Sroh.

Mandu Khel (600; Kharmana river).—A section of Nasrazai, Masuzai, Lashkarzai, Orakzais. Samil. Headman; Muhammad Shah.

Mangalai (5).—A minor fraction of Aghzan, Zira Khel, Amzoni, Mallizad, Dawaris. Headman; Piyao Muhammad.

Mangali (4).—A minor fraction of Chuttan, Zira Khel, Amzoni, Mallizad, Dawaris. Headman; Dadai.

Mangals (8,000; hills between Khost and Zurmat).—This tribe touches the British border near the Peiwar Kotal.

Mangat Khel.—A minor fraction of Sardi Khel, Bakka Khel (1000), Wali Khel, Utmanzai, Darwesh Khel, Wazirs. Headman; Mauladad Khan.

Mangi Khel (200).—A minor fraction of Bada Khel, Datti Khel, Galeshahi, Shaman Khel, Mahsuds. Headmen; Ali Khan, Daulat, Shamdai, Saleh.

Mangizai (395; near Quetta), A section of Bazai, Karun Khel, Sanatia, Kakars. Headman; Saidal.

Mangizai (300; West of Dera Ghazi Khan and Zhob).—Nomadic, a division of Laharzai, Musa Khels. Headmen; Jamal (Lalizai), Mian Khan (Daozai), Mehr Ban (Neknamzai), Alikan (Khadizai), Dadu (Brahimzai) Zhobai (Sadozai), Gul Khan (Malikzai), Mirbaz (Ahmadzai).

Mani Khel (1,000; Mastura valley and Landuki pass).—One of the four divisions of the Muhammad Khel, Orakzais. Gar. Shiah.

Manizai (West of Dera Ghazi Khan District).—A section of Maghduzai, Ahmadzai, Balil Khel, Musa Khels. Headman; Balu Khan.

Manjam Kor.—A minor fraction of Hakim Khel, Sharagh Khel, Kaddam Khel, Feroz Khel, Mashi Khel, Mannia Khel, Hassan Khel, Mitha Khan Khel, Kuki Khel (4,500), Afridis. Gar. Headmen; Abbas, Hakim, Nazir.

Mankalzai (40).—A division of Haripal, Sheranis. Headman; Haripal.

Mannia Khel.—A section of Hassan Khel, Mitha Khan Khel, Kuki Khel (4,500), Afridis. Gar. Headman; Khaista Khan is the leading man.

MANOZAI (29).—A division of Palao, Lunis. Headmen; Rahman (Ahmadzai), Alam Khan (Isazai), Karm Khan (Baozai).

MANSUM KHEL (Bannu District).—A minor fraction of Barmi Khel, Khandar Khan Khel, Hathi Khel (2,000), Shin Khel, Ahmadzai, Darwesh Khel Wazirs.

MANSUR (1,500).—A clan of the Gaduns.

MANUN KHEL (90; Black Mountain).—A sub-division of Hasanzai, Isazai, Yusafzais. Headman; Khadi.

MANUZAI (391).—A division of Oba Khel, Sheranis.

MANZAR KHEL (80).—A minor fraction of the Aziz Khel, Nazar Khel, Aimal Khel, Bahlolzai, Mahsuds. Headmen; Samandar, Maman, Kadir Shah.

MANZAR KHEL (360; Tochi river).—A sub-division of Ibrahim Khel, Utmanzai, Darwesh Khel Wazirs. Headmen; see Ali Khel, Daolatan Khel, and Sikandar Khel.

MANZOR KHEL—A minor fraction of Tor Khel, Umarzai (600), Shin Khel, Ahmadzai, Darwesh Khel Wazirs. Headmen; Jamal Din, Adal Khan, Alam Khan, Senian.

MARCHI KHEL.—A minor fraction of Abdul Khel, Bora Khel (1,000), Mohmit Khel, Utmanzai, Darwesh Khel Wazirs.

MARDAN KHEL.—A sub-division of Sultan-ka-Khel, Bar Ranizai, Akozai—Yusufzai Swatis.

MARDANZAI (120).—A section of Isa Khel, Ahmad Khel, Oba Khel, Sheranis.

MARDANZAI (1,000).—A section of Jalalzai, Alizai, Sanzar, Kakars.

MARAT KHEL (6).—A section of Zhao Khel, Tapiai, Tappizad, Dawaris. Headman; Ahmad Shah.

MAREGHUTZAI (500).—A sub-division of Kebzai, Sanzar, Kakars. Headman; Banga (Zakariazai).

Margan (15).—A minor fraction of Machi Khel, Shumi Khel, Palli Khel, Manazai, Alizai, Mahsuds. Headmen; Aliband, Shaistam.

Marhel (135).—A clan of the Sheranis. Headman; Kakar Khan.

Marid Khel.—A minor fraction of Mian Khel, Janakhori (800), Hassan Khel, Adam Khel, Afridis.

Mari Kor.—A section of Hatai Kor, Muhammad Khan Kor, or 'Bar' Burhan Khel, Pandiali, Mohmands. Headmen; Nazrai, Khalid, Razo.

Marizai (150).—A clan of the Isots. Headman; Muhammad Yar (Adamzai.)

Marizai (West of Dera Ghazi Khan District).—A section of Malizai, Ahmadzai, Balil Khel, Musa Khels. Headman; Wudan.

Marjan Khel.—A section of Utmanzai, Adinzai, Khwazazai, Akozai—Yusufzai Swatis.

Marjanzai (21; Thal—Chotiali).—A division of Drigzai, Lunis. Headmen; Alif Khan (Husezai), Mir Gul (Umrzai), Karm Khan (Jitianai), Azmat (Ishkun).

Markhozai.—A division of Alizai, Utman Khels.

Marki Khel (80).—A section of Matti Khel, Galeshahi, Shaman Khel, Mahsuds. Headmen; Azam, Shah Zaman.

Marki Khel Kalan.—A section of Musara Khel, Ashazi, Iliaszai, Bunerwals.

Marki Khel Khurd.—A section of the Musara Khel, Ashazi, Iliaszai, Bunerwals.

Marobi (120).—A section of Sultanai, Shabi Khel, Alizai, Mahsuds. Headman; Kaisar.

Maromat.—A minor fraction of Takhmal Khel, Nazar Khel, Star Ali Khan Khel, Sarki Khel, Madda Khel (1,600), Ibrahim Khel, Utmanzai, Darwesh Khel Wazirs.

Maror Khel.—A minor fraction of Pira Khel, Jamal Khel, Malik Shahi (400), Wali Khel, Utmanzai, Darwesh Khel Wazirs. Headman; Hussaini.

Marozai (Zhob).—A minor fraction of Ibrahimzai, Shadozai, Ali Khel, Sanzar, Kakars.

Marpani (82).—A sub-division of Ismailalagh, Spin, Tarins. Headman; Sher Khan.

Marsai (30).—A minor fraction of the Garerai, Shumi Khel, Palli Khel, Manazai, Alizai, Mahsuds. Headmen; Taku, Shakal, Gulzar.

Marsid Khel.—A minor fraction of Kalla Khel (700), Ashu Khel, Hassan Khel, Adam Khel, Afridis.

Maruf Khel.—A minor fraction of Basi Khel, Kamal Khel, Sahib Jan, Aka Khel, (1,800), Afridis. Samil.

Maruf Khel.—A sub-division of Wargare, Dana, Battannis.

Marufzai (100).—A section of Brahimzai, Yahia Khel, Sen Khel, Sheranis.

Marufzai (21).—A sub-division of Malezai, Rakanwal, Lunis. Headmen; Dilwas (Marufzai), Bangi (Bangizai).

Marwas Khel.—A sub-division of the Zanka Khel, Ali Khels (3,000), "Hamsayas" of the Orakzais, ⅓ Shiah. Gar. Headman; Nur Hussian.

Marwat.—A minor fraction of Sulimani Khel, Ismail Khel, Bozi Khel (1,600), Ibrahim Khel, Utmanzai, Darwesh Khel Wazirs.

Maryam Khel (35).—A section of Ghalib Khel, Badanzai, Shaman Khel, Mahsuds. Headman; Nawaz.

Maryam Khel (79).—A sub-division of Darpa Khel, Mallizad, Dawaris. Headmen; Didar, Yar Muhammad, Mazad, Pachi, Zerdast, Mirai, Shamali, Niazi, Lagar Shah.

Masa (2,000; Zhob).—A division of (Northern) Sanzar, Kakars.

Masal Kor (Hills north-west of Michni).—A minor fraction of Asaf Khel Dalkha Kor, Dadu Khel, Tarakzai, Mohmands. Headmen; see **Asaf Khel.**

Masan Khel.—A sub-division of the Akhel (600), Ismailzai, Orakzais. Gar. Headmen; Muhammad Sher, Makhmad Mir, Yara, Kabir.

Masaud Kor (North-east of the Bedmanai pass).—A division of Safis, who are a vassal clan of the Mohmands.

Masaud Kor (Kam Shilman).—A minor fraction of Asaf Khel, Dalkha Kor, Dadu Khel, Tarakzai, Mohmands.

Masazai or **Machazai** (100).—A section of Jalalzai, Alizai, Sanzar, Kakars.

Masha Khel (25; Dera Ismail Khan District).—Nomadic, a section of Sein Khel, Mian Khel, Lohana, Pawindahs.

Mashaki.—A minor fraction of Shakal Khel (100), Haibat Khel, Jawaki, Adam Khel Afridis.

Mashi Khel.—A minor fraction of Mannia Khel, Hassan Khel, Mitha Khan Khel Kuki Khel (4,500) Afridis' Gar. Headmen; Musa Khan, Khaista Khan.

Masizai.—A section of Hani, Panezun, Sanzar, Kakars.

Massar Khel (50).—A sub-division of Boba. Dana, Battannis.

Mastai Kor.—A minor fraction of Rami Khel, Kadai Kor, Gandab, Halimzai, Mohmands. With them live a small section of the Yusuf Khel. Headman; Kanzal.

Mastal Khel.—A minor fraction of Makki Khel, Kattia Khel, Hassan Khel, Mitha Khan Khel, Kuki Khel (4,500) Afridis. Gar. Headmen; see Makki Khel.

Masti Khel.—A minor fraction of Karmandi Khel, Khwaja Khel, Miamai, Kabul Khel (2,600), Wali Khel, Utmanzai, Darwesh Khel Wazirs.

Masti Khel (Wana).—A minor fraction of Tojiya Khel (1,600), Bomi Khel, Nasra Din, Kalu Khel, Ahmadzai, Darwesh Khel Wazirs.

Masti Khel.—A minor fraction of Babur Khel, Keimal Khel, Urmuz Khel, Sipah (1,200), Afridis. Samil. Headman; Khanezaman.

Masti Khel.—A sub-division of Kambar Khel, Kambar Khel (4,500), Afridis. Gar. Headmen; Muhammad Yar, Fakir, Galistan, Gul Shah, Rahmat.

Masti Khel (1,125; Kharmana river).—A section of Landizai, Masuzai, Lashkarzai, Orakzais. Gar. Headman; Arsala Khan.

Mast Khel (Bajaur).—A division of Isazai, Tarkanis.

Mastu Khel (1,500; Kurram).—A division of Sargalli, Turis.

Masuzai (5,000; Kharmana river, close to Kurram).—The largest of the three divisions of the Lashkarzai, Orakzais. Some authorities, however, regard them as a separate clan. ½ Gar, and ½ Samil. Much split up by factions.

Matani.—A sub-division of the Khoja Hawas Khel, Ali Khels (3,000), "Hamsayas" of the Orakzais. Gar. ⅛ Shiah.

Mati Khel.—A minor fraction of Drepillari, Sarki Khel, Madda Khel (1,600), Ibrahim Khel, Utmanzai, Darwesh Khel Wazirs.

Matiwal (45; Dera Ismail Khan District).—Nomadic, a minor fraction of Waruki, Sein Khel, Mian Khel, Lohana, Pawindahs. Headman; see Mian Khel.

Matkai.—A section of Malik Shahi (400), Wali Khel, Utmanzai, Darwesh Khel Wazirs. Headmen; Torabas, Marota, Pirwal, Umar Khel, Achegul.

Mat Khan Khel.—A division of Kambar Khel (4,500), Afridis. Gar. Headmen; Sher Khan, Hamid, Nurai, Mihrdin, Gattai and Matta.

Matkhwazai.—A division of Salar, Gaduns.

Matta.—A division of Mandal, Utman Khels.

Matta Khel.—A section of Ghalib Khan Khel, Malikdin Khel, Malikdin Khel (4,000), Afridis. Samil. Headmen: see Nathu Khel.

Matta Kor.—A minor fraction of Sroh, Busha Khel, Kamali, Halimzai, Mohmands. Headman; Khanizaman.

Matti Khel (110).—A sub-division of Galeshahi, Shaman Khel, Mahsuds.

Matun (1,000 ; Samil Valley, Khost).—A clan of Khostwals.

Matubizai (1,300).—A sub-division of Bar Sulizai, Baizai, Akozai—Yusufzai Swatis.

Mauli Khel (30).—A minor fraction of Sharri Khel, Kasim Khel, Chahar Khel, Shaman Khel, Mahsuds. Headmen; Fattehroz, Alijan.

Mawal Khel (760).—A section of Haibat Khel, Jawaki, Adam Khel, Afridis.

Mayan Khel.—A minor fraction of Dod Khel, Mir Hasani, Macha, Madda Khel (1,600), Ibrahim Khel, Utmanzai, Darwesh Khel Wazirs.

Mayar Khel (80 ; Gomal).—A division of Miani, Sheranis.

Mayub Khel.—A minor fraction of Saadat Khel, Drepillari, Sarki Khel, Madda Khel (1,600), Ibrahimzai, Darwesh Khel Wazirs.

Mazadin Khel.—A minor fraction of Jamaldin Khel, Wadin Khel, Khazzar Khel, Star Ali Khan Khel, Sarki Khel, Madda Khel (1,600), Ibrahim Khel, Utmanzai, Darwesh Khel Wazirs.

Mazai Kor (Bohai Dag).—A sub-division of Maimana Khel, Khwaezai, Mohmands. Headman ; Saifuddin.

Mazak Khel.—A minor fraction of Khairak Khel, Wadin Khel, Khazzar Khel, Star Ali Khan Khel, Sarki Khel, Madda Khel (1,600), Ibrahim Khel. Utmanzai, Darwesh Khel, Wazirs.

Mazeed Khel.—A minor fraction of Sikandar Khel, Kandai, Isa Khel, Pandiali, Mohmands.

Mazen Khel.—A minor fraction of Pridai (150), Ashu Khel, Hassan Khel, Adam Khel, Afridis.

Mazid Khel.—A minor fraction of Hati Khel, Mali (or Muli) Khel, Salarzai, Iliaszai, Bunerwals.

Mehtar Khel.—A minor fraction of Mushakki, Macha, Madda Khel (1,600), Ibrahim Khel, Utmanzai, Darwesh Khel Wazirs.

Mehtarzai (960).—A subdivision of Harun Khel, Saristia, Kakars. Headman ; Sirdar Habo Khan.

Mekbal.—A minor fraction of Shugai, Tori Khel (2,670), Ibrahim Khel, Utmanzai, Darwesh Khel Wazirs. Headman ; Gul Husain.

Mekhiani or Chalgari (727).—A division of Spin, Tarins. Headmen ; Mauladad, Azim, Ahad.

Menzai (Saiads ; 16).—A division of Drigzai, Lunis.

Metrak Khel.—A minor fraction of Pir Muhammad Khel, Ismail Khel, Bozi Khel, Madda Khel (1,600), Ibrahim Khel, Utmanzai, Darwesh Khel Wazirs.

Mewadav Khel.—A minor fraction of Pir Muhammad Khel, Ismail Khel, Bozi Khel, Madda Khel (1,600), Ibrahim Khel, Utmanzai, Darwesh Khel Wazirs.

Mewa Khel (25).—A section of Palali, Tapiai, Tappizad Dawaris. Headmen ; Gul Ahmad, Muhammad Khan, Amir Khan.

Mia Khel—A minor fraction of Bar Khozhai, Khaddar Khel (770), Mohmit Khel, Utmanzai, Darwesh Khel, Wazirs. Headman ; Saidigai.

Miadda Khel.—A minor fraction of Mandi Khel (Langi), Mad Khozhai, Khaddar Khel (700), Mohmit Khel, Utmanzai, Darwesh Khel Wazirs. Headman ; Magule.

Miamai.—A section of Kabul Khel (2,600), Wali Khel, Utmanzai, Darwesh Khel Wazirs. Headmen ; Mezhai, Surkam, Gulbat Khan, Mehr Ali.

Mian.—Any Mussalman holy man ; and often his descendants.

Miana (Miranzai, Vihowa).—A Trans-Indus tribe, numbers of which are found scattered along the frontier, some living with the Bangash, others with the Khetrans, etc.

Miandad Kor.—A minor fraction of Farid Khel, Firoz Khel, Mashi Khel, Hassan Khel, Mitha Khan Khel, Kuki Khel (4,500), Afridis. Gar. Headmen ; see Rahim Kor.

Mian Gul Khel (Bannu District).—A minor fraction of Kundi, Pirba Khel, Hathi Khel (2,000), Shin Khel, Ahmadzai, Darwesh Khel Wazirs.

Miani.—A section of Dreplara, Shakhi, Waraspun, Battannis.

Mianir Khel (60).—A minor fraction of the Walidad Khel, Lalli Khel, Abdullai, Aimal Khel, Bahlolzai, Mahsuds. Headman ; Saleh Shah.

Mianis (240 ; Gomal).—A clan of Sheranis.

Mianis (390 ; Gomal).—One of the lesser Pawindah trading tribes.

Mian Khan Khel (Bannu District).—A minor fraction of Jiraki, Pirba Khel, Hathi Khel (2,000), Shin or Sani Khel, Ahmadzai, Darwesh Khel Wazirs. Headman ; Gulbagh.

Mian Khel.—A minor fraction of Baghdad Khel, Keimal Khel, Urmuz Khel, Sipah (1,200), Afridis. Samil. Headmen ; Amirai, Fakir.

Mian Khel.—A minor fraction of Amar Khel, Annai (1,000), Budai, Zakha Khel, Afridis. Headman ; Bangai.

Mian Khanzai.—See Baranzai.

Mian Khel.—A section of Janakhori (800), Hassan Khel, Adam Khel, Afridis.

Mian Khel (16).—A minor fraction of Bizodai, Malikshai, Aimal Khel, Bahlolzai, Mahsuds. Headman ; Khatkai.

Mian Khel (1,400 ; Ghazni and Derajat).—A division of the Lohana, Pawindahs. Headman ; Azim Khan.

Mihr Din Kor.—A minor fraction of Yardil Kor, Kadai Kor, Gandab, Halimzai, Mohmands. Headmen ; Shah Jehan, Nawab Khan.

Mihr Khan Khel (10 ; Dera Ismail Khan District). Nomadic, a minor fraction of Aka Khel, Isot Khel, Mian Khel, Lohana, Pawindahs. Headman ; see Mian Khel.

MIHR KHAN KHEL.—A minor fraction of Balli Khel, Shadi Khel, Bora Khel (1,000), Mohmit Khel, Utmanzai, Darwesh Khel Wazirs. Headman; Kippat Khan.

MILA KHEL.—A section of Zargun Khel (300), Galai, Adam Khel, Afridis.

MINA KHEL.—A minor fraction of Malik Shahi, Jani Khel (1,000), Wali Khel Utmanzai, Darwesh Khel, Wazirs. Headmen; Piyao Khan.

MINA KHEL (35).—A section of Gurbuzai, Darpa Khel, Mallizad, Dawaris. Headmen; Shahzada, Shadi Khel, Shahdarra, Manzar Khel.

MINTAR KHEL.—A minor fraction of Muhammad Khel, Hassan Khel (400), Mohmit Khel, Utmanzai, Darwesh Khel Wazirs. Headmen; Misrai, Kabul, Khugalgai, Saadat Beg, Fazal Shah, Gulaband.

MIR AHMAD KHEL (140; Black Mountain).—A subdivision of Hasanzai, Isazai, Yusufzais. Headmen; Sherdad, Jehandad.

MIR AHMAD KHEL.—A minor fraction of Aka Khel, Ismailzai, Daulatzai, Malizai, Bunerwals.

MIR AHMAD KHEL.—A subdivision of Alisherzai (3,000), Lashkarzai, Orakzais. Samil. Headman; Zira Shah.

MIR AHMAD KHEL.—A section of Ibrahim Khel, Gadaizai, Iliaszai, Bunerwals.

MIR AHMAD KHEL (MIR Hussain Khel).—A subdivision of the Firoz Khel (1,000), Daulatzai, Orakzais. Samil. Headman; Sherbaz.

MIR AHMAD KHEL.—A minor fraction of Mir Ahmad Khel, Mir Hussain Khel, Firoz Khel (1,000). Daulatzai, Orakzais. Samil. Headman; Sherbaz.

MIRA KHEL.—A section of Zargun Khel (300), Galai, Adam Khel, Afridis.

MIRA KHEL.—A minor fraction of Ali Khel, Shugai, Tori Khel (2,670), Ibrahim Khel, Utmanzai, Darwesh Khel Wazirs. Headman; Galand.

MIRA KHEL.—A minor fraction of Balli Khel, Shadi Khel, Bora Khel (1,000), Mohmit Khel, Utmanzai, Darwesh Khel Wazirs.

MIRA KHEL.—A minor fraction of Mad Khozhai, Khaddar Khel (770), Mohmit Khel, Utmanzai, Darwesh Khel Wazirs. Headmen; Watanrai, Sanobar, Rakhm Shah.

MIRA KHEL (10).—A minor fraction of Charkhil, Charkhil, Land, Malakh, Mallizad, Dawaris. Headman; Id Muhammad.

MIRAK KHEL (Dakka, Girdi and Peshawar valley, and Upper Helmand).—Nomadic, a sub-division of Utmanzai, Kuchi, Mohmands.

MIRAK KOR.—A minor fraction of Daud Khel, Kadai Kor Gandab, Halimzai, Mohmands. Headmen; Mirak, Suleiman, Muhammad Habib.

MIR ALI.—A minor fraction of Dre Pillari, Tori Khel (2,670), Ibrahim Khel, Utmanzai, Darwesh Khel Wazirs. Headman; Shahzadin.

MIRALI KHEL.—A minor fraction of Mirkalan Khel (900), Musa Khel, Mamuzai, Lashkarzai, Orakzais. Gar.

MIR ALI KHEL.—A minor fraction of Idia Khel, Jani Khel (1,000), Wali Khel, Utmanzai, Darwesh Khel Wazirs. Headmen; Zarghun Shah, Gul Ghafar, Akaldin.

MIR ALI KHEL (200).—A minor fraction of Abrahim Khel, Ali Karan, Mamuzai, Lashkarzai, Orakzais. Gar. Headman; Rahman.

MIR ALI KHEL.—A sub-division of the Bazoti (500), Daulatzai, Orakzais. Samil. Headman; Safarali.

MIRANIS; see SHERANIS.

MIRAM KHEL (8).—A section of Zhao Khel, Tapiai, Tappizad, Dawaris. Headman; Sheikh Amin.

MIRAM SHAH (179).—A division of Tappizad, Dawaris. Headmen; Din Muhammad, Khoja Azam, Bahawan, Mir Bosh, Nakar, Mongol, Gulbat.

MIRAN KHEL.—A minor fraction of Karim Khel, Jamal Khel, Malik Shahi (400), Wali Khel, Utmanzai, Darwesh Khel Wazirs. Headman; Taghar.

MIRAN KHEL.—A section of Sheikhmal Khel, Kambar Khel, Kambar Khel (4,500), Afridis. Gar. Headmen; Mirzada, Wazir, Muddah Nur, Mast Ali, Sher Gul.

MIRAN KHEL.—A sub-division of Karna Khel, Malikdin Khel (4,000), Afridis. Samil. Headmen; see Yar Muhammad Khel.

MIRANZAI (67).—A division of Palao, Lunis. Headmen; Paind Khan (Khanikzai), Sher Khan (Karimdadzai), Umar (Narizai), Gulraz (Janguzai), Ramzan (Shikar Khanzai).

MIR ASAN KHEL.—A section of Babu Khel, Adinzai, Khwazazai, Akozai—Yusafzai Swatis.

MIRAS KHEL.—A minor fraction of Ismail Khel (150), Kimat Khel Jawaki, Adam Khel, Afridis.

MIRAZIS KHEL (Near Landuki pass).—A sub-division of the Bar Muhammad Khel, (1000), Muhammad Khel, Orakzais. Gar. Shiah.

MIRBASH KHEL.—A minor fraction of Shakal Khel (100), Haibat Khel Jawaki, Adam Khel, Afridis.

MIRBASH KHEL.—A minor fraction of Ismail Khel (150), Kimat Khel, Jawaki, Adam Khel, Afridis.

MIR BAZ KOR.—A minor fraction of Rani Khel, Kadai Kor, Gandab, Halimzai, Mohmands. Headman; Sarkai.

MIRBEG KHEL.—A section of the Kambar Khel, Bazoti (500) Daulatzai, Orakzais. Samil.

MIRBEG KHEL.—A minor fraction of Pirwal Khel, Tatar Khel or Akhorwal, Hassan Khel, Adam Khel, Afridis.

MIRBEG KHEL (Bannu District).—A minor fraction of Tori Khel, Musa Khel, Hathi Khel (2,000), Shin Khel, Ahmadzai, Darwesh Khel Wazirs. Headman; Shah Tamoz.

MIRDAD KHEL (Kuram).—A sub-division of Duperzai, (1,600), Chardai, Turis.

MIRDAD KHEL (88).—A minor fraction of the Abdul Rahman Khel, Sher Khel, Haibat Khel, Nana Khel, Bahlolzai, Mahsuds.

MIRDAD KOR.—A sub-division of the Bazid Khel Sheikhans (3,000), "Hamsayas" of the Orakzais. Samil. Headman; Alidad.

MIRDADZAI (West of Dera Ghazi Khan District).—A section of Jalalzai, Hasan Khel, Balil Khel, Musa Khels. Headman; Lawang.

MIRGHAT KHEL.—A minor fraction of Basi Khel, Kamal Khel, Sahib Jan, Aka Khel (1,800), Afridis. Samil.

MIR GHARAB.—A minor fraction of Takhmal Khel, Nazar Khel, Star Ali Khan Khel, Sarki Khel, Madda Khel (1,600), Ibrahim Khel, Utmanzai, Darwesh Khel Wazirs.

MIR HASANI.—A minor fraction of Macha, Madda Khel (1,600), Ibrahim Khel, Utmanzai, Darwesh Khel Wazirs. Headmen; Mirza Shah and Shah Badan.

MIR HASSAN KHEL.—A section of the Mir Ahmad Khel (Mir Hussain Khel), Firoz Khel (1,000), Daulatzai, Orakzais. Samil. Headman; Lal Khan.

MIR HUSSAIN KHEL.—A sub-division of the Firoz Khel (1,000) Daulatzai, Orakzais. Samil. Headman; Zain Khan.

MIRI KHEL.—A division of Aka Khel (1,800), Afridis. Samil.

MIRI KHEL.—A section of Pakhai (1,000), Budai, Zakha Khel Afridis. Samil. Headmen; see Fatteh Khel and Mitha Khel.

MIRI KHEL.—A minor fraction of Nekki Khel, Hasan Khel, Pakhai (1,000), Budai, Zakha Khel Afridis. Samil. Headman; Wali Muhammad Khan.

MIRI KHEL.—A section of Suran Khel, Babakri, Sipah (1,200), Afridis. Samil. Headmen; Abdulla, Sahib Gul.

MIRI KHEL (120).—A section of Land, Malakh, Mallizad, Dawaris. Headmen; Khojai, Muhammad Akbar.

MIR KALAN KHEL (900).—A section of the Musa Khel, Mamuzai, Lashkarzai, Orakzais. Gar. Headman; Mulla Abdul Kadir Akhun.

MIR KALAN KHEL (170).—A minor fraction of Dreplara Khusrogi, Nasruddin, Zakha Khel Afridis. Samil. Headmen; Jamrez, Ali Mast, Zaidulla, Arjumand Shah, Purdil, Mirza Khan, Nurulla.

MIRKHA KHEL (60).—A section of Baromai, Shabi Khel, Alizai, Mahsuds. Headmen; Khoidad, Tarai.

MIR KHAN KHEL.—A subdivision of Ali Khel, Bar Ranizai, Akozai—Yusufzai Swatis.

MIR KHAN KHEL (12).—A minor fraction of Khoidadai, Malikshai, Aimal Khel, Bahlolzai, Mahsuds. Headmen; Hassani, Shabbaz.

MIR KHAN KHEL (25).—A minor fraction of the Pirdad Khel, Abdul Rahman Khel, Sher Khel, Haibat Khel, Nana Khel, Bahlolzai, Mahsuds. Headman; Mitha.

MIR KHAN KHEL.—A section of Madda Khel, Sher Gulla, Aka Khel (1,800), Afridis. Samil.

MIR KHAN KHEL.—A minor fraction of Durar (300), Khusrogi, Nasruddin, Zakha Khel Afridis. Samil. Headmen; see Bucha Khel sub-section.

MIR KHAN KHEL.—A minor fraction of Asat Khel, Wuzi Khel (800), Mohmit Khel, Utmanzai, Darwesh Khel Wazirs. Headman; Jama Gul.

MIR KHAN KHEL.—A minor fraction of Adam Khel, Nazar Khel, Star Ali Khan Khel, Sarki Khel, Madda Khel (1,600), Ibrahim Khel, Utmanzai, Darwesh Khel Wazirs.

MIR KHAN KHEL.—A section of Usman Khel, Sikandar Khel, Kuki Khel (4,500), Afridis. Gar. Headman; Nazir.

MIR KHANZAI (5).—A subdivision of Walainai, Rakanwal, Lunis. Headman; see Walainai.

MIR KHEL (Khanki river).—A sub-division of Khadizai (200), Ismailzai. Orakzais. Samil. Headman; Gulla,

MIR KHONI (12).—A sub-division of Khaddi, Mallizad, Dawaris. Headmen; Gulanur and Mad Azam.

MIR KULLI KHEL.—A sub-division of Bazoti (500), Daulatzai, Orakzais. Samil. Headman; Ghulam Raza.

MIRMAN KHEL.—A minor fraction of Dosalli, Wuzi Khel (800), Mohmit Khel, Utmanzai, Darwesh Khel Wazirs.

MIROB KHEL (Bannu District) —A minor fraction of Taos Khel, Pirba Khel, Hathi Khel (2,000), Shin Khel, Ahmadzai, Darwesh Khel Wazirs. Headman; Pilawar Khan.

MIRO KHEL.—A sub-division of Mamuzai, Mishtis (3,000), "Hamsayas" of the Orakzais. Samil. Headman; Hayat Khan.

MIRO KHEL (Daradar valley). —A sub-division of Mamuzai (200), Ismailzai, Orakzais. Samil. Headman; Khan Mir.

MIRO KHEL.—A sub-division of Shamozai, Khwazazai, Akozai—Yusufzai Swatis.

MIRO KHEL.—A minor fraction of Panjpai, Musa Khel, Nurizai, Malizai, Bunerwals.

MIRO KHEL.—A sub-division of Sepah, Baezai Mohmands. Headmen; Sultan Said, Ghulam Hassan, Shafa Alam, Janan.

MIRON (42).—A section of Nawar Khel, Miran Shah, Tappizad, Dawaris. Headmen; Rezan Shah, Shah Badan.

MIROSH KHEL (60).—A minor fraction of Shammal, Hassu Khel, Tor, Mallizad, Dawaris. Headmen; Nakib and Fazal Din.

MIR SAID KHEL (400; Kharmana river)—A minor fraction of the Mandu Khel, Nasrazai, Masuzai, Lashkarzai, Orakzais. Samil. Headman; Mir Hussain.

MIR SAIAD KOR (Pipal).—A sub-division of Hassan Khel, Dawezai, Mohmands. Headman; see Dawezais.

MIR SAID KHEL.—A minor fraction of Sanzal or Sanyal Khel, Kamal Khel, Sahib Jan, Aka Khel (1,800), Afridis. Samil.

Mir Wais Khel.—A minor fraction of Panjpai, Musa Khel, Nurizai, Malizai, Bunerwals.

Mirwas Khel.—A sub-division of Shamezai, Khwazazai, Akozai—Yusufzai Swatis.

Mirwaz Khel (Mastura valley).—A sub-division of Mani Khel (1,000), Muhammad Khel, Orakzais. Gar. Shiah.

Mirwaz Khel. (7)—A minor fraction of Mitha Khel, Badiwai, Khalli Khel, Shaman Khel, Mahsuds. Headman; Khangul.

Mirzabeg Khel.—A sub-division of Mat Khan Khel, Kambar Khel (4,500), Afridis. Gar. Headmen; Sher Khan, Hamid and Nurai.

Mirzai (300).—A section of Mehtarzai, Harun Khel, Sanatia, Kakars. Headmen; Sirdar Habo Khan (Headman of Mehtarzais), Alif, Aziz, Saodagar, Paio, Mulla, Kamal Ali.

Mirzai (1,000).—A sub-division of Alizai, Sanzar, Kakars. Headman; Shah Karez.

Mirza Khel.—A minor fraction of Mir Khan Khel, Asat Khel, Wuzi Khel (800), Mohmit Khel. Utmanzai, Darwesh Khel Wazirs.

Mirza Khel.—A minor fraction of Said Khel, Umarzai (600), Shin Khel, Ahmadzai, Darwesh Khel Wazirs.

Mirza Khel.—A minor fraction of Muhammad Khel (700), Isperka, Kalu Khel, Ahmadzai, Darwesh Khel Wazirs. Headman; Daulat Khan.

Mirza Khel (500).*—One of the four clans of the Chamkannis. The Mirza Khel and Darre Khel are sometimes known collectively as the Khwaja Khel.

Mirza Khel.—A sub-division of Kandahari, Safis, who are a vassal clan of the Mohmands

Mirzis.—See **Zmarais.**

Mishak Khel.—A minor fraction of Karun Khel, Asad Khel, Mitha Khan Khel, Kuki Khel (4,500), Afridis. Gar. Headmen; Abdul Aziz, Gulistan, Sherzaman, Muhammad Amin.

---

* Includes Darre Khel.

MISHRI KHEL.—A minor fraction of Jalal Khel, Mali (or Muli) Khel, Salarzai, Iliaszai, Bunerwals.

MISHTI (3,000; Mastura valley down to British territory near Hangu).—One of the four "Hamsaya" clans of the Orakzais. They are a powerful clan and are looked up to by the others as leaders in important questions. Samil.

MISHWANIS.—See MUSHWANIS.

MISRI KHEL.—A minor fraction of Samna Khel, Ghuli Khel, Ambar Khel, Mat Khan Khel, Kambar Khel (4,500), Afridis. Gar. Headmen; see Khojal Khel.

MISRI KHEL.—A section of Bosti Khel (150), Galai, Adam Khel, Afridis.

MISRI KHEL.—A section of the Umar Khan Khel, Alisherzai (3,000), Lashkarzai, Orakzais. Samil. Headman; Madda Shah.

MISRI KHEL.—One of the subdivisions of the Hassanzai, Mishti (3,000), "Hamsayas" of the Orakzais. Samil.

MISRI KHEL (13).—A minor fraction of Khuttay, Taib Khel, Amzoni, Mallizad, Dawaris. Headman; Gul Habib.

MISRI KHEL (10).—A minor fraction of Shadi Khel, Lar Lorai, Land, Malakh, Mallizad, Dawaris. Headman; Kaimat Khan.

MITA KHEL (35).—A section of Issuri, Tor, Tappizad, Dawaris. Headmen; Muin Shah, Dolai, Shah Baram, Jalar Khan Sahib.

MITA KHEL.—A minor fraction of Kharmanj Khel, Khwaja Khel, Miamai, Kabul Khel (2,600), Wali Khel, Utmanzai, Darwesh Khel Wazirs.

MITHA KHAN KHEL.—A division of Kuki Khel (4,500), Afridis. Gar.

MITHA KHEL (186).—A section of the Badiwai, Khali Khel, Shaman Khel, Mahsuds.

MITHA KHEL (60).—A minor fraction of Shammal, Hassu Khel, Tor, Mallizad, Dawaris. Headmen; Fakir Shah, Mauzar Khan, Shah Salim, Nawi.

MITHIS (300; North-west of Dera Ismail Khan District).—One of the lesser Pawindah tribes.

MITHU KHEL.—A minor fraction of the Barid Khel, Sturi Khel (400), Alizai (Sturi Khel), Daulatzai, Orakzais. Samil. Headman; Badshah Kalandar.

MITTAH KHAN KHEL (Close to Ublan pass).—A sub-division of the Sipah (400), Muhammad Khel, Orakzais. Gar. Shiah.

MITTI KHEL.—A minor fraction of the Khamar Khel, Gidi Khel, Manazai, Alizai, Mahsuds.

MIYAN KHEL.—A minor fraction of Malik Shahi, Jani Khel (1,000), Wali Khel, Utmanzai, Darwesh Khel Wazirs. Headman; Sahib Gul.

MIYAMI KHEL (20).—A minor fraction of Abdul Rahman Khel, Muhammad Khel, Malakh, Mallizad, Dawaris. Headmen; Gul Kadam, Ghulam Shahzada.

MIYAN KHEL (30).—A section of Malli Khel, Idak, Tappizad, Dawaris. Headmen; Nazar Shah Azid.

MIZRAI (28).—A division of Rakanwal, Lunis. Headmen; Lashkar Saiad, Bahadur.

MIZRIS.—See ZMARAIS.

MOBARAK KHEL.—A minor fraction of Bash Khel (150), Sheraki Galai, Adam Khel, Afridis.

MOBIN.—A minor fraction of Takhmal Khel, Nazar Khel, Star Ali Khan Khel, Sarki Khel, Madda Khel (1,600), Ibrahim Khel, Utmanzai, Darwesh Khel Wazirs.

MOGAL BARA KHAN KHEL.—A minor fraction of Khwaja, Khadin Khel, Ashazai, Iliaszai, Bunerwals.

MOGAL KHEL.—A minor fraction of Yunas Khel, Bosti Khel (150), Galai, Adam Khel, Afridis.

MOGHALGAI (60).—A section of Bibizai, Shabi Khel, Alizai, Mahsuds. Headmen; Zarpiyao, Matta.

MOGHAL KHEL (100).—A section of Pathanai, Shabi Khel, Alizai, Mahsuds. Headman; Shahzad.

MOGHAL KHEL.—A minor fraction of Manzar Khel, Tor Khel, Umarzai (600), Shin Khel, Ahmadzai,

Darwesh Khel Wazirs. Headman; Senian.

Moghal Khel.—A minor fraction of Pira Khel, Mir Hasani, Macha, Madda Khel (1,600). Ibrahim Khel, Utmanzai, Darwesh Khel Wazirs.

Moghal Khel.—A minor fraction of Dani Khel, Matkai. Malikshahi (400), Wali Khel, Utmanzai, Darwesh Khel Wazirs. Headman; Achegul.

Moghal Khel (Bannu District). A minor fraction of Daulat Khel, Ali Khel, Musa Khel, Hathi Khel (2,000), Shin Khel, Ahmadzai, Darwesh Khel Wazirs.

Moghul Khel.—A minor fraction of Usman Khel, Shanai (750), Budai, Zakha Khel Afridis. Samil. Headmen; Mihr Din, Bawar, Sultan Mir, Gul Shah.

Mohabat Khel.—A minor fraction of Kandao Khel (400), Ashu Khel, Hassan Khel, Adam Khel, Afridis.

Mohil Khel.—A minor fraction of Shekhai, Annai (1,000), Budai, Zakha Khel, Afridis. Samil. Headmen; see Rahim Khel and Ahmad Beg Khel.

Mohib Khel.—A minor fraction of Sarmast Khel, Badi Khel, Dardoni, Wuzi Khel (800), Mohmit Khel, Utmanzai, Darwesh Khel Wazirs. Headman; Bozi.

Mohmand Khel.—A minor fraction of Daulat Khel, Ghaib Khan Khel, Malikdin Khel, Malikdin Khel (4,000), Afridis. Samil. Headmen; see Daulat Khel.

Mohmand Khel.—A minor fraction of Kattia Khel, Hassan Khel, Mitha Khan Khel, Kuki Khel (4,500), Afridis. Gar. Headmen; Kambar, Boner, Kaddam Khan, Boghi, Saidal, Ghanni, Torbaz, Mirwali.

Mohmands (16,000 to 18,000; hills north-west of Peshawar, between the Swat and Kabul rivers).—A Pathan tribe of pure Afghan descent. They have four main divisions, *viz*., Tarakzai, Halimzai, Baezai and Khwaezai. A fringe of affiliated clans, (the Kukkozai, Dawezai, and Utmanzai) surrounds the tribe; it is further hedged in, on the slopes of the Tatara Ranga, by the vassal clan of the Mullagoris, and towards Bajaur by the Safis. The Isa Khel and Burhan Khel of Pandiali were originally branches of the Tarakzai, but are now quite distinct. The chiefs, who are recognized as Khans of the Mohmands, are those of Lalpura, Goshta and Pandiali. Of these the most important are the Khans of Lalpura. The holder of the Lalpura Khanship is Akbar Khan, who is at present at Kabul, under surveillance.

Mohmit Khan Khel.—A minor fraction of Tor, Jani Khel (1,000), Wali Khel, Utmanzai, Darwesh Khel Wazirs. Headman; Amaldad.

Mohmit Khel (2,970).—One of the three great divisions of the Utmanzai clan of the Darwesh Khel Wazirs, the other two divisions being the Ibrahim Khel and the Wali Khel. Headman; Kippat Khan. Bora Khel is the leading man.

Momaddi (35).—A sub-division of Zerakki, Mallizad, Dawaris. Headmen; Pir Muhammad and Masal.

Momin Khel (60).—A minor fraction of Sher Khel, Haibat Khel, Nana Khel, Bahlolzai, Mahsuds. Headmen; Mir Ajal, Bare Khan, Malang Khan.

Morcha Khel (Lalpura, Kam, Dakka, etc., on the Kabul river).—A minor fraction of Durma Kor, Shah Mansur Khel, Dadu Khel, Tarakzai, Mohmands. They are the Khan (or chief) Khel of the Mohmands, and it is from them that the Khans of Lalpura are invariably selected; see Mohmands.

Morgai Kor.—A section of Hatai Kor, Muhammad Khan Kor, or 'Bar' Burhan Khel, Pandiali, Mohmands.

Morib Khel.—A minor fraction of Kata Gran, Shugai, Tori Khel (2,670), Ibrahim Khel, Utmanzai, Darwesh Khel Wazirs. Headman; Makam.

Morib Khel.—A minor fraction of Usman Khel, Takti Khel, Bakka Khel (1,000) Wali Khel, Utmanzai, Darwesh Khel Wazirs. Headmen; Khojamir, Mazalmir, Islam Khan.

Mot Khel.—A minor fraction of Shadi Khel, Bora Khel (1,000), Mohmit Khel,

Utmanzai, Darwesh Khel Wazirs.

Mowa Khel.—A minor fraction of Indus Khel, Drepillari, Sarki Khel, Madda Khel (1,600), Ibrahim Khel, Utmanzai, Darwesh Khel Wazirs.

Mozadin Tabar.—A minor fraction of Mamun Kor, Kandai, Isa Khel, Pandiali, Mohmands. Headmen ; see Kandai.

Mubarak Khel.—A minor fraction of Mirghat Khel, Basi Khel, Kamal Khel, Sahib Jan, Aka Khel, (1,800), Afridis. Samil.

Mubarak Shah.—A minor fraction of Khizar Khel, Mintar Khel, Muhammad Khel, Hassan Khel (400), Mohmit Khel, Utmanzai, Darwesh Khel Wazirs. Headman ; Saadat Beg.

Mubarak Shahi (225).—A division of Mallizad, Dawaris. Headmen ; Sheikh Mansur is the leading man ; see also Shujawal and Hakim Khel.

Mudah Khel.—A sub-division of Khadakzai, Khwazazai. Akozai—Yusufzai Swatis.

Mughul Khel.—A sub-division of Barmi Khel, Kamrai or Kamar Khel (600), Afridis. Samil. Headmen ; Hafiz Samandar, Firoz Khan, Anar, Bahadur Shah, Sifat Shah, Sheradin, Zardad, Mir Ali.

Muhammad Khan Kor.—A sub-division of Burhan Khel Pandiali, Mohmands ; they are also known as 'Bar,' Burhan Khel.

Muhammad Khel (Goshta). A sub-division of the Khadi Khel, Khwaezai Mohmands. Headmen ; Mir Muhammad Khan, Barkat Khan, Yusuf Khan.

Muhammad Khel.—A minor fraction of Ismail Khel, Makhozai, Nasuzai, Iliaszai, Bunerwals.

Muhammad Khel (Khanki river).—A sub-division of the Khadizai (200), Ismailzai, Orakzais. Samil. Headman ; Mirak.

Muhammad Khel (120).—A minor fraction of the Machi Khel, Shumi Khel, Palli Khel, Manazai, Alizai, Mahsuds. Headman ; Shah Salim.

Muhammad Khel (2,480 ; Mastura valley and Landuki pass).—One of the four clans of the Orakzais. They are much under the influence of Saiads. Gar. Shiah.

MUHAMMAD KHEL.—A section of Zargun Khel (300), Galai, Adam Khel, Afridis.

MUHAMMAD KHEL (700; migratory).—A section of Isperka, Kalu Khel, Ahmadzai, Darwesh Khel Wazirs. Headmen; Muhammad Jan, Daulat Khan, Habib Gul, Jan, Nur Muhammad, Shah Kamran, Katamir, Pir Muhammad, Wasila Khan.

MUHAMMAD KHEL.—A section of Hassan Khel (400), Mohmit Khel, Utmanzai, Darwesh Khel Wazirs. Headmen; Misrai, Kabul, Khusalgai Saadat Beg, Fazal Shah, Gulaband, Gulbat Shah, Sippar.

MUHAMMAD KHEL (18).—A sub-division of Khaddi, Mallizad, Dawaris. Headmen; Mazid Khan, Madazan.

MUHAMMAD KHEL (12).—A section of Nana Khel, Tapiai, Tappizad, Dawaris. Headmen; Musa, Ahmad Khan.

MUHAMMAD KHEL (701).—A sub-division of Malakh, Mallizad, Dawaris. Headmen; Khan Muhammad Khan, Fazal Din, Makhmad, Shah Azam, *alias* Bich, Balrang, Ghanam Shah, Habib Shah.

MUHAMMAD PIR.—A section of Alizai, Darpa Khel, Mallizad, Dawaris. Headman; Muhammad Pir.

MUHAMMAD YAR KOR.—A minor fraction of Rami Khel, Kadai Kor, Gandab, Halimzai, Mohmands. Headman; Mahba Din.

MUHAMADZAI (271).—A subdivision of Ahmad Khel, Oba Khel, Sheranis.

MUHAMMADZAI (Peshawar District).—A tribe who live in Hashtnagar: they are also known as Mohmandzai or Mamanzai.

MUHAMMADZAI—see MAMUZAI ZAIMUKHTS.

MUIA (800).—One of the divisions of Waraspun, Battanis. Headmen; Ahmad Shah (Mandi Khel), Didari (Dari Khel), Isof Khan (Khwad Khel).

MUKHBALS; see MAKHBALS.

MULA KHEL.—A section of Aya Khel, Ashazai, Iliaszai, Bunerwals.

MULA KHEL (520; north-west of Dera Ismail Khan District).—One of the lesser Pawindah trading tribes.

MULAZAI (240).—A section of Panizai, Harun Khel, Sanatia, Kakars. Headman; Mushkai.

MULLAGAN (80).—A sub-division of Tor, Mallizad' Dawaris. Headmen; Muhammad Amin, Fazalli.

MULLAGAN (14).—A minor fraction of Ipi, Haidar Khel, Tor, Tappizad, Dawaris. Headman; Mir Alam.

MULLAGORI KOR.—A minor fraction of Rajai Khel, Yusuf Khel, Isa Khel, Pandiali, Mohmands.

MULLAGORIS (400; Tartara). —A vassal clan of the Mohmands.

MULLA KHEL.—One of the two sub-divisions of the Umarzai Sheikhans (3,000), "Hamsayas" of the Orakzais. Samil. Headman; Rahman.

MULLA KHEL (Dir).—A section of Sultan Khel, Sesada, Malizai, Yusufzais.

MULLAH KHEL.—A sub-division of Bahram-ka-Khel, Bar Ranizai, Akozai—Yusufzai Swatis.

MULLAH KOR.—A minor fraction of Sultan Khel, Hamza Khel, Gandab, Halimzai, Mohmands. Headman; Lalajan.

MULLAH KOR.—A minor fraction of Sroh, Busha Khel, Kamali, Halimzai, Mohmands. Headman; Khanizaman.

MULTANI KHEL.—A section of Zakku Khel, Sikandar Khel, Kuki Khel (4,500), Afridis. Gar. Headmen; Taus, Said Gul.

MURADI KHEL (350).—A section of Dalkha Kor, Dadu Khel, Tarakzai, Mohmands. Headmen; Multan, Najai, Muhammad Hassan (Shahi Kor), Achuk (Takhai Kor), Akbar, Madda Khan, Mir Ali.

MURADU KHEL.—A section of Azi Khel, Ali Khel, Bar Ranizai, Akozai—Yusufzai Swatis.

MURSENZAI (West of the Dera Ghazi Khan District).—A section of Malizai, Ahmadzai, Balil Khel, Musa Khels. Headman; Rahman.

MUSA KHEL.—A minor fraction of Narmi Khel, Bakka Khel (1,000), Wali Khel, Utmanzai, Darwesh Khel

Wazirs. Headman; Banai Khan.

Musa Khel.—A minor fraction of Misri Khel, Bosti Khel (150), Galai, Adam Khel, Afridis.

Musa Khel—A sub-division of Yar Ali Khel, Kamrai Khel (600) Afridis. Samil.

Musa Khel (Bannu District).—A section of Hathi Khel (2,000), Shin Khel, Ahmadzai, Darwesh Khel Wazirs. Headmen; Adam Khan, Shah Tamoz.

Musa Khel (Bajaur).—A division of Isazai, Tarkanis.

Musa Khel (2,840).—A section of the Allaiwals.

Musa Khel.—A minor fraction of Warkam Khel, Aib Khel, Salarzai, Iliaszai, Bunerwals.

Musa Khel.—A section of Makhozai, Nasozai, Iliaszai, Bunerwals.

Musa Khel.—A sub-division of Nurizai, Malizai, Bunerwals.

Musa Khel (1,500).—A subdivision of Kuz Sulizai, Baizai, Akozai—Yusufzai Swatis.

Musa Khel.—A section of Sen Khel, Gadaizai, Iliaszai, Bunerwals.

Musa Khel.—A section of Aya Khel, Ashazai, Iliaszai, Bunerwals.

Musa Khel (15; Dera Ismail Khan District).—Nomadic, a minor fraction of Pasani, Isot Khel, Mian Khel, Lohana, Pawindahs. Headman; see Mian Khel.

Musa Khel (Pawindahs, 12; Dera Ismail Khan District).—Nomadic, a minor fraction of Zakori, Sein Khel, Mian Khel, Lohana, Pawindahs. Headmen; see Mian Khel.

Musa Khel (1,800).—A subdivision of Sepah, Baizai, Mohmands.

Musa Khel (7).—A minor fraction of Umarzai, Zira Khel, Amzoni, Mallizad, Dawaris. Headman; Malak Khan.

Musa Khel (12).—A subdivision of Khaddi, Mallizad Dawaris. Headman; Didar.

Musa Khels (4,670; west of Dera Ghazi Khan District).—A large tribe of Pathans, said to be descended from a younger brother of the ancestor of the Kakar tribe.

MUSAKKI.—A section of Wuzi Khel (800), Mohmit Khel, Utmanzai, Darwesh Khel Wazirs.

MUSAKKI (260).—A sub-division of Tor, Mallizad, Dawaris. Headmen; see Tukar Khel, Ladi Khel, Shahabdin Khel, and Shabi Khel.

MUSA KOR (Bohai Dag).—A sub-division of Maimana Khel, Khwaezai, Mohmands. Headman; Saifur.

MUSAM KHEL.—A minor fraction of Sikandar Khel, Manzar Khel (360), Ibrahim Khel, Utmanzai, Darwesh Khel Wazirs. Headman; Lal Khan.

MUSARA KHEL.—A sub-division of Ashazai, Iliaszai, Bunerwals.

MUSAZAI (85; Dera Ismail Khan District).—Nomadic, a section of Sein Khel, Mian Khel, Lohana. Pawindahs. Headmen; see Mian Khel.

MUSAZAI (West of Dera Ghazi Khan District).—A subdivision of Hamzazai, Balil Khel, Musa Khels. Headman; Dari Khan.

MUSAZAI (20).—A division of Oba Khel, Sheranis.

MUSAZAI.—A division of Mansur, Gaduns.

MUSHAKKI.—A minor fraction of Macha, Madda Khel (1,600), Ibrahim Khel, Utmanzai, Darwesh Khel Waziris. Headmen; Ware Khan of Surram, Barlai of Tsapparai.

MUSHWANIS. (250; Sharod).—A small tribe of Saiads divided into five clans; *viz.*, Sarkozais, Panjpais, Chichazais, Muhammad Khels, and Mian Khanzais. A few Mushwanis live with the Utmanzais of the Hazara border. The clans, etc., of the Mushwanis are not separately indexed in this Dictionary.

MUTAKAI (500; south of junction of Jandol and Bajaur streams).—One of the eight clans of the Utman Khels.

MUZI KHEL.—A minor fraction of Mushakki, Macha, Madda Khel (1,600), Ibrahim Khel, Utmanzai, Darwesh Khel Wazirs.

N

NABI KHEL (13).—A sub-division of Boya, Tappizad, Dawaris. Headman; Katawaz.

NAHAKKI or YUSAF KOR (80).—A section of Ibrahim Khel, Kamali, Halimzai, Mohmands.

NAHAR (Dera Ghazi Khan District and Khetran Hills).—A Pathan tribe. Headman; Khan Muhammad.

NAIM SHER KOR (Khanki river).—A sub-division of Khadizai (200), Ismailzai, Orakzais, Samil. Headman; Mira Khan.

NAKRIZ (126).—A section of Shujawal, Mubarak Shahi, Mallizad, Dawaris. Headmen; Zarif, Maula Hassan, Moghlay and Mala.

NAKSHBAND KHOR (Khanki valley).—A sub-division of Sada Khel (10), Ismailzai, Orakzais. Samil. Headman; Said Salam.

NANA KHEL.—A minor fraction of Balli Khel, Shadi Khel, Bora Khel (1,000), Mohmit Khel, Utmanzai, Darwesh Khel Wazirs.

NANA KHEL.—A minor fraction of Idar Khel, Ali Khel, Khaddar Khel (770), Mohmit Khel, Utmanzai, Darwesh Khel Wazirs. Headman; Ziarai.

NANA KHEL.—A minor fraction of Manzar Khel, Tor Khel, Umarzai (600), Shin Khel, Ahmadzai, Darwesh Khel Wazirs. Headman; Adal Khan.

NANA KHEL.—A minor fraction of Mir Khan Khel, Asat Khel, Wuzi Khel (800), Mohmit Khel, Utmanzai, Darwesh Khel Wazirs.

NANA KHEL (40; Dera Ismail Khan District).—Nomadic, a minor fraction of Zakori, Sein Khel, Mian Khel, Lohana, Pawindahs. Headman; see Mian Khel.

NANA KHEL (142).—A subdivision of Tapiai, Tappizad, Dawaris. Headmen; Adil Shah, Azim Khan, Gulshahdad, Musa, Khamid, Hazrat Pir.

NANDAR KHEL.—A minor fraction of Jaipali, Kabul Khel (2,600), Wali Khel, Utmanzai, Darwesh Khel Wazirs.

NANDIHARIS (1,000; Nandihar valley, north of Hazara District).—A tribe of Swati origin. Headmen; Samandar Khan, Mozuffar Khan.

NANI KHEL (11).—A section of Alizai, Darpa Khel, Mallizad, Dawaris. Headman; Suliman Khel.

NANI KHEL (30).—A minor fraction of Lar Lorai, Land. Malakh, Maliizad, Dawaris. Headmen; Sanobar Khan, Walibaz, Madigai.

NANU KHEL (70; Black Mountain).—A sub-division of Hasanzai, Isazai, Yusufzais. Headman; Fakir.

NARAIZAI.—A division of Kukkozai, who are a vassal clan of the Mohmands.

NARANG KHEL.—A minor fraction of Bolaki Khel, Tatar Khel or Akhorwal (300), Hassan Khel, Adam Khel, Afridis.

NARMI KHEL (Bannu and Shawal).—A section of Bakka Khel (1,000), Wali Khel, Utmanzai, Darwesh Khel Wazirs. Headmen; Banai Khan, Shah Nawaz, Ghainadin, Pilod Khan.

NASAR KHEL.—A minor fraction of Ghani Khel, Mir Hasani, Macha, Madda Khel (1,600), Ibrahim Khel, Utmanzai, Darwesh Khel Wazirs.

NASAR KHEL.—A minor fraction of Sanni Khel, Zargun Khel (300), Galai, Adam Khel, Afridis.

NASAR KHEL (9).—A section of Zhao Khel, Tapiai, Tappizad, Dawaris. Headman; Gula Din.

NASARS (7,500; move yearly from Khorasan into Derajat).—A trading clan, one of the wealthiest of the Pawindah tribe. They are divided into (1) Jalal Khel, (2) Ushi Khel, (3) Par Khel, (4) Alambeg Khel, (5) Banu Khel, (6) Yahaya Khel, (7) Kamal Khel, (8) Daud Khel, (9) Musazai, (10) Tangi Khel, (11) Saru Khel. (12) Niamat Khel.

NASARZAI.—A division of Anjra Khel, Zmarais. Headman; Ghairat Khan.

NASI KOR.—A sub-division of Azim Khan Kor, Umar Khan Khel, Alisherzai, (3,000) Orakzais. Samil.

NASIR KOR.—A minor fraction of Rasul Kor, Wali Beg Kor, Gandab, Halimzai, Mohmands. Headmen; Hassan, Ghulam Nabbi, Mehr Gul.

NAS KHEL (500 ; Bori, Zhob) —A division of the (Southern) Sanzar, Kakars.

NASRA DIN (7,210).—A sub-division of Kalu Khel, Ahmadzai, Darwesh Khel Wazirs. Headmen ; see Shadi Khel and Bomi Khel.

NASRAT KHEL (Cis-Indus, and on the north-eastern borders of Buner).—A sub-division of the Chagarzai, Malizai, Yusufzais. They do not belong to Buner proper.

NASRAT KHEL.—A section of Ghalib Khan Khel, Malikdin Khel, Malikdin Khel (4,000), Afridis. Samil. Headmen ; see Nathu Khel.

NASRAT KHEL (80 ; Black Mountain).—A sub-division of Hasanzai, Isazai, Yusufzais. Headmen; Gujar Khan, Sahaid.

NASRAZAI (650 ; Kharmana river).—A sub-division of Masuzai, Lashkzarai, Orakzais. ½ Gar, ½ Samil. Headman ; Mir Ahmad Shah.

NASRI KHEL.—A minor fraction of Bachagai, Tor, Jani Khel (1,000), Wali Khel, Utmanzai, Darwesh Khel Wazirs. Headman ; Gulbaz.

NASRI KHEL.—A minor fraction of Mushakki, Macha (1,600), Ibrahim Khel, Utmanzai, Darwesh Khel Wazirs.

NASRI KHEL (10).—A minor fraction of Bar Kaum, Hassu Khel, Tor, Mallizad, Dawaris. Headman ; Gul Sahib.

NASR KHEL (302).—A section of Haidar Khel, Tor, Tappizad, Dawaris. Headmen ; Gul Khan, Lalo Khan.

NASRUDDIN (1,200 to 1,500). —A division of Zakka Khel Afridis. Samil. Headmen ; see Habib, Paindai, and Khusrogi.

NASRUDIN KHEL (1,500 ; Maidan, Dir).—A sub-division of Sesada, Malizai, Yusafzais. Headmen ; Khans of Robat and Fam, Jan of Bargulai, and Barun.

NASUZAI (2,000 ; western and eastern slopes of Duma mountain).—One of the four divisions of Iliaszai, Bunerwals.

NATHU KHEL.—A section of Ghalib Khan Khel, Malikdin Khel, Malikdin Khel (4,000), Afridis. Samil.

Headmen ; Sultan Muhammad Khan, Feroz Khan, Yar Muhammad Khan, Muhammad Raza, Alam Khan, Gholai, Kasim, Hamid, Said Ghulam, Majid Akhundzada, Miran, Mir Alam, Mir Azim, Mir Salim, Mir Ahmad, Nur Jan.

NATOZAI (2,000 ; Zhob).—A division of (Northern) Sanzar, Kakars.

NAWAB KOR.—A minor fraction of Rahmatai Kor, Kadai Kor, Gandab, Halimzai, Mohmands. Headman ; Nausher Khan.

NAWAR KHEL (125).—A subdivision of Miram Shah, Tappizad, Dawaris. Headmen ; Din Muhammad, Khoja Azam, Bahawan, Mir Bosh.

NAWAR KHEL (30).—A section of Nawar Khel, Miram Shah, Tappizad, Dawaris. Headmen ; Bahawan, Nalakh, Tani.

NAWAR KHEL (10).—A section of Zira Khel, Amzoni, Mallizad, Dawaris. Head man ; Azam Shah.

NAWAZ KHEL.—A minor fraction of Sanni Khel, Zargun Khel (300), Galai, Adam Khel, Afridis.

NAZAI KHEL.—A minor fraction of Aziz Khel, Shadi Khel, Bora Khel (1000), Mohmit Khel, Utmanzai, Darwesh Khel Wazirs.

NAZAL KHEL.—A minor fraction of Marchi Khel, Abdul Khel, Bora Khel (1,000), Mohmit Khel, Utmanzai, Darwesh Khel Wazirs.

NAZARBEG KHEL (British territory).—A minor fraction of Budin Khel (100), Shadi Khel, Nasra Din Khel, Kalu Khel, Ahmadzai, Darwesh Khel Wazirs. Headman ; Mir Alam.

NAZAR KHEL.—A minor fraction of Star Ali Khan Khel, Sarki Khel, Madda Khel (1,600), Ibrahim Khel, Utmanzai, Darwesh Khel Wazirs. Headmen ; Kadam Khan, Nabbi Khan.

NAZHI KHEL.—A minor fraction of Pira Khel, Mir Hasani, Macha, Madda Khel (1,600), Ibrahim Khel, Utmanzai, Darwesh Khel Wazirs.

NAZI KHEL.—A section of Abdal Khel, Urmuz Khel, Sipah (1,200), Afridis. Samil. Headman ; J mma.

Nazi Khel.—A minor fraction of Moghul Khel, Usman Khel, Shanai (750), Zakha Khel Afridis. Samil. Headmen; Mihr Din, Bawar, Sultan Mir, Gul Shah.

Nazir Khel.—A minor fraction of Sanni Khel, Zargun Khel (800), Galai, Adam Khel, Afridis.

Nazo Khel.—A sub-division of Aimal Khan Khel, Zanka Khel (3,000), "Hamsayas" of the Orakzais. Gar. Shiah.

Nazo Khel.—A sub-division of the Khoja Hawas Khel, Ali Khels (3,000), "Hamsayas" of the Orakzais. Gar. ½ Shiah.

Nazr Ali Khel.—A section of Maddi Khel, Utmanzai, Bar Ranizai, Akozai—Yusufzai Swatis.

Nekam Khel.—A minor fraction of Bizen Khel (700), Shadi Khel, Nasra Din, Kalu Khel, Ahmadzai, Darwesh Khel Wazirs. Headman; Timar Khan.

Nekbol (4).—A minor fraction of Chuttan, Zira Khel, Amzoni, Mallizad, Dawaris. Headman; Manganai.

Neknamzai (West of Dera Ghazi Khan District).—A sub-division of Hamzazai, Balil Khel, Musa Khels. Headman; Shambi.

Neknamzai (West of Dera Ghazi Khan District).—A sub-division of Mangizai, Laharzai, Musa Khels. Headman; Mehrban.

Nekpi Khel (4,000; a valley of the same name on right bank of Swat).—A division of Khwazazai, Akozai—Yusufzai Swatis. Headman; Yusuf Khan.

Nekzam Khel.—A section of Tor Sapar (350), Galai, Adam Khel, Afridis.

Nekzam Khel.—A minor fraction of Walli Khel, Ali Khel, Sheikhmal Khel, Kambar Khel, Kambar Khel (4,500). Afridis. Gar. Headman; Saleh Muhammad.

Nezam Khel (26).—A section of Hakim Khel, Mubarak Shahi, Mallizad, Dawaris. Headman; Nazam Khan.

Niamat Khel (150).—A division of Tatta, Battannis. Headmen; Kushal Khan (Kaka), Marwut (Agzar),

Mir Azar (Shahgul), Raddat (Bassia), Binak (Firoz).

NIAMAT KHEL.—A minor fraction of Waruka Ali Khan Khel, Sarki Khel, Madda Khel (1,600), Ibrahim Khel, Utmanzai, Darwesh Khel Wazirs.

NIAST KHEL; A section of Aya Khel, Ashazai, Iliaszai, Bunerwals.

NIAZIS (980; Khorasan and the Derajat).—Migratory, a Pawindah tribe divided as follows:—(1) Mamrez Khel, (200); (2) Nurkkhan Khel, (170); (3) Mahsud Khel, (230); (4) Ali Khel, (120); (5) Mala Khel, (260). There are four other clans of this tribe, *viz.*, Isa Khels (1,600), Kamar Mashani (30), Kundi (360), and Sarhang (1,200), who are settled in British territory in Isa Khel, Kalabagh, Mianwali, Bannu, etc.

NIKKI KHEL.—A minor fraction of Hassan Khel, Pakhai (1,000), Budai, Zakha Khel Afridis. Samil. Headmen; see Miri Khel, Ahmad Khel, Lal Khel and Kazian Kor.

NOKUZAI (450; West of Dera Ghazi Khan District).—A division of Laharzai, Musa Khels. Headmen; Baiak, Bazi, Khan Daoran (Dodazai), Khatal, Momin, Mulla Nadar, Hasan (Kabalzai).

NOR KHAL.—A minor fraction of Balal Khel, Hassan Khel (400), Mohmit Khel, Utmanzai, Darwesh Khel Wazirs. Headman; Ghulam Jan.

NOZAI (250).—A clan of Isots Headman; Mahmud Khan.

NOZAI (100; west of Dera Ghazi Khan).—A division of Laharzai, Musa Khels. Headmen; Shahbaz (Dawizai), Sheran (Bashanizai), Gulsher (Isazai), Mendak (Jalalzai).

NURAK KHEL (Talash and Dush Khel, Dir).—A subdivision of the Ausa Khel, Malizai, Yusufzais.

NURAK KHEL.—A sub-division of Sarsa, Tatta, Battannis.

NURI KHEL (10).—A section of Utman, Miram Shah, Tappizad, Dawaris. Headman; Mongul.

NURIZAI (1,200; southern corner of the Buner valley).—One of the three division of Malizai. Bunerwals.

NUR KHAN KHEL (20 ; Dera Ismail Khan District).—Nomadic, a minor fraction of Aka Khel, Isot Khel, Mian Khel, Lohana, Pawindahs.

NUR MAKHMAD KHEL.—A minor fraction of Sulimani Khel, Ismail Khel, Bozi Khel, Madda Khel (1,600), Ibrahim Khel, Utmanzai, Darwesh Khel Wazirs.

NUR MUHAMMAD KHEL.—A section of Ghaibi Khel, Bahram-ka Khel, Bar-Ranizai, Akozai—Yusufzai Swatis.

NUR MUHAMMAD KHEL.—A minor fraction of Tor Khel, Asad Khel, Mitha Khan Khel, Kuki Khel (4,500), Afridis. Gar. Headmen ; Razai, Islamdin.

NUROZAI (Gomal).—A division of Miani, Sheranis.

NURWEZ KHEL.—A sub-division of the Khwaja Hawas Khel, Ali Khels (3,000), "Hamsayas" of the Orakzais. Gar. ⅓ Shiah.

O

OBA KHEL (1,633).—A clan of the Sheranis. Headman ; Azim Khan.

OJI KHEL (10).—A section of Muhammad Khel, Malakh, Mallizad, Dawaris. Headmen ; Habib Shah, Muhammad Said.

ORAKZAIS (27,800 ; Tirah, the mountainous district north-west of Kohat, and immediately south of the Afridi country, down to the Miranzai valley).—One of the most important of the tribes on the North-West Frontier. It may be noted that the Muhammad Khel clan, as also portions of the Alizais and Ali Khels, are Shiahs.

OZBAKAI (41).—A sub-division of Shingi, Bahlolzai, Mahsuds.

OZI (50).—A sub-division of Zerakki, Mallizad, Dawaris. Headmen ; Salamai, and Nabat Shah.

P

Pabbi Khel.—A sub-division of Kambar Khel, Kambar Khel (4,500), Afridis. Gar. Headmen; Muhammad Sher, Khwaja Ali, Yaro, Nurai, Sherai, and Sher.

Padai Kor.—A sub-division of the Dawat Khel, Khwaezai, Mohmands. Headman; Bara Khan.

Padmi (33).—A section of Taib Khel, Amzoni, Mallizad Dawaris. Headmen; Faizullah, Merai.

Padshah Khel.—A minor fraction of Ya Khel, Babu Khel, Adinzai, Khwazazai, Akozai—Yusufzai Swatis.

Pagal Kor or Kadal Kor.—A minor fraction of Daud Khel, Kadai Kor, Gandab, Halimzai, Mohmands. Headmen; Yakub, Allah Mit.

Pagal Kor or Wali Beg Kor.—A minor fraction of Rasul Kor, Wali Beg Kor, Gandab, Halimzai, Mohmands. Headmen; Shere Zaman, Gul Hassan, Ghulam Jan.

Pahar Khel.—A minor fraction of Dre Nami, Balal Khel, Hassan Khel (400), Mohmit Khel, Utmanzai Darwesh Khel Wazirs. Headman; Malak Din.

Pah Khel (Bohai Dag).—A sub-division of Khadi Khel, Khwaezai, Mohmands. Headmen; Gudai, Muhammad.

Paia Khel.—A section of Janakhori (800), Hassan Khel, Adam Khel, Afridis.

Paia Khel (200).—A section of Taru Khel, Boba, Dana, Battannis.

Paie (350).—A clan of the Allaiwals.

Pai Khel.—A minor fraction of Kundai, Tor Khel, Umarzai (600), Shin Khel, Ahmadzai, Darwesh Khel Wazirs. Headman; Ghallai.

Pat Khel (60; Dera Ismail Khan District.).—Nomadic, a minor fraction of Umrzai, Sein Khel, Mian Khel, Lohana, Pawindahs. Headmen; see Mian Khel.

PAINDA.—A minor fraction of Madak, Bada, Asil, Ismailzai, Utman Khels.

PAINDAI (940).—A sub-division of Nasruddin, Zakha Khel Afridis. Samil. Headmen; Abdulla Mir, Shahbaz, Mir Kasim, Sher Ali, Bazai, Afzal, Lal Mir, Khair Muhammad.

PAINDA KHEL (170; Black Mountain.).—A sub-division of Akazai, Isazai, Yusufzais. Headmen; Zarif Khan, Abdulla, Sahaid.

PAINDA KHEL.—A section of Alisher Khel, Gadaizai, Iliaszai, Bunerwals.

PAINDA KHEL (300).—A section of Khidrzai, Ahmad Khel, Oba Khel, Sheranis.

PAINDA KHEL.—A minor fraction of Manak Khel, Bakhshi Khel, Madda Khel (1,600), Ibrahim Khel, Utmanzai, Darwesh Khel Wazirs.

PAINDA KHEL.—A section of Macha Khel, Bahram-ka-Khel, Bar Ranizai, Akozai —Yusufzai Swatis.

PAINDA KHEL (200; British territory).—A minor fraction of Shadi Khel, Nasra Din, Kalu Khel, Ahmadzai, Darwesh Khel Wazirs. Headmen; Gulbaz, Sarwar Khan.

PAINDA KHEL.—A sub-division of Shamozai, Ismailzai, Utman Khels. Headmen; Ayub Khan, Mir Saiad.

PAINDA KHEL.—A sub-division of Shamozai, Ismailzai, Utman Khel.

PAINDA KHEL (3,900; left bank of the Panjkora river, Dir).—A sub-division of Sesada, Malizai, Yusufzais. Headmen; Rahmatulla of Barkhand; Mir Afzal of Samkut, Gul Abdulla of Bandai, Abid Khan of Dorial, and Saiad Kamal of Akhagram.

PAINDI KHEL.—A sub-division of Barmi Khel, Kamrai Khel (100) Afridis. Samil. Headman; Daulat.

PAIO KHEL.—A minor fraction of Khazzar Khel, Star Ali Khan Khel, Sarki Khel, Madda Khel (1,600), Ibrahim Khel, Utmanzai, Darwesh Khel Wazirs.

PAIPALI.—A section of Kabul Khel (2,600), Wali Khel, Utmanzai, Darwesh Khel Wazirs.

PAIPALI (13).—A sub-division of Banda, Tappizad, Dawaris. Headman ; Ghonsamir.

PAKAN KHEL (30).—A section of Urmuz, Tor, Mallizad, Dawaris. Headmen ; Alam Din, Kotan, Hassan Muhammad, Ishak.

PAKHAI (1,000).—A sub-division of Budai, Zakha Khel Afridis. Samil. Headmen ; see Wali Khel, Saddo Khel, Hassan Khel, Shekhwal, Sikandar Khel, and Mir Khel.

PAKHAI.—A minor fraction of Mahmadai, Ashu Khel (1,400), Hassan Khel, Adam Khel, Afridis.

PAKHZAI.—A sub-division of Hamzazai, Sanzar, Kakars.

PALALI (76).—A sub-division of Tapiai, Tappizad, Dawaris. Headmen ; Mir Baz, Mir Alam, Gul Ahmad, Fatteh Mir.

PALAO (246 ; Anambar and Chotiali.).—A clan of Lunis. For Headmen ; see Bahu, Sadozai, Miranzai, Manozai.

PAL KHEL.—A section of Mandazai, Daulatzai, Malizai, Bunerwals.

PALLI KHEL (1,325).—The most important of the four sub-divisions of the Manazai, Alizai, Mahsuds.

PANAKZAI.—A minor fraction of Sikandar Khel, Abdul Khel, Bora Khel (1,000), Mohmit Khel, Utmanzai, Darwesh Khel Wazirs.

PANEZUN (Peshin).—A division of Sanzar, Kakars.

PANI.—A tribe living at Sibi and Sanga, who claim to be Kakars.

PANIZAI (2,325).—A sub-division of Harun Khel, Sanatia, Kakars. Headman ; Sirdar Ibrahim Khan.

PANIZUN (500).—A division of (Western) Sanzar, Kakars.

PANJGOL.—A division of Nandihari, Swatis.

PANJI KHEL (10).—A minor fraction of Bizodai, Malikshai, Aimal Khel, Bahlolzai, Mahsuds. Headman ; Saleh Din.

PANJMIRAL.—A division of Nandihari, Swatis.

PANJPAL.—A section of Musa Khel, Nurizai, Malizai, Bunerwals.

PANJPAI (Buner).—A subdivision of Nasuzai, Iliaszai, Bunerwals.

PANJ PILARA (330).—A section of Abdullai, Aimal Khel, Bahlolzai, Mahsuds.

PANZAI (West of Dera Ghazi Khan District).—A section of Dodarai, Nokuzai, Laharzai, Musa Khels. Headman; Baiak.

PARA KHEL (50).—A minor fraction of the Shami Khel, Palli Khel, Manazai, Alizai Mahsuds. Headmen; Gulamir, Kotas Khan, and Sanjrai.

PARANCHAS (Kohat and Peshawar districts, Kabul, Bokhara).—A tribe of merchants who are settled in various parts of the frontier districts.

PARATE KHEL—A minor fraction of Madda Khel, Miamai, Kabul Khel (2,600), Utmanzai, Darwesh Khel Wazirs.

PARDESI KOR.—A minor fraction of the Rajai Khel, Yusuf Khel, Isa Khel Pandiali, Mohmands. Headmen; see Isa Khel.

PAREZ KHEL (60).—A section of the Manderi, Idak, Tappizad, Dawaris. Headmen; Zarmak, Kundai, Said Alam, Zergul.

PAREZ KHEL (57).—A subdivision of Tapiai, Tappizad, Dawaris. Headmen; Abdulla, Fatteh Khan, Zarar.

PARIARIS (400; Black Mountain).—Divided into Saiads (100), Chagarzais, Bazi Khels (200), Gujars, etc., (100).

PARIT KHEL (6).—A sub-division of Khaddi, Mallizad, Dawaris. Headman; Tawan.

PAR KHEL (Tartara).—A division of Mullagoris, who are a vasssal clan of the Mohmands.

PARSHAI.; A minor fraction of Madak, Bado, Asil, Ismailzai, Utman Khels.

PASANI (115; Dera Ismail Khan District).—Nomadic, a section of Isot Khel, Mian Khel, Lohana, Pawindahs.

PASHA KHEL (5).—A sub-division of Khaddi, Mallizad, Dawaris. Headman; Gul Azam.

Pashezai.—A division of Umrzai Musa Khels. Headman; Shahozai.

Pashmin Khel.—A minor fraction of Paipali, Kabul Khel (2,600), Wali Khel, Utmanzai, Darwesh Khel Wazirs.

Past Khel (300; Loargai).—A division of Ali Sher Khel, Shinwaris.

Pastranis.—A tribe said to inhabit the northern most hills of the Dera Ghazi Khan District. No other information available.

Pathanai (200).—A sub-division of Shabi Khel, Alizai, Mahsuds.

Patol Khel (Shakai).—A minor fraction of Khanda Khan Khel, Hathi Khel, Shin Khel, Ahmadzai, Darwesh Khel Wazirs. Headman; Landai.

Patozai (West of Dera Ghazi Khan District).—A section of Maghdtizai, Ahmadzai, Balil Khel, Musa Khels. Headman; Halim.

Patu Khel.—A minor fraction of Mawal Khel (760), Haibat Khel, Jawaki, Adam Khel, Afridis.

Pawindahs (30,000; between Khorasan and India).—The name applied in the Derajat to all those migratory Pathan tribes who come down to British territory in winter, returning, as summer approaches, to Afghanistan. The leading Pawindah clans are:—Nasars, Suliman Khels, Kharotis, Mian Khels and Dautanis. Of less importance are:—Niazis, Mula Khels, Mithis, Kundis, Tarakis, Tokhis and Andars.

Payan Khel.—A minor fraction of Hassan Khel, Pakhai (1,000), Budai, Zakha Khel, Afridis. Samil. Headmen; Zarin, Sharabat, Saidai, Mir Din, Madrai, Nadir, Gulab Shah.

Payao Khel.—A section of the Chawar Khel, Bazoti, (500) Daulatzai, Orakzais. Samil.

Payavi Khel (Samana and Khanki valley).—A sub-division of Rabia Khel (700), Ismailzai, Orakzais. Samil. Headmen; Zamin, Mastan, Sahib Khan, Gul Ahmad, Ghulam Shah, etc.

Pechi Saiads (45).—A division of (Western) Sanzar, Kakars (Hamsayas).

Peghozai (200; Kuz Totai).—One of the eight clans of Utman Khels.

Pesha Kor (Pipal).—A sub-division of Hassan Khel, Dawezai, Mohmands.

Pila Khel.—A minor fraction of Shugai, Tori Khel (2,670), Ibrahim Khel, Utmanzai, Darwesh Khel Wazirs. Headmen; Khonai, Pir Hussain.

Pira Khel.—A minor fraction of Boza Khel, Tor Khel, Umarzai (600), Shin Khel, Ahmadzai, Darwesh Khel Wazirs.

Pira Khel.—A minor fraction of Jamal Khel, Malak Shahi (400), Wali Khel, Utmanzai, Darwesh Khel Wazirs. Headmen; Hussaini, Zariband, Gulla Khan, Pergai, Sulemani.

Pira Khel.—A section of Kanezai, Kattagram, Tatta, Battannis.

Pira Khel.—A minor fraction of Marjan Khel, Utmanzai, Adinzai, Khwazazai, Akozai—Yusufzai Swatis.

Pira Khel.—A minor fraction of Mir Hasani, Macha, Madda Khel (1,600), Ibrahim Khel, Utmanzai, Darwesh Khel Wazirs.

Pirakzai (105).—A section of the Khidrzai, Ahmad Khel, Oba Khel, Sheranis.

Pirali (15).—A sub-division of Banda, Tappizad, Dawaris. Headman; Shadak, Alima Khan.

Piral Khel (18).—A minor fraction of Ipi, Haidar Khel, Tor, Tappizad, Dawaris. Headmen; Sahibdin, Lal Khan.

Piran (6).—A sub-division of Zerakki, Mallizad, Dawaris. Headman; Khataki.

Piran Dangar Khel (150).—A section of Muhammad Khel, Malakh, Mallizad, Dawaris. Headmen; Badrang, Ghanam Shah.

Pirat Khel (10).—A minor fraction of the Barumi Khel, Khoidad Khel, Gidi Khel, Manazai, Alizai, Mahsuds. Headman; Shahleh.

Pirba Khel (Bannu District).—A section of Hathi Khel (2,000), Shin Khel,

Ahmadzai, Darwesh Khel Wazirs. Headmen; Musharrab Khan, Gulbagh, Pilwar Khan, Dangir Khan.

PIRDAD KHEL (125).—A minor fraction of Abdul Rahman Khel, Sher Khel, Haibat Khel, Nana Khel, Bahlolzai, Mahsuds.

PIR KHEL.—A minor fraction of Khuniya Khel (200), Shadi Khel, Nasra Din, Kalu Khel, Ahmadzai, Darwesh Khel Wazirs. Headman; Lalo Khan.

PIR MUHAMMAD KHEL (43).—A section of the Haidrai, Chahar Khel, Shaman Khel, Mahsuds.

PIR MUHAMMAD KHEL.—A minor fraction of Ismail Khel, Bozi Khel, Madda Khel (1,600), Ibrahim Khel, Utmanzai, Darwesh Khel Wazirs.

PIRU KHEL.—A section of Ghaibi Khel, Babakri, Sipah (1,200), Afridis. Samil. Headmen; Ashraf.

PIRWAL KHEL (800; Loargai).—A division of Ali Sher Khel, Shinwaris. Headman; Nawab.

PIRWAL KHEL.—A section of Tatar Khel or Akhorwal (300), Hassan Khel, Adam Khel, Afridis.

PIRZADA.—The descendant of a Pir, or Mussalman spiritual guide.

POI KHEL (81).—A section of Muhammad Khel, Malakh, Mallizad, Dawaris. Headmen; Shadazam *alias* Bich, Ghulam Jan, Juma Khan, Pirnam.

POPALZAI.—A section of Hani, Panezun, Sanzar, Kakars.

POS KHEL (25).—A minor fraction of Padmi, Taib Khel, Amzoni, Mallizad, Dawaris. Headmen; Mirai, Saddagul, Ajam Shah.

POS KILLA (50).—A minor fraction of Dangar Khel, Piran Dangar Khel, Muhammad Khel, Malakh, Mallizad, Dawaris. Headman; Ghanam Shah, Lal Shah, Sher Ali.

POS KILLA (20).—A section of Khojrai, Darpa Khel, Mallizad, Dawaris. Headmen; Shah Hussein, Muhammad Yar, Mianwar, Makhmad.

Pos Parez Khel (20).—A section of Tapiai, Tappizad, Dawaris. Headmen; Abdulla, Nazir Muhammad.

Potia Khel.—Another name for the Alizai, Mahsuds.

Potiya Khel.—A minor fraction of Khuniya Khel (200), Shadi Khel, Nasra Din, Kalu Khel, Ahmadzai, Darwesh Khel Wazirs. Headmen; Bhittani Khan, Mihrwal.

Poliya Khel.—A minor fraction of Titar Khel, Khan Khel, Takhti Khel, Bakka Khel (1,000), Wali Khel, Utmanzai, Darwesh Khel Wazirs. Headman; Mian Khel.

Pridai (150).—A section of Ashu Khel, Hassan Khel, Adam Khel, Afridis.

Pub Khel (40).—A minor fraction of Poi Khel, Muhammad Khel, Malakh, Mallizad, Dawaris. Headmen; Shadazam, *alias* Bich, Ghulam Jan.

R

Rabia Khel (700; Samana and Khanki valley).—The largest division of the Ismailzai, Orakzais. Samil. Headman; Muhammadin.

Rab Khel (Kharmana river).—A minor fraction of Abdul Mirzi (410), Landaizai, Masuzai, Lashkarzai, Orakzais. Gar. Headman; Musa.

Raggi Khel (Bannu District).—A minor fraction of Baik Khel, Khandar Khan Khel, Hathi Khel (2,000), Shin Khel, Ahmadzai, Darwesh Khel Wazirs.

Raghzai (60).—A section of Taib Khel, Amzoni, Mallizad, Dawaris. Headmen; Said Akbar, Mokhsein, Janak, Pir Badshah, Khairan.

Rahdo Kor.—A minor fraction of Ranra Khel, Shafi Khel, Walibeg Kor, Gandab, Halimzai, Mohmands. Headman; Gudai.

Rahimdad Khel (29).—A minor fraction of Abdul Rahman Khel, Sher Khel, Haibat Khel, Nana Khel, Bahlolzai, Mahsuds.

Rahimdad Khel.—A minor fraction of Bash Khel (150), Sharaki, Galai, Adam Khel, Afridis.

Rahimdad Khel.—A minor fraction of Basi Khel, Kamal Khel, Sahib Jan, Aka Khel, (1,800), Afridis. Samil.

Rahimdad Khel (45).—A section of Ghalib Khel, Badanzai, Shaman Khel, Mahsuds. Headmen; Zarpiyao, Fakir Shah.

Rahimdad Kor.—A minor fraction of Asaf Khel, Dalkha Kor, Dadu Khel, Tarakzai, Mohmands.

Rahim Khel.—A minor fraction of Talagh Khel, Kaddam Khel, Feroz Khel, Mashi Khel, Mannia Khel, Hassan Khel, Mitha Khan Khel, Kuki Khel (4,500), Afridis. Gar. Headman; Khaza Khan.

Rahim Khel.—A minor fraction of Mohib Khel, Shekhai, Annai (1,000), Budai, Zakha Khel, Afridis. Samil. Headmen; Khwas Khan, Dadrai, Gholai, Mozam Din.

Rahim Khel.—Another name for the Sarki Khel.

Rahim Kor.—A minor fraction of Farid Khel, Feroz Khel, Mashi Khel, Mannia Khel, Hassan Khel, Mitha Khan Khel, Kuki Khel, (4,500), Afridis. Gar. Headmen; Mulla Nazir, Mirwal, Said Gul.

Rahim Kor.—A minor fraction of Sultan Khel, Hamza Khel, Gandab, Halimzai, Mohmands. Headman; Muhammad Ghaus.

Rahimzai.—A section of Mirzai, Alizai, Sanzar, Kakars.

Rahman Khel.—A minor fraction of Shakal Khel (100), Haibat Khel, Jawaki, Adam Khel, Afridis.

Rahman Kor (Confines of Bajaur).—A division of Gorai, Utman Khels.

Rahmanzai (4).—A sub-division of Zakarzai, Rakanwal, Lunis.

Rahmat Kor.—A section of Musa Khel, Sipah, Baezai, Mohmands. Headmen; Saiad Azim, Hassim, Alazai Hadi Gul.

Rahmatal Kor.—A section of Kadai Kor, Gandab, Halimzai, Mohmands. Headmen; Naushere Khan, Abdul Kadir, Ghulam Jan, Samo.

RAHRA KHEL.—A minor fraction of Sher Khan Khel, Umar Khan Khel, Malikdin Khel, Malikdin Khel (4,000), Afridis. Samil. Headmen; see Gholai.

RAIBAT KHEL (Bannu District.)—A minor fraction of Ali Khel, Musa Khel, Hathi Khel (2,000), Shin Khel, Ahmadzai, Darwesh Khel Wazirs.

RAISANI (114).—A sub-division of Ismailalagh, Spin, Tarins. Headman; Panid Khan.

RAJAI KHEL (Danish Kol).—A section of Yusuf Khel, Isa Khel, Pandiali, Mohmands. Headmen; Kach Kol, Chat.

RAJAK KHEL.—A minor fraction of Bar Khozhai, Khaddar Khel (770), Mohmit Khel, Utmanzai, Darwesh Khel Wazirs. Headman; Hukm Shah.

RAJJI KHEL (50).—A minor fraction of Malai, Dachi Khel, Palli Khel, Manazai, Alizai, Mahsuds. Headmen; Said Muhammad, Mir Shah Jehan.

RAJJI KHEL.—A minor fraction of Mintar Khel, Muhammad Khel, Hassan Khel (400), Mohmit Khel, Utmanzai, Darwesh Khel Wazirs. Headman; Gulaband.

RAJJI KHEL (25).—A section of Rana Khel, Tapiai, Tappizad, Dawaris. Headmen; Hazrat Pir, Fatteh Mir, Mirab.

RAKANWALS (286; Thal-Chotiali).—A clan of Lunis. Headmen; see Malezai, Ladu, Walainai, Mizrai, Saiadan, Zakarzai.

RAMI KHEL.—A section of Kadai Kor, Gandab, Halimzai, Mohmands.

RAMSHER KHEL.—A section of Durbi Khel, Kambar Khel, Kambar Khel (4,500), Afridis. Gar. Headmen; Muhammad Sher, Khwaja Ali, Yaro and Nurai.

RANA KHEL (70; Dera Ismail Khan District).—Nomadic, a minor fraction of Umrzai, Sein Khel, Mian Khel, Lohana, Pawindahs.

RANGI KHEL.—A minor fraction of Idar Khel, Ali Khel, Khaddar Khel (770), Mohmit Khel, Utmanzai,

Darwesh Khel Wazirs. Headman; Sakhe Man.

Ranizai, Bar (4,800; Left bank of the Swat river).—One of the three clans of Akozai—Yusufzai Swatis. Headman; Khan of Aladand.

Ranizai, Sam (3,200; South of Shakot and Digar, and north of Mardan).—A division of Bar Ranizai, Akozai —Yusufzai Swatis.

Note.—Originally servants of the Bar Ranizai, but now independent.

Ranra Khel.—A minor fraction of Shati Khel, Ali Beg Kor, Gandab, Halimzai, Mohmands.

Rasman Khel (20).—A minor fraction of Charkhil, Charkhil, Land, Malakh, Mallizad, Dawaris. Headmen; Gul Rahman, Gulzar.

Rasul Khel (80; Black Mountain).—A section of Aziz Khel, Akazai, Isazai, Yusufzais.

Rasul Khel.—A minor fraction of Haibtanai, Tori Khel (2,670), Ibrahim Khel, Utmanzai, Darwesh Khel, Wazirs. Headman; Miandad.

Rasul Khel.—A section of Taru Khel, Boba, Dana, Battannis.

Rasul Kor.—A section of Wali Beg Kor, Gandab, Halimzai, Mohmands.

Raza Khel.—A minor fraction of Gadia Khel, Tatar Khel, or Akhorwal (300), Hassan Khel, Adam Khel. Afridis.

Raza Khel.—A section of Kulla Khel, Malikdin Khel, Malikdin Khel (4,000), Afridis. Samil. Headmen; see Bakhmali Khel.

Raza Khel.—A minor fraction of Samna Khel, Ghuli Khel, Ambar Khel, Mat Khan Khel, Kambar Khel (4,500), Afridis. Gar. Headmen; see Khojal Khel.

Razo Khel (15).—A subdivision of Khaddi, Mallizad, Dawaris. Headmen; Kotai and Rahim Shah.

Razoni.—A section of Wuzi Khel (800), Mohmit Khel, Utmanzai, Darwesh Khel Wazirs.

Redan Khel (6).—A minor fraction of Kharmach Khel, Malai, Shingi, Bahlolzai, Mahsuds. Headman; Atamir.

Rekhmina Kor (Danish Kol).—A minor fraction of Rajai Khel, Yusuf Khel, Isa Khel, Pandiali, Mohmands.

Reshmin Khel.—A minor fraction of Madda Khel, Miamai, Kabul Khel (2,600), Utmanzai, Darwesh Khel Wazirs. Headman; Mezhai.

Reshmin Khel.—A minor fraction of Sikandar Khel, Abdul Khel, Bora Khel (1,000), Mohmit Khel, Utmanzai, Darwesh Khel Wazirs. Headman; Sheikh.

Reshmin Khel (8).—A minor fraction of Bar Kaum, Hassu Khel, Tor, Mallizad, Dawaris. Headmen; Painda Khan, Nezam Gul.

Richbin Khel.—A minor fraction of Kemal Khel, Babu Khel, Adinzai, Khwazazai, Akozai—Yusufzai Swatis.

Rozi Khel (25).—A section of Zhao Khel, Tapiai, Tappizad, Dawaris. Headman; Isab Khan.

Rozi Khel.—A minor fraction of Ali Khel, Musa Khel, Hathi Khel (2,000), Shin Khel, Ahmadzai, Darwesh Khel Wazirs.

Rukhan Khel.—A minor fraction of Kandao Khel (400), Ashu Khel, Hassan Khel, Adam Khel, Afridis.

Rustam Khel.—A section of Hasan Khel, Gadaizai, Iliaszai, Bunerwals.

Rustam Kor.—A sub-division of Bazid Khel Sheikhans (3,000), "Hamsayas" of the Orakzais. Samil. Headman; Mustamand.

S

Saadat Khel.—A minor fraction of Drepillari, Sarki Khel, Madda Khel (1,600), Ibrahim Khel, Utmanzai, Darwesh Khel Wazirs.

Sabak Khel.—A section of Shadi Khel, Bobak, Dana, Battannis.

Saba Kor.—A section of Khalil Khel, Kasim Khel, Tarakzai, Mohmands.

Sabari; (2,000; Shamil valley, Khost).—A clan of the Khostwals.

Sabat Kor.—A minor fraction of Ali Khan Khel, Ali Karan,

Mamuzai (3,500), Lashkarzai, Orakzais. Gar. Headman; Feroz Khan.

SAB KHEL.—A minor fraction of Shekhai, Annai (1,000), Budai, Zakha Khel, Afridis. Samil. Headmen; Kattia Mir Khel, Fateh Khel, Sahib Khel.

SABITZAI (100).—A section of Shadzai, Alizai, Sanzar, Kakars. Headman; Bagai.

SABITZAI.—A minor (Hamsaya) fraction of Saiadzai, Barakzai, Targhari, Sanzar, Kakars.

SABOGAI.—A minor fraction of Sadda Khel (300), Isperka, Kalu Khel, Ahmadzai. Darwesh Khel Wazirs, Headman; Ahmad Gul.

SABURAI KHEL (Mastura river).—A sub-division of the Mani Khel (1,000), Muhammad Khel, Orakzais. Gar. Shiah.

SADA KHEL (80; Khanki valley). A sub-division of Rabia Khel (700), Ismailzai, Orakzais. Samil. Headman; Nakshband.

SADAK KHEL.—A minor fraction of Maruf Khel, Basi Khel, Kamal Khel, Sahib Jan, Aka Khel, (1,800), Afridis. Samil.

SADAKZAI (West of Dera Ghazi Khan District).—A subdivision of Hamzazai, Balil Khel, Musa Khels. Headman; Macha.

SADAZAI (10).—A sub-division of Malezai, Rakanwal, Lunis. Headman; see Malezai.

SADDA KHEL (35).—A minor fraction of Mirdad Khel, Abdul Rahman Khel, Sher Khel, Haibat Khel, Nana Khel, Bahlolzai, Mahsuds. Headman; Dakkas.

SADDA KHEL (300; Bannu and Shakai).—A section of Isperka, Kalu Khel, Ahmadzai, Darwesh Khel Wazirs. Headmen; Zalim Khan, Ahmad Gul.

SADDO KHEL.—A section of Pakhai (1,000), Budai, Zakha Khel, Afridis. Samil. Headman; Zarin, Sharabat, Saidai, Mirdin, Madrai, Nadir, Gulab Shah.

SADDO KHEL.—A sub-division of Mamozai, Mishtis (3,000), "Hamsayas" of the Orakzais. Samil. Headman; Fakir.

SADIANZAI (52).—A division of Palao, Lunis.

Sadi Khel.—A small division of Tatta, Battannis.

Sadikzai.—A minor (Hamsaya) fraction of Hosenzai, Barakzai, Targhari, Sanzar, Kakars.

Sadin (Babukarrah valley, Bajaur).—A division of Salarzai, Tarkanis.

Sado Kor or Nazar Kor (Bohai Dag).—A sub-division of Maimana Khel, Khwaezai, Mohmands. Headmen; Sado, Ahmad.

Sadozais.—A clan of Popalzai Duranis, which furnished the first independent Shahs of the Durani dynasty, (A. D. 1747), the Barakzais furnishing the Amirs. The line of the Shahs was overthrown in the third generation (A. D. 1834), after a protracted period of anarchy and dissension, which broke out on the death (A. D. 1773) of Ahmad Shah Durani, the founder of Afghan national independence. See also Duranis, and Bar Duranis.

Sadozai (110).—A section of Karmozai, Ahmad Khel, Sen Khel, Sheranis.

Sadozai (40).—A minor fraction of Haidarzai, Natozai, Dumar, Sanzar, Kakars.

Sadozai.—A minor (Hamsaya) fraction of Hasanzai, Barakzai, Targhari, Sanzar, Kakars.

Sadozai (56; Anambar).—A division of Palao, Lunis.

Sadozai (West of Dera Ghazi Khan District).—A section of Jalalzai, Hasan Khel, Balil Khel, Musa Khels. Headman; Mian.

Sadozai (West of Dera Ghazi Khan District).—A sub-division of Mangizai, Laharzai, Musa Khels. Headman; Zhobai.

Saemanzai.—A minor fraction of Masezai, Hani, Panezun, Sanzar, Kakars.

Safar Khel.—A minor fraction of Ghulam Khel (300), Haibat Khel, Jawaki, Adam Khel, Afridis.

Safarza.—A sub-division of the Hamzazai, Sanzar, Kakars.

Safarzai (50).—A section of Bazai, Harun Khel, Sanatia, Kakars. Headman; Ikhbal.

Safarzai.—A minor fraction of Shamozai, Hamzazai, Arbu Khel, Sanzar, Kakars.

Safis.—A vassal clan of the Mohmands, who are probably Kafir converts to Islam. Headmen; Shamsai, Sherdil, Mazim, Musai, Khanpur, Jangrez, Zarapai Mian Khan, Abbas.

Sah (110).—A sub-division of Yahia, Sen Khel, Sheranis.

Sahab Kor (Loi Shilman).—A section of Durma Kor, Shah Mansur Khel, Tarakzai, Mohmands.

Sahib Jan.—A division of Aka Khel (1,800), Afridis. Samil.

Sahib Khan Kor.—A section of Hatai Kor, Muhammad Khan Kor, or Bar Burhan Khel, Pandiali, Mohmands.

Sahib Khel.—A section of the Umar Khan Khel, Alisherzai (3,000), Lashkarzai, Orakzais. Samil. Headman; Kasim Khan.

Sahib Khel.—A minor fraction of Sab Khel, Shekhai, Annai (1,000), Budai, Zakha Khel, Afridis. Samil. Headmen; Mulla Faiz Muhammad, Mulla Ali Muhammad, Ahmad.

Sahib Khel (30; Dera Ismail Khan District).—Nomadic, a minor fraction of Aba Khel, Isot Khel, Mian Khel, Lohana, Pawindahs. Headman; see Mian Khel.

Sahibzai (160; Gomal).—A division of Miani, Sheranis.

Sahogi (70).—A minor fraction of the Kimat Khel, Haidar Khel, Tor, Tappizad, Dawaris. Headmen: Mad Akbar, Jalal.

Saiads.—A true Saiad is the descendant of Ali, the son-in-law of Muhammad, by Fatima, Muhammad's daughter. Many of the Pathan tribes, such as the Bangash of Kohat, and the Mishwanis of the Hazara border, claim Saiad origin. The apostles who completed the conversion of the Pathans to Islam where called Saiads if they came from the west, and Shekhs if from the east; hence doubtless, many false claims to Saiad origin. In Afghanistan the Saiads have much of the commerce in their hands, as their holy character allows them to pass unharmed where other Pathans would infallibly be murdered.

SAIAD.—A section of Manzar Khel (360), Ibrahim Khel Utmanzai, Darwesh Khel, Wazirs. Headman; Anwar Shah.

SAIADS (230; Black Mountain)—A sub-division of Hasanzai, Isazai, Yusufzais. Headmen; Saiad Azim Shah, Bahadur Shah.

SAIAD AHMAD.—A sub-division of Alisherzai (3,000,) Lashkarzai, Orakzais. Samil. Headman; Rayaz.

SAIADAN (7).—A division of Rakanwal, Lunis. Headman; Alam Shah.

SAIADANZAI (3).—A sub-division of Zakarzai, Rakanwal Lunis. Headmen; see Zakarzai.

SAIAD ALI KHEL (Mahaban).—A section of Hasan Khel, Mada Khel, Isazai, Yusufzais. Headman; Sher Khan.

SAIADGIS (430; Wazristan).—A clan of Saiads who inhabit Zowe, Shawal and the Toch,i Dawarghar, Ka nibogh and the Dandi plain, north of Miram Shah. There are also some Saiadgis across the frontier in Birmal, of whom little is known. The divisions of the Saiadgis are known by the names of the localities they inhabit, as above. The Saiadgis of Kanibogh and of Shawal are pastoral in their habits, and all are on good terms with the Darwesh Khel. Headmen; Zalmai (Dandi plain) is the leading man; others are Mir Sahib (Zowe), Gulbagh (Shawal), Ghamir (Dawarghar).

SAIAD KHAN NMASI (320).—A section of the Ali Karan, Mamuzai, Lashkarzai, Orakzais. Gar.

SAIAD KHEL (120; Dera Ismail Khan District).—Nomadic, a section of Isot Khel, Mian Khel, Lohana, Pawindahs. Headmen; see Mian Khel.

SAIAD KAHNZAI.—A section of Maizai, Nas Khel, Sanzar, Kakars.

SAIAD TIRIMZAI (580).—A clan of the Allaiwals.

SAIADZAI (5).—A sub-division of Mizrai, Rakanwal, Lunis. Headmen; see Mizrai.

SAIADZAI (120).—A (Hamsaya) section of the Barakzai, Targhari, Sanzar,

Kakars. Headmen; Kalandar of Takhor, and Rahmatulla of Bagh.

SAIADZAI (200).—A section of Sarangzai, Harun Khel, Sanatia, Kakars. Headman; Sirdar Bai, chief of all the Sarangzais.

SAIADZAI (200).—A section of Mehtarzai, Harun Khel, Sanatia, Kakars. Headman; Aziz.

SAIDAN DANGAR KHEL (40).—A section of Shujawal, Mubarak Shahi, Mallizad, Dawaris. Headmen; Hussain Shah, Sheikh Kabir, Sheikh Sadi.

SAIDGAI.—A minor fraction of Khan Khel, Takhti Khel, Bakka Khel (1000), Wali Khel, Utmanzai, Darwesh Khel Wazirs. Headman; Gul Khatni.

SAID KHEL (Bannu, Kuram).—A section of Umarzai (600), Shin Khel, Ahmadzai, Darwesh Khel Wazirs. Headman; Pirmal Khan.

SAIFALI.—A section of Kabul Khel (2,600), Wali Khel, Utmanzai, Darwesh Khel Wazirs. Headman; Kotan Khan.

SAIFALI KHEL (Bannu District).—A minor fraction of Dodi Khel, Khandar Khan Khel, Hathi Khel, Shin Khel, Ahmadzai, Darwesh Khel Wazirs.

SAINI KHEL.—A minor fraction of Narmi Khel, Bakka Khel (1,000), Wali Khel, Utmanzai, Darwesh Khel Wazirs. Headmen; Shah Nawaz.

SAINI KHEL.—A minor fraction of Titar Khel, Khan Khel, Takhti Khel, Bakka Khel (1,000), Wali Khel, Utmanzai, Darwesh Khel Wazirs. Headmen; Khan Badshah, Khazan Khan.

SAIN KHEL (70; Black Mountain).—A section of Aziz Khel, Akazai, Isazai, Yusufzais.

SAINZAI (Gomal).—A division of Miani, Sheranis.

SAKA KHEL (30).—A section of Salimkai, Khadi Khel, Shaman Khel, Mahsuds. Headmen; Haji Muhammad, Halal.

SAKKI KHEL.—A sub-division of Mamozai, Mishtis (3,000), "Hamsayas" of the Orakzais. Samil. Headman; Shahzu.

Salami Khel.—A minor fraction of Kundai, Tor Khel, Umarzai (600), Shin Khel, Ahmadzai, Darwesh Khel Wazirs. Headman; Zaid Gul.

Salar (1,300).—One of the two clans of the Gaduns.

Salarzai (1,600; Western Buner).—A division of Iliaszai, Bunerwals. Headman; Hastam Khan, now an old man.

Salarzai.—A minor fraction of Shamozai, Hamzazai, Arbu Khel, Sanzar, Kakars.

Salarzais (4,000; Babukarrah valley, Bajaur).—One of the four clans of the Tarkanis. Headmen; Khan of Pashat, and Samad Khan of Matta Shah.

Salemi Khel (8; Dera Ismail Khan District).—Nomadic, a minor fraction of Aba Khel, Isot Khel, Mian Khel, Lohana, Pawindahs. Headman; see Mian Khel.

Salemi Khel.—A sub-division of Umar Khel, Tatta, Battannis. Headman; Sher Muhammad.

Salem Khanzai (West of Dera Ghazi Khan District).—A section of Jalalzai, Hasan Khel, Balil Khel, Musa Khels. Headman; Khoidad.

Salezai (27).—A division of Rakanwal, Lunis.

Salih Khel (40).—A minor fraction of Shinki Khel, Babakki, Hassu Khel, Tor, Mallizad, Dawaris. Headmen; Gul Hassan, Gul Raihan.

Salih Kor.—A minor fraction of Rahmatal Kor, Kadai Kor, Gandab, Halimzai, Mohmands. Headmen; Abdul Kadir, Ghulam Jan.

Salimi Khel (140).—A minor fraction of the Dachi Khel Palli Khel, Manazai, Alizai, Mahsuds.

Salim Kai (125).—A sub-division of Khadi Khel, Shaman Khel, Mahsuds.

Salim Kai (60).—A minor fraction of Panj Pilara, Abdullai, Aimal Khel, Bahlolzai, Mahsuds. Headman; Rozadin.

SALIM KHAN KOR.—A sub-division of "Kuz" or "Khrappawal" Burhan Khel, Pandiali, Mohmands. Headman; Gulzar Shah.

SALIMONAI (35).—A minor fraction of the Abdul Khel, Langar Khel, Khoidad Khel, Gidi Khel, Manazai, Alizai, Mahsuds. Headman; Nirla Khan.

SALO KOR.—A minor fraction of Sroh, Busha Khel, Kamali, Halimzai, Mohmands. Headman; Khanizaman.

SALWA KHEL (40).—A section of Mullagan, Tor, Mallizad, Dawaris. Headman; Muhammad Amin.

SAMADINZAI (456).—A sub-division of Isa Khel, Sanatia, Kakars. Headman; Malikdad Muhammad.

SAMAND (59).—A division of Drigzai, Lunis.

SAMEL (or Ismail) KHEL.—A sub-division of Shamozai, Khwazazai, Akozai—Yusufzai Swatis.

SAMILZAIS (Bajaur).—One of the four clans of the Tarkanis.

SAMKORI (270).—A clan of Allaiwals.

SAMNA KHEL.—A minor fraction of Ghuli Khel, Ambar Khel, Mat Khan Khel, Kambar Khel (4,500), Afridis. Gar. Headman; see Khojal Khel.

SAMOZAI.—(Mastura, Khanki and Miranzai valleys).—One of the three divisions of the Sheikhans, "Hamsayas" of the Orakzais. Samil. Headman; Sharab.

SANATIAS (7,373; Kalat, Peshin, and Upper Zhob).—A clan of Kakars. Headmen; Guldad (Shamozai), Sirdar Habo Khan (Mehtarzai), Sirdar Bai Khan (Saranzai), Baidula (Sarangzai), Sirdar Ibrahim Khan (Panizai), Malikdad Muhammad (Samadinzai).

SANDUZAI (West of the Dera Ghazi Khan District).—A section of Kabalzai Nokuzai, Laharzai, Musa Khels. Headman; Momin.

SANGARAI (25).—A section of Bazid Khel, Jawaki, Adam Khel, Afridis.

Sangar Khel (Danish Kol).—A section of Yusaf Khel, Isa Khel, Pandiali, Mohmands. Headmen ; Zaidullah, Guldost.

Sani Khel ; see **Shin Khel**.

Sanizai (300 ; Bar and Kuz Totai).—One of eight clans of the Utman Khels.

Sanni Khel.—A section of Zargun Khel (300), Galai, Adam Khel, Afridis.

Sanyal Khel, or **Sanzal Khel** ; see **Sanzal Khel**.

Sanzal Khel, or **Sanyal Khel**.—A section of Kamal Khel, Sahib Jan, Aka Khel (1,800), Afridis. Samil.

Sanzar or **Saran Khel** (31,659 ; Bori, Zhob and Thal Chotiali).—The most powerful of the five Kakar clans. They are divided into southern, western, and northern Sanzars. The southern number some 7,565, the western (mostly Hamsayas) 3,994, and the northern (termed Zhobis) 18,600. Headmen ; Sirdar Shah Jehan, Dost Muhammad, Saifulla.

Sar Khan.—A minor fraction of Nekzam Khel, Tor Sapar (350), Galai, Adam Khel, Afridis.

Sar Khel.—A minor fraction of Makki Khel, Kattia Khel, Hassan Khel, Mitha Khan Khel, Kuki Khel (4,500), Afridis. Gar. Headmen ; see Makki Khel.

Sarangzai (1,290).—A subdivision of Harun Khel, Sanatia, Kakars. Headman ; Sirdar Bai Khan.

Sarar.—A section of Tara Khel, Muia, Waraspun, Battannis.

Sarbadal Kor.—A minor fraction of Muradi Khel, Dalkha Kor, Dadu Khel, Tarakzai, Mohmands.

Sarbadar Khel.—A subdivision of Mat Khan Khel, Kambar Khel (4,500), Afridis. Gar. Headmen ; Sher Khan, Hamid, Nurai.

Sarbar Khel (1,200).—A section of Bazid Khel, Jawaki, Adam Khel, Afridis.

Sargalli.—(2,500 ; Kurram). —The smaller of the two clans of the Turis.

Sardari Khel (40).—A minor fraction of Pirdad Khel, Abdul Rahman Khel, Sher Khel, Haibat Khel, Nana Khel, Bahlolzai, Mahsuds. Headmen; Allahdad, Shahzal.

Sardi Khel (Bannu and Shawal).—A section of Bakka Khel (1,000), Wali Khel, Utmanzai, Darwesh Khel Wazirs. Headmen; Ashraf Khan, Khaki Shah, Gulak Khan, Rasul Shah, Landak, Mauladad Khan, Banai.

Sargan Kor.—A minor fraction of Ismail, Khadin Khel, Ashazai, Iliaszai, Bunerwals.

Sargarrai Kor (Bohai Dag).—A sub-division of Khadi Khel, Khwaezai, Mohmands. Headmen; Akram, Aziz Khan.

Sargul Khel.—A minor fraction of Pirwal Khel, Tatar Khel, or Akhorwal, Hassan Khel, Adam Khel, Afridis.

Sarkani Khel.—A sub-division of Shamozai, Ismailzai, Utman Khels. Headmen; Dost Muhammad, Mohrdil, Muhammad Akram.

Sarkani Khel (Arang).—A sub-division of Shamozai, Ismailzai, Utman Khels.

Sarkhi Khel.—A minor fraction of Mira Khel, Mad Khozhai, Khaddar Khel (770), Mohmit Khel, Utmanzai, Darwesh Khel Wazirs. Headman; Rakhm Shah.

Sarki Khel.—A section of Madda Khel (1,600), Ibrahim Khel, Utmanzai, Darwesh Khel Wazirs. Headmen; Sadda Khan, Alambe, and Shadam Khan are the leading men; see also Madda Khel, Ali Khan Khel, and Drepillari.

Sarki Khel.—A sub-division of Akhel (600), Ismailzai, Orakzais. Gar. Headmen; Malik Maddu, Mir Khan, Said Gul, Nur Ayaz, Said Shah, Sher Ali.

Sarmashai (50).—A section of Salimkai, Khaki Khel, Shaman Khel, Mahsuds. Headmen; Namar, Pasti, Ghazo.

Sarmast Khel.—A minor fraction of Machi Khel, Abdul Khel, Bora Khel, (1,000), Mohmit Khel, Utmanzai, Darwesh Khel Wazirs.

Sarmast Khel.—A minor fraction of Yunas Khel, Bosti Khel (150), Galai, Adam Khel, Afridis.

Sarmast Khel.—A minor fraction of Mian Khel, Janakhori (800), Hassan Khel, Adam Khel, Afridis.

Sarmast Khel.—A minor fraction of Badi Khel, Dardoni, Wuzi Khel (800), Mohmit Khel, Utmanzai, Darwesh Khel Wazirs. Headmen; Bozi, Wazir Khan, Nakir Khan.

Sarmast Khel (70).—A minor fraction of the Gega Khel, Sher Khel, Haibat Khel, Nana Khel, Bahlolzai, Mahsuds. Headmen; Muhammad Afzal, Mianwal.

Sarni Khel.—A sub-division of Shamozai, Ismailzai, Utman Khels. Headman; Badol.

Sarni Khel (Arang).—A sub-division of Shamozai, Ismailzai, Utman Khels.

Sarsa (100).—A division of Tatta, Battannis. Headmen; Sher Khan (Jalal Khel), Lawat (Nurah Khel).

Saru Khel (Kurram).—A sub-division of Duparzi (1,600), Chardai, Turis.

Saru Khel (30; Dera Ismail Khan District).—Nomadic, a minor fraction of Aka Khel, Isot Khel, Mian Khel, Lohana, Pawindahs. Headmen; see Mian Khel.

Sarwar Khel.—A minor fraction of Nekzam Khel, Tor Sapar (350), Galai, Adam Khel, Afridis.

Sattal Khel.—A minor fraction of Ghulam Khel (300), Haibat Khel, Jawaki, Adam Khel, Afridis.

Saur Khel.—A minor fraction of Ali Khel (100), Ashu Khel, Hassan Khel, Adam Khel, Afridis.

Sebujni (2,000; Ningolai to the Harnawai stream).—A division of Khwazazai, Akozai — Yusufzai Swatis. Headman; Jalal Khan.

Sed Khel.—A division of Samilzai, Tarkanis.

Sein Khel (600; Dera Ismail Khan District).—Nomadic, a sub-division of Mian Khel, Lohana, Pawindahs. Headman; Azim Khan.

Sehani (54).—A sub-division of Ismailalagh, Spin, Tarins. Headman; Isa Khan.

Sen.—A section of Khakizai, Ashazai, Iliaszai, Bunerwals.

Sen Khel (1,540).—A clan of Sheranis.

Sen Khel.—A sub-division of Abba Khel, Tatta, Battannis.

Sen Khel.—A sub-division of Gadaizai, Iliaszai, Bunerwals.

Senzai.—A section of Kanezai, Kattagarm, Tatta, Battannis. Headmen; Khajak, Haan.

Senzai.—A section of Kesu, Woruke, Dana, Battannis.

Senzai (Bajaur).—One of the divisions of Isazai, Tarkanis.

Senzai (Bajaur).—A small aboriginal tribe, living at Senzai, two miles north of Mundah, in Jandol.

Sepah.—A sub-division of Kandahari Safis, who are a vassal clan of the Mohmands

Sepah.—A division of Baezai, Mohmands.

Seegu Khel (or Siyu).—A section of Panjpai, Nasuzai, Iliaszai, Bunerwals.

Sewanai Kor (Bohai Dag).—A sub-division of Khadi Khel, Khwaezai, Mohmands. Headman; Painda Khan.

Shabadin Khel (20).—A section of Palali, Tapiai, Tappizad, Dawaris. Headmen; Mir Alam or Mir Alani, Gumbat.

Shaba Khel.—A sub-division of Ali Khel, Bar Ranizai, Akozai—Yusufzai Swatis.

Shabak Khel (10).—A minor fraction of Kharmach Khel, Malai, Shingi, Bahlolzai, Mahsuds. Headman; Fatteh Khan.

Shabar Khel.—A minor fraction of Sarmast Khel, Badi Khel, Dardoni, Wuzi Khel (800), Mohmit Khel, Utmanzai, Darwesh Khel Wazirs. Headman; Nakir Khan.

Shabbar Khel.—A minor fraction of Kharmanj Khel, Khwaja Khel, Miamai, Kabul Khel (2,600), Wali Khel, Utmanzai, Darwesh Khel Wazirs. Headman; Gulbat Khan.

Shabaz Khel (15).—A minor fraction of Idal Khel, Muhammad Khel, Malakh, Mallizad, Dawaris. Headman ; Kazi.

Shabezai (80).—A section of Isa Khel, Ahmad Khel, Oba Khel, Sheranis.

Shabi Khel (1,270).—A division of the Alizai, Mahsuds.

Shabil Khel.—A minor fraction of Umar Khel, Annai (1,000), Budai, Zakha Khel, Afridis. Headmen ; Shahaba Din, Bolak, Arab.

Shabozai.—A sub-division of Arbu Khel, Sanzar, Kakars.

Shabzai (Zhob).—A section of Ibrahimzai, Shadozai, Ali Khel, Sanzar, Kakars.

Shadak Khel (6).—A section of Boya, Tappizad, Dawaris. Headman ; Tor.

Shadak Kor.—A minor fraction of Hyatai Kor, Shah Mansur Khel, Dadu Khel, Tarakzai, Mohmands. Headman ; Sofi.

Shadaks.—A minor fraction of Muhammad Khel (700), Isperka, Kalu Khel, Ahmadzai, Darwesh Khel Wazirs. Headmen ; Katamir.

Shadat Kor.—A sub-division of Maimana Khel, Khwaezai, Mohmands. Headman ; Mira Jan.

Shadi Khel (200).—A sub-division of Bobak, Dana, Battannis. Headman ; Batur of Bagh.

Shadi Khel (75 ; Dera Ismail Khan District).—Nomadic, a section of Isot Khel, Mian Khel, Lohana, Pawindahs. Headman ; see Mian Khel.

Shadi Khel (1,800 ; British territory, Wana and Gumatti. Some fractions migrate to Baddar).—A section of Nasra Din, Kalu Khel, Ahmadzai, Darwesh Khel, Wazirs. Headmen ; Sarwar Khan, Amin Khan, Jalal Khan, Timar Khan, Nazir Khan, Gul Adam, Sahib Khan, Gulbaz, Sawar Khan, Mir Alam, Bhittani Khan, Mihrwah, Lalo Khan.

Shadi Khel.—A minor fraction of Sikander Khel, Manzar Khel (360), Ibrahim Khel, Utmanzai, Darwesh Khel Wazirs. Headman ; Maddi Khan.

SHADI KHEL.—A section of Bora Khel (1,000), Mohmit Khel, Utmanzai, Darwesh Khel Wazirs. Headman; Kippat Khan.

SHADI KHEL.—A minor fraction of Boza Khel, Tor Khel, Umarzai (600), Shin Khel, Ahmadzai, Darwesh Khel Wazirs.

SHADI KHEL.—A minor fraction of Balal Khel, Hassan Khel (400), Mohmit Khel, Utmanzai, Darwesh Khel Wazirs. Headmen; Piyao Khan, Badde Fakir, Khan Ghazat.

SHADI KHEL (25).—A subdivision of Banda, Tappizad Dawaris. Headmen; Shabol, Nazr Muhammad.

SHADI KHEL (9).—A minor fraction of Ipi, Haidar Khel, Tor, Tappizad, Dawaris. Headmen; Guldad, Salim.

SHADI KHEL (40).—A minor fraction of Lar Lorai, Land, Malakh, Mallizad, Dawaris. Headmen; Bazar Din, Kimat Khan, Fakir Muhammad.

SHADIZAI.—A section of Ahmad Khel, Targhari, Sanzar, Kakars.

SHADOZAI.—A minor (Hamsaya) fraction of the Hasanzai, Barakzai, Targhari, Sanzar, Kakars.

SHADOZAI (275).—A minor fraction of Bulozai, Panizai Harun Khel, Sanatia, Kakars. Headmen; Ali Muhammad, Ramzan, Faiz Muhammad.

SHADZAI (3,900).—A sub-division of Alizai, Sanzar, Kakars. Headmen; Ali (Aktarzai), Saiad Rahmat (Ali Khel), Hamzai (Daolatzai), Bagai (Sebitzai).

SHAGU KOR.—A minor fraction of Ambora Khel, Sanzal Khel, Kamal Khel, Sahib Jan, Aka Khel (1,800), Afridis. Samil.

SHAHAB DIN KHEL (60).—A section of Musakki, Tor, Mallizad, Dawaris. Headmen; Hassan, Sawan, Gul Raihan, Mihr Gul.

SHAHAB KHEL.—A minor fraction of Manzar Khel, Tor Khel, Umarzai (600), Shin Khel, Ahmadzai, Darwesh Khel Wazirs. Headman; Jamal Din.

SHAHABUDDIN KHEL (90).—A minor fraction of Garerai, Shumi Khel, Malli

Khel, Manazai, Alizai, Mahsuds. Headmen; Zafar, Isab, Kabul, Zarmast.

SHAH ALAM KHEL (128).—A section of the Kasim Khel, Chahar Khel, Shaman Khel, Mahsuds.

SHAHBANA KOR.—A minor fraction of Sultan Khel, Hamza Khel, Gandab, Halimzai, Mohmands. Headman; Nurai.

SHAHBAS KHEL.—A minor fraction of Mir Said Khel, Sanzal Khel, Kamal Khel, Sahib Jan, Aka Khel (1,800), Afridis. Samil.

SHAHBAZ KHEL (40).—A minor fraction of Bizodai, Malikshai, Aimal Khel, Bahlolzai, Mahsuds. Headmen; Zobar, Asal Khan, Akbar Khan.

SHAHBAZ KOR. (Danish Kol).—A minor fraction of Rajai Khel, Yusaf Khel, Isa Khel, Pandiali, Mohmands.

SHAHBEG KHEL.—A minor fraction of Tor Khel, Asad Khel, Mitha Khan Khel, Kuki Khel (4,500), Afridis. Gar. Headmen; Razai and Islamdin.

SHAHBEG KHEL.—A minor fraction of Fatteh Khel, Mir Khel, Pakhai (1,000), Budai, Zakha Khel, Afridis. Samil. Headmen; Muhammad Nur, Muhammad Shah, and Kamr Din.

SHAHBUDINZAI (West of Dera Ghazi Khan District).—A sub-division of Hamzazai, Balil Khel, Musa Khels. Headman; Kalandar.

SHADAD KHEL.—A section of the Kambar Khel, Bazoti (500), Daulatzai, Orakzais. Samil.

SHAHDAD KHEL.—A division of Mutakai, Utman Khels.

SHAHDOZAIS (200).—A small Pathan tribe, said to be an offshoot of the Kakars. Headman; Jehangir.

SHAHGUL KHEL.—A sub-division of Niamat Khel, Tatta, Battannis. Headman; Mir Azar.

SHAHGUL KOR.—A minor fraction of Rasul Kor, Wali Beg Kor, Gandab, Halimzai, Mohmands. Headmen; Khalid, Ghulam Din, Kalandar.

SHAHI KHEL (15 ; Dera Ismail Khan District).—Nomadic, a minor fraction of Saiad Khel, Isot Khel, Mian Khel, Lohana, Pawindahs. Headmen ; see Mian Khel.

SHAHI KHEL (80 ; Black Mountain).—A section of Barat Khel, Akazai, Isazai, Yusufzais.

SHAHI KHEL.—A minor fraction of Ghulam Khel (300), Haibat Khel, Jawaki, Adam Khel, Afridis.

SHAHI KHEL (40).—A section of Musakki, Tor, Mallizad, Dawaris. Headmen ; Niamidar, Azmat, Gul Sahib, Kippat.

SHAHI KHEL (8).—A minor fraction of Padmi, Taib Khel, Amzoni, Mallizad, Dawaris. Headman ; Faizullah.

SHAHI KOR.—A minor fraction of Muradi Khel, Dalkha Kor, Dadu Khel, Tarakzai, Mohmands. Headman ; Muhammad Hassan.

SHAHI KOR (Kharmana river).—A minor fraction of the Ash Khel (580), Khwaja Khel, Masuzai, Lashkarzai, Orakzais. Samil. Headman ; Sabzulla.

SHAH JAHAN KHEL.—A minor fraction of Jambai Khel, Waruka, Ali Khan Khel, Sarki Khel, Madda Khel, (1,600), Ibrahim Khel, Utmanzai, Darwesh Khel Wazirs.

SHAH KHEL.—A section of Ibrahim Khel, Gadaizai, Iliaszai, Bunerwals.

SHAH MANSUR KHEL (1,300).—A section of Dadu Khel. Tarakzai, Mohmands.

SHAH MIRI.—A minor fraction of Dre Pillari, Tori Khel (2,670), Ibrahim Khel, Utmanzai, Darwesh Khel Wazirs. Headman ; Khari.

SHAH MUHAMMAD KHEL.—A minor fraction of Pira Khel, Jamal Khel, Malik Shahi (400), Wali Khel, Utmanzai, Darwesh Khel Wazirs. Headman ; Pirgai.

SHAHMAL KHEL.—A minor fraction of Firoz Khel, Tor Sapar (350), Galai, Adam Khel, Afridis.

SHAHNUR KOR.—A minor fraction of Zaman Khel, Makki Khel, Kattia Khel, Hassan Khel, Mitha Khan Khel, Kuki Khel (4,500), Afridis. Gar.

Shahozai (West of Dera Ghazi Khan District).—A division of Umarzai, Musa Khels. Headman ; Shahozai.

Shahozai (100).—A sub-division of Yahia, Sen Khel, Sheranis.

Shahul Khel (40).—A sub-division of Ismail Khel, Manazai, Sheranis.

Shahwali Khel.—A minor fraction of Sikandar Khel, Abdul Khel, Bora Khel (1,000), Mohmit Khel, Utmanzai, Darwesh Khel Wazirs.

Shahwaz Khel.—A sub-division of the Khwaja Hawas Khel, Ali Khel (3,000), "Hamsayas" of the Orakzais. Gar. ½ Shiah.

Shaib Khel.—A section of the Mir Ahmad Khel, Alisherzai (3,000), Lashkarzai, Orakzais. Samil.

Shaib Khel.—A minor fraction of Dani Khel, Matkai, Malikshahi (400), Wali Khel, Utmanzai, Darwesh Khel, Wazirs. Headman ; Marota.

Shaikh Bazid (Wana).—A minor fraction of Zalli Khel (3,000), Bomi Khel, Nasra Din, Kalu Khel, Ahmadzai, Darwesh Khel Wazirs.

Shaikh Khel.—A section of Aib Khel, Salarzai, Iliaszai, Bunerwals.

Shaikh Khel.—A minor fraction of Kambir (or Kambo) Khel, Aib Khel, Salarzai, Iliaszai, Bunerwals.

Shaikh Khels (Talash valley, and Dush Khel, in Dir).—A division of Ausa Khel (Malizai) Yusafzais. In combination with the Nurak Khels they can muster some 1,500 fighting men.

Shakal Khel (100).—A section of Haibat Khel, Jawaki, Adam Khel, Afridis.

Shakhar Khel.—A minor fraction of Musakki, Wuzi Khel (800), Mohmit Khel, Utmanzai, Darwesh Khel Wazirs. Headman ; Kaloni.

Shakhar Khel (Bannu District).—A minor fraction of Kundi, Pirba Khel, Hathi Khel (2,000), Shin or Sani Khel, Ahmadzai, Darwesh Khel Wazirs. Headman ; Dangir Khan.

SHAKHI (230).—A division of Waraspun, Battannis. Headmen; Saidal (Ismailak); Jandar (Chalak Khel), Ahmad Khan (Fateh Khel).

SHAKHIRYA KHEL.—A minor fraction of Khojal Khel (600), Shadi Khel, Nasra Din, Kalu Khel, Ahmadzai, Darwesh Khel Wazirs.

SHAKHUL KHEL.—A minor fraction of Mir Husani, Macha, Madda Khel (1,600), Ibrahim Khel, Utmanzai, Darwesh Khel Wazirs.

SHAKKI KHEL (60).—A subdivision of the Band Khel, Bahlolzai, Mahsuds. Headman; Rahimdád.

SHAKRZAI (40).—A section of Land Amand, Ahmad Khel, Oba Khel, Sheranis.

SHALMAI KOR.—A minor fraction of Rami Khel, Kadai Kor, Gandab, Halimzai, Mohmands. Headmen; Khan Shere, Zainullah.

SHAMAK KHEL (420).—A section of the Abdullai, Aimal Khel, Bahlolzai, Mahsuds.

SHAMAL KHEL.—A minor fraction of Pirwal Khel, Tatar Khel or Akhorwal, Hassan Khel, Adam Khel, Afridis.

SHAMALI KHEL.—A sub-division of the Akhel (600), Ismailzai, Orakzais. Gar. Headman; Mákhodi.

SHAMAMZAI (300).— A section of the Baranzai, Kebzai, Sanzar, Kakars. Headmen; Jamal, Behai, Paio.

SHAMAN KHEL (1,928).—A clan of Mahsuds.

SHAMERAI (140).—A sub-division of the Manazai, Alizai, Mahsuds.

SHAMEZAI (34).—A division of Rakanwal, Lunis.

SHAMEZAI (4,000; Harhawai stream to Kohistan).—A division of Khwazazai, Akozai—Yusufzai Swatis. Headman; Hussain Khan of Asharai.

SHAMI KHEL.—A minor fraction of Shugai, Tori Khel, (2,600), Ibrahim Khel, Utmanzai, Darwesh Khel Wazirs. Headmen; Hakim, Musa, Hashim Khan.

SHAMIL (1,000; Shamil valley, Khost).—A clan of the Khostwals.

SHAMIZAI (West of Dera Ghazi Khan District).—A section of Kudizai, Ahmadzai, Balil Khel, Musa Khels. Headman; Lal Khan.

SHAMMAL (210).—A section of Hassu Khel, Tor, Mallizad, Dawaris. Headmen; Madda Khan, Gul Hassan, Mir Kazam, Nakib, Fazal Din, Fakir Shah, Manzar Khan, Shah Salim, Nawi.

SHAMMI KHEL (40).—A section of Nana Khel, Tapiai, Tappizad, Dawaris. Headmen; Adil Shah, Pirdil.

SHAMOZAI (8,000; Arang, south of Bajaur).—A division of Ismailzai, Utman Khels.

SHAMOZAI (174).—A subdivision of Harun Khel, Sanatia, Kakars. Headmen; Nur Muhammad (Iliaszai), Guldad (Lalakzai, and headman of all the Shamozais.)

SHAMOZAI.—A section of Hamzazai, Arbu Khel, Sanzar, Kakars. Headmen; Shah Alam (Mahrizai), Soba Khan (Kashmirzai), Palo (Mirakzai, headman of all the Hamzazais).

SHAMOZAI (2,000; Swat river).—A division of Khwazazai, Akozai—Yusufzai Swatis.

SHAMSHA KHEL.—A minor fraction of Mawal Khel (760), Haibat Khel, Jawaki, Adam Khel, Afridis.

SHAMSHER KHEL.—A minor fraction of Idia Khel, Jani Khel (1,000), Wali Khel, Utmanzai, Darwesh Khel Wazirs. Headman; Zarghun Shah.

SHAMSHER KHEL (18).—A sub-division of Khaddi, Mallizad, Dawaris. Headmen; Fatteh Khan, Wati.

SHAMSI KHEL (100).—A minor fraction of the Jalal Khel, Sher Khel, Haibat Khel, Nana Khel, Bahlolzai, Mahsuds. Headmen; Karim, Kargah.

SHAMSI KHEL (Wana).—A minor fraction of Tojiya Khel (1,600), Bomi Khel, Nasra Din, Kalu Khel, Ahmadzai, Darwesh Khel Wazirs.

SHAMSI KHEL (25).—A minor fraction of the Ali Khel, Haidar Khel, Tor, Tappizad, Dawaris. Headman; Abizar.

SHAMSO KOR.—A sub-division of Masand Safis who are a vassal clan of the Mohmands.

SHAN KHEL (80).—A division of Tatta, Battannis. Headman; Mir Azim (Bilal).

SHANAI or SHAN KHEL (750).—A division of Zakha Khel Afridis. Samil. Headmen; Said Khan, Mihr Din, Bawar, Sultan Mir, Gul Shah, Khanzad, Langar, Khandin, Said Khan.

SHARAGH KHEL.—A minor fraction of Kaddam Khel, Feroz Khel, Mashi Khel, Mannia Khel, Hassan Khel, Mitha Khan Khel, Kuki Khel (4,500), Afridis. Gar. Headmen: Abbas; Hakim; Nazir.

SHARAK KHEL.—A minor fraction of Sadda Khel (300), Isperka, Kalu Khel, Ahmadzai, Darwesh Khel Wazirs. Headman; Zalim Khan.

SHARAKI (200).—A sub-division of Galai, Adam Khel, Afridis.

SHARBAT KHEL.—A minor fraction of Paipali, Kabul Khel (2,600), Wali Khel, Utmanzai, Darwesh Khel Wazirs.

SHARIF KHEL.—A minor fraction of Kata Gran, Shugai, Tori Khel (2,670), Ibrahim Khel, Utmanzai, Darwesh Khel Wazirs. Headman; Muhammad Gul.

SHARIF KHEL.—A section of the Chawar Khel, Bazoti (500), Daulatzai, Orakzais. Samil.

SHARIF KHEL (10).—A section of Hakim Khel, Mubarak Shahi, Mallizad, Dawaris. Headmen; Ahmadnur. Badidar.

SHARRI KHEL (55).—A section of Kasim Khel, Chahar Khel, Shaman Khel, Mahsuds.

SHATI KHEL.—A section of Wali Beg Kor, Gandab, Halimzai, Mohmands.

SHATKAI (60).—A section of Malik Dinai, Manazai, Alizai, Mahsuds. Headman; Bozak.

SHATO KHEL (Pipal).—A subdivision of Babakai Kor, Dawezai, Mohmands. Headman; Mohmandai.

SHAWAL KHEL.—A minor fraction of Shadi Khel, Balal Khel, Hassan Khel (400), Mohmit Khel, Utmanzai, Darwesh Khel Wazirs. Headman; Piyao Khan.

SHEIKH AFZAL (Wana).—A minor fraction of Gangi Khel (800—400 in Wana), Bomi Khel, Nasra Din Khel, Kalu Khel, Ahmadzai, Darwesh Khel Wazirs.

SHEIKH ALI.—A minor fraction of Narmi Khel, Bakka Khel (1,000), Wali Khel, Utmanzai, Darwesh Khel Wazirs. Headman; Ghainadin.

SHEIKHAN (3,000; Mastura, Khanki, and Miranzai valleys).—A "Hamsaya" clan of the Orakzais. Samil.

SHEIKHAN (15).—A sub-division of Khaddi, Mallizad, Dawaris. Headman; Zarogha Din.

SHEIKH ALI.—A minor fraction of Mushakki, Masha, Madda Khel (1,600), Ibrahim Khel, Utmanzai, Darwesh, Khel Wazirs.

SHEIKH BUDIN.—A minor fraction of Sardi Khel, Bakka Khel (1,000), Wali Khel, Utmanzai, Darwesh Khel Wazirs. Headmen; Ashraf Khan, Khaki Shah, Gulak Khan.

SHEIKHBUDIN KHEL.—A minor fraction of Wadin Khel, Khazzar Khel, Star Ali Khan Khel, Sarki Khel, Madda Khel (1,600), Ibrahim Khel, Utmanzai, Darwesh Khel Wazirs.

SHEIKH KHEL (Bajaur).—A division of the Isazai, Tarkanis.

SHEIKHMAL KHEL.—A subdivision of Kambar Khel, Kambar Khel (4,500), Afridis. Gar. Headmen; Jan Muhammad, Muhammad Amir.

SHEKMAL KHEL (600; Loargai).—A division of Ali Sher Khel, Shinwaris.

SHEIKHMALI KHEL (200).—A minor fraction of Abrahim Khel, Ali Karan, Mamuzai, Lashkarzai, Orakzais. Gar. Headman; Said Ahmad.

SHEIKHNUR KHEL.—A minor fraction of Jambai Khel, Waruka Ali Khan Khel, Sarki Khel, Madda Khel (1,600), Ibrahim Khel, Utmanzai, Darwesh Khel Wazirs.

Sheikh Umrai.—A minor fraction of Pira Khel, Jamal Khel, Malik Shahi (400), Wali Khel, Utmanzai, Darwesh Khel Wazirs. Headman; Sulemani.

Sheikhwadi.—A minor fraction of Shadi Khel, Bora Khel (1,000), Mohmit Khel, Utmanzai, Darwesh Khel Wazirs.

Shekh.—An Arabic word meaning elder or chief. It is a title properly confined to tribes of Arab descent, but is very commonly used to denote a *convert to Islam*.

Shekhai (100; Trans frontier).—A division of the Ali Sher Khel, Shinwaris.

Shekhai.—A section of Annai (1,000), Budai, Zakha Khel, Afridis. Samil Headman; Khwas Khan.

Sahekh Khel.—A minor fraction of Khusalai, Tori Khel (2,670), Ibrahim Khel, Utmanzai; Darwesh Khel Wazirs. Headman; Shahmak.

Shekh Ali Khel.—A division of Kamrai or Kamar Khel (600), Afridis. Samil. Headmen; Mulla Amir Shah, Mulla Akhundzada, Sher Wali.

Shekan.—A minor fraction of Kasim Khel, Suran Khel Babakri, Sipah (1,200), Afridis. Samil. Headmen; see Kasim Khel.

Shekh Barid Khel (70).—A minor fraction of the Nikarrab Khel, Khoidad Khel, Gidi Khel, Manazai, Alizai, Mahsuds. Headman; Sab Khan, Piyao.

Shekhan.—A minor fraction of Karun Khel, Asad Khel, Mitha Khan Khel, Kuki Khel (4,500), Afridis. Gar. Headmen; Gulab, Alam Sher, Sherai, Ghulam Ali, Khairdad, Alladad Fakir, Abbas.

Shekhu Khel (20; Dera Ismail Khan District)—Nomadic, a minor fraction of Baloch Khel, Isot Khel, Mian Khel, Lohana, Pawindahs. Headmen; see Mian Khel.

Shekwal.—A section of Pakhai (1,000), Budai, Zakha Khel, Afridis. Samil. Headmen; Sher Ali, Mirza, Samundar, Payao.

SHEKHZAI.—A minor fraction of Masezai, Hani, Panezun, Sanzar, Kakars.

SHEORANIS; see SHERANIS.

SHER.—A sub-division of the Khwaja Hawas Khal, Ali Khels (3,000), Hamsayas of the Orakzais. Gar. ½ Shiah.

SHER AHMAD KHEL.—A minor fraction of Saifali, Kabul Khel (2,600), Wali Khel, Utmanzai, Darwesh Khel Wazirs.

SHERAKAI.—A minor fraction of Dreplara, Paindai (940), Nasruddin, Zakha Khel, Afridis. Samil. Headmen; Chikkun, Tamas, Anwar, Nazr Din.

SHER ALI KHEL (20).—A minor fraction of the Nekzan Khel, Sher Khel, Haibat Khel, Nana Khel, Bahlolzai, Mahsuds. Headman; Alam.

SHERANIS, also called Sheoranis and Miranis (4,500; country around Takht-i-Suleman).—A tribe of Pathans. Headmen; Nika, Azim Khan.

SHERANZAI (50).—A minor fraction of Babuzai, Natozai, Dumar, Sanzar, Kakars.

SHERBAZ KHEL.—A section of Tor Sapar (350), Galai, Adam Khel, Afridis.

SHER DARI KHEL (150).—A minor fraction of the Jalal Khel, Sher Khel, Haibat Khel, Nana Khel, Bahlolzai, Mahsuds.

SHERGA KHEL.—A section of Utmanzai, Adinzai, Khwazazai, Akozai—Yusufzai Swatis.

SHERGUL KHEL.—A minor fraction of Yunas Khel, Bosti Khel (150), Galai, Adam Khel, Afridis.

SHER GULLA.—A division of Aka Khel (1,800), Afridis. Samil.

SHERI KHEL.—A minor fraction of Baghdad Khel, Keimal Khel, Urmuz Khel, Sipah (1,200), Afridis. Samil. Headman; Lal Muhammad.

SHER KHAN KHEL.—A minor fraction of Kharmanj Khel, Khwaja Khel, Miamai, Kabul Khel (2,600), Wali Khel, Utmanzai, Darwesh Khel Waziris.

SHER KHAN KHEL.—A minor fraction of Umar Khan Khel, Malikdin Khel, Malikdin Khel (4,500), Afridis. Samil. Headmen; see Kutti Khel.

SHER KHAN KHEL.—A minor fraction of Kasim Khel (250), Kimat Khel, Jawaki, Adam Khel, Afridis.

SHER KHAN KHEL.—A minor fraction of Mohmand Khel, Kattia Khel, Hassan Khel, Mitha Khan Khel, Kuki Khel (4,500), Afridis. Gar. Headmen; Kambar, Boner and Kaddam Khan.

SHER KHAN KHEL.—A minor fraction of Musa Khel, Makhozai, Nasuzai, Iliaszai, Bunerwals.

SHER KHAN KHEL (16).—One of the two sections of the Malla Khel, Chahar Khel, Shaman Khel, Mahsuds. Headmen; Shahid Khan, Zarpiyao.

SHER KHEL.—A minor fraction of Kambir (or Kambo) Khel, Aib Khel, Salarzai, Iliaszai, Bunerwals.

SHER KHEL (1,020).—A section of the Haibat Khel, Nana Khel, Bahlolzai, Mahsuds.

SHER KHEL.—A minor fraction of Targali, Muhammad Khel, Hassan Khel (770), Mohmit Khel, Utmanzai, Darwesh Khel Wazirs.

SHER KHEL.—A minor fraction of Dre Nami, Balal Khel, Hassan Khel (400), Mohmit Khel, Utmanzai, Darwesh Khel Wazirs. Headman; Niyaz Muhammad.

SHER KHEL.—A minor fraction of Buha Khel, Maddu Khel, Asad Khel, Mitha Khan i Khel, Kuki Khel (4,500), Afridis. Gar. Headmen; Mulla Nazir, Mirwal, Said Gul.

SHER KHEL.—A minor fraction of Gharu Khel, Ashraf Khel, Kamal Khel, Sahib Jan, Aka Khel (1,800), Afridis. Samil.

SHER KHEL.—A sub-division of Mat Khan Khel, Kambar Khel (4,500), Afridis. Gar. Headmen; Sher Khan, Hamid, and Nurai.

SHER KHEL.—A minor fraction of Ahmad Beg Khel, Mohib Khel, Shekhai, Annai (1,000), Budai, Zakha Khel, Afridis. Samil. Headmen; Shahzada, Arsala, Aligul.

SHER KHEL (30).—A minor fraction of Kimat Khel, Haidar Khel, Tor, Tappizad, Dawaris. Headmen; Nasar Khan, Banocha Khan, Khanai.

SHER MUHAMMAD KHEL.—A minor fraction of Mir Hasani, Macha, Madda Khel (1,600), Ibrahim Khel, Utmanzai, Darwesh Khel Wazirs.

SHERPAN KHEL.—A section of Mandazai, Daolatzai, Malizai Bunerwals.

SHERZAI.—A minor fraction of the Ali Khanzai, Hamzazai, Arbu Khel, Sanzar, Kakars.

SHERZAI KHEL.—A section of Hasan Khel, Gadaizai, Iliaszai, Bunerwals.

SHILMANI MOHMANDS (300; Loi and Kam Shilman).—These are really sections of the Shah Mansur Khel and the Masaud Kor, Dadu Khel, Tarakzais and Halimzai Mohmands in Loi Shilman; in Kam Shilman there is a minor fraction of Asaf Khel, Dalkha Kor, Dadu Khel, Tarakzai, Mohmands.

SHIN or SANI KHEL (3,400; British territory, Shakai, and Wana).—A division of Ahmadzai, Darwesh Khel Wazirs. Headmen; see Hathi Khel, Sirki Khel, and Umarzai.

SHINGI (585).—A division of the Bahlolzai, Mahsuds.

SHINKI KHEL.—A section of Sultan Khel, Sher Gulla, Aka Khel (1,800), Afridis. Samil.

SHINKI KHEL (155).—A minor fraction of Babakki, Hassu Khel, Tor, Mallizad, Dawaris. Headmen; Faujdar, Mad Afzal, Karar, Gul Hassan, Gul Raihan.

SHINSARAI KOR.—A minor fraction of Hyatai Kor, Shah Mansur Khel, Dadu Khel, Tarakzai, Mohmands. Headman; Saiyid Rasul.

SHINWARIS; see ALI SHER KHEL.

SHIRAK KHEL.—A minor fraction of Mawal Khel (760), Haibat Khel, Jawaki, Adam Khel. Afridis.

SHIRAK KHEL.—A sub-division of the Hassanzai, Mishtis (3,000), "Hamsayas" of the Orakzais. Samil. Headman; Langar.

Shir Khel (18).—A sub-division of Zerakki, Mallizad, Dawaris. Headmen; Gulapir, Khangul.

Shiri Khel or Alizai (500; Mastura river).—A division of the Daulatzai, Orakzais. Samil. ⅓ Shiah.

Shita Khel (60).—A section of Issuri, Tor, Tappizad, Dawaris. Headmen; Samand Khan, Dinai, Nadam, Minai.

Shkundi Khel (25; Mastura river).—A sub-division of the Alizai (or Sturi Khel), Daulatzai, Orakzais. Samil. Shiah. Headman; Dalil Khan.

Sho Muhammad Khel (16).—A minor fraction of the Barumi Khel, Khoidad Khel, Gidi Khel, Manazai, Alizai, Mahsuds. Headman; Aligul.

Shobak Khel (20).—A minor fraction of the Rahimdad Khel, Abdul Rahman Khel, Sher Khel, Haibat Khel, Nana Khel, Bahlolzai, Mahsuds. Headmen; Shale, Shazal.

Shodi Khel (16).—One of the five sections of the Ghalib Khel, Badanzai, Shaman Khel, Mahsuds. Headman; Akbar Khan.

Shogi Khel.—A minor fraction of Umar Khel, Ali Khel, Khaddar Khel (770), Mohmit Khel, Utmanzai, Darwesh Khel Wazirs. Headman; Nazarka.

Shomar Khel (14).—A minor fraction of the Rahimdad Khel, Abdul Rahman Khel, Sher Khel, Haibat Khel, Nana Khel, Bahlolzai, Mahsuds. Headmen; Gandapur, Panai.

Shomai (25).—A minor fraction of the Garri Khel, Baran Khel, Chahar Khel, Shaman Khel, Mahsuds. Headmen; Lal Gul, Mauladad.

Shpalkai Khel.—A section of Zargun Khel (800), Galai, Adam Khel, Afridis.

Shudakka (50).—A minor fraction of Gita Khel, Muhammad Khel, Malakh, Mallizad, Dawaris. Headmen; Sawan, Ahmad Din.

Shugai.—A section of Tori Khel (2,670), Ibrahim Khel. Utmanzai, Darwesh Khel Wazirs. Headmen; Ilias and Madd (Muhammad) Akbar.

Shui Khel.—A minor fraction of Narmi Khel, Bakka Khel (1,000), Wali Khel, Utmanzai, Darwesh Khel Wazirs. Headman; Pilod Khan.

Shuja Khel.—A minor fraction, of Kata Gran, Shugai, Tori Khel (2,670), Ibrahim Khel, Utmanzai, Darwesh Khel Wazirs. Headman; Khonamir.

Shujawal (28).—A section of Shujawal, Mubarak Shahi, Mallizad, Dawaris. Headmen; Sheikh Mansur, Salih Khan, Asad Khan.

Shujawal (126).—A sub-division of Mubarak Shahi, Mallizad, Dawaris. Headmen; Sheikh Mansur, Salih Khan, Shahmadi, Zarif, Maula Hassan, Idak, Mir Kazam, Hussain Shah, Shaikh Kabir.

Shumi Khel (895).—A section of Palli Khel, Manazai, Alizai, Mahsuds.

Sidzai (9).—A sub-division of Ladu, Rakanwal, Lunis. Headman; see Ladu.

Sikandar Khel (Daradar valley).—A sub-division of Mamuzai (200), Ismailzai, Orakzais. Samil. Headman; Mir Ahmad.

Sikandar Khel.—A section of Kandai, Isa Khel, Pandiali, Mohmands.

Sikandar Khel.—A section of Manzar Khel (360), Ibrahim Khel, Utmanzai, Darwesh Khel Wazirs. Headmen; Lal Khan, Ayaz Khan, Maddi Khan.

Sikandar Khel.—A division of Kuki Khel (4,500), Afridis. Gar. Headmen; Mir Alam, Rahmatulla, Nazir, Guljai, Taus, Said Gul.

Sikandar Khel.—A section of Pakhai (1,000), Budai, Zakha Khel, Afridis. Samil. Headmen; Band Ali, Muhammad Azim.

Sikandar Khel (25).—A section of Palali, Tapiai, Tappizad, Dawaris. Headmen; Baz, Khanzam, Zabta Khan.

Sikandar Khel.—A minor fraction of Khuniya Khel (200), Shadi Khel, Nasra Din, Kalu Khel, Ahmadzai, Darwesh Khel Wazirs.

Sikandar Khel.—A minor fraction of Sikandar Khel, Manzar Khel (360), Ibrahim Khel Utmanzai, Darwesh Khel, Wazirs. Headman; Ayaz Khan.

Sikandar Khel.—A section of Abdul Khel (1,000), Mohmit Khel, Utmanzai, Darwesh Khel, Wazirs.

Sikandar Kor.—A minor fraction of Kamal Khel, Maddu Khel, Asad Khel, Mitha Khan Khel, Kuki Khel (4,500), Afridis. Gar. Headmen; Muhammad Amin, Gul Jan, Budai, Langar.

Siman (20).—A section of Malli Khel, Idak, Tappizad, Dawaris. Headmen; Said Shah, Azim Khan, Jamal Din.

Siman Khel (6).—A section of Palali, Tapiai, Tappizad, Dawaris. Headman; Fatteh Mir.

Sin, Suin or Siun (1,000).—A clan of the Kakars.

Sini Khel.—A minor fraction of Khizar Khel, Mintar Khel, Muhammad Khel, Hassan Khel (400), Mohmit Khel, Utmanzai, Darwesh Khel Wazirs. Headman; Khugalgal.

Sini Khel.—A section of Khuniya Khel (200), Shadi Khel, Nasra Din, Kalu Khel, Ahmadzai, Darwesh Khel Wazirs.

Sini Khel (8).—A minor fraction of Khuttay, Taib Khel, Amzoni, Mallizad, Dawaris. Headman; Nazar Khan.

Sini Khel (25).—A minor fraction of Lar Lorai, Land, Malakh, Mallizad, Dawaris. Headmen; Akub, Balyam, Said Muhammad.

Sin Khur.—A minor fraction of the Khoidadzai, Shadzai, Alizai, Sanzar, Kakars.

Sinki Khel.—A minor fraction of Shadi Khel, Balal Khel, Hassan Khel (400), Mohmit Khel, Utmanzai, Darwesh Khel Wazirs. Headman; Badde Fakir.

Sipah (1,200; Bara valley and Kajurai).—One of the six Khyber Afridi clans. Samil. Headmen; Sher Muhammad, Shah Murad, Suliman Shah.

SIPAH (400; Mastura valley, and Landuki pass.)—A division of the Muhammad Khel, Orakzais. Gar. Shiah.

SIPAH (610).—A section of the Ali Karan, Mamuzai, Lashkarzai, Orakzais. Gar. See Azad Khel.

SIRGIRI or SARGHARI (200; Peshin).—A small Kakar clan. Headman; Sultan Muhammad.

SIRKI KHEL (800 [400 in, Wana], Bannu, Wana and Birmal).—A sub-division of Shin Khel, Ahmadzai, Darwesh Khel Wazirs. Headmen; Lajmir Khan, Band Khan, Madazan, Zargar Khan. These Maliks are responsible for the Gomal.

SIRKI KHEL (15).—A minor fraction of Gita Khel, Muhammad Khel, Malakh, Mallizad, Dawaris. Headman; Watanai.

SIRKI KHEL (20).—A minor fraction of Taos Khel, Sogi Khel, Muhammad Khel, Malakh, Mallizad, Dawaris. Headmen; Pirat Shah, Zargul.

SKHALI KHEL.—A minor fraction of Bai Khel, Firozai, Chagarzai, Malizai, Bunerwals.

SMEL KHEL.—A minor fraction of Bai Khel, Firozai, Chagarzai, Malizai, Bunerwals.

SOB KHEL.—A minor fraction of Jambai Khel, Waruka Ali Khan Khel, Sarki Khel, Madda Khel (1,600), Ibrahim Khel, Utmanzai, Darwesh Khel Wazirs.

SOGI KHEL (140).—A section of Muhammad Khel, Malakh, Mallizad, Dawaris. Headmen; Khan Muhammad Khan, Makhmad.

SORA KHEL (70).—A minor fraction of the Goga Khel, Sher Khel, Haibat Khel, Nana Khel, Bahlolzai, Mahsuds. Headman; Shahid Khan.

SPAIGI (30).—A minor fraction of Abdul Rahman Khel, Muhammad Khel, Malakh, Mallizad, Dawaris. Headmen; Hakim Khan, Wazir Azam.

SPEKIS; see SPAIGI, for which it is another name.

SPIN KHEL (15).—A section of Zhao Khel, Tapiai, Tappizad, Dawaris. Headman; Zariband.

SROH (120).—A section of Busha Khel, Kamali, Halimzai, Mohmands.

STAR ALI KHAN KHEL.—A name sometimes applied to the Khazzar Khel and Nazar Khel, minor fractions of the Ali Khan Khel, Sarki Khel, Madda Khel (1,600), Ibrahim Khel, Utmanzai, Darwesh Khel Wazirs. Headmen; Sadda Khan, Alambe and Shadam Khan.

STURI KHEL (400, Mastura river).—A sub-division of Alizai, or Sturi Khel, Daulatzai, Orakzais. Samil.

SUDAN KHEL (350; Bannu to Shakai, and Birmal)—A section of Isperka, Kalu, Khel, Ahmadzai, Darwesh Khel Wazirs. Headmen; Jalandar Shah and Mani Khan.

SULAIMAN KHEL (Khanki valley).—A sub-division of the Sada Khel (80), Ismailzai, Orakzais. Samil.

SULEIMAN KHEL.—A section of Sheikhmal, Kambar Khel, Kambar Khel (4,500), Afridis. Gar. Headmen; Mulla Walli, Azizulla.

SULEMANI.—Sometimes said to be a section of Khaddar Khel (770), but in reality a section of Wuzi Khel, Mohmit Khel, having land among the Khaddar Khels. Headmen; Sahib Din and Gul Sahib.

SULEMANI.—A section of Wuzi Khel (800), Mohmit Khel, Utmanzai, Darwesh Khel Wazirs.

SULIMANI KHEL.—A minor fraction of Ismail Khel, Bozi Khel, Madda Khel (1600), Ibrahim Khel, Utmanzai, Darwesh Khel Wazirs.

SULIMAN KHEL.—A sub-division of Bahram-ka-Khel, Bar Ranizai, Akozai—Yusufzai Swatis.

SULIMAN KHEL (320).—A section of Targhari, Sanzar, Kakars.

SULIMAN KHELS (9,220; between Kalat-i-Ghilzai and Jalalabad).—The most numerous and powerful of the Pawindah trading tribes.

SULIMAN MAHAMADZAI (300).—A section of Arozai, Ahmad Khel, Sen Khel, Sheranis.

SULIMANZAI.—A division of Salar, Gaduns.

SULTAN-KA-KHEL (700; east and south of the Swat-Panjkora junction).—A division of Bar Ranizai, Akozai—Yusafzai Swatis.

SULTAN KHEL.—A minor fraction of Kharmanj Khel, Khwaja Khel, Miamai, Kabul Khel (2,600), Wali Khel, Utmanzai, Darwesh Khel Wazirs. Headman; Surkam.

SULTAN KHEL.—A section of Abdul Khel, Urmuz Khel, Sipah (1,200), Afridis. Samil. Headman; Sher Jan.

SULTAN KHEL.—A section of Suran Khel, Babakri, Sipah (1,200), Afridis. Samil. Headmen; Niaz Karim, Iran, Gul Muhammad.

SULTAN KHEL.—A sub-division of Sher Gulla, Aka Khel (1,800), Afridis. Samil.

SULTAN KHEL.—A section of Annai (1,000), Budai, Zakha Khel Afridis. Samil. Headman; Bangai.

SULTAN KHEL.—A minor fraction of Ghulam Khel (300), Haibat Khel, Jawaki, Adam Khel, Afridis.

SULTAN KHEL.—A minor fraction of Hassan Khel, Pakhai (1,000), Budai, Zakha Khel, Afridis. Samil. Headmen; Mehrban, Mad Afzal, Mohabbat Sardar, Nurai.

SULTAN KHEL (Near Ublan pass).—A section of the Sipah (400), Muhammad Khel, Orakzais. Gar. Shiah.

SULTAN KHEL (Mahaban).—A section of Hassan Khel, Mada Khel, Isazai, Yusufzais. Headmen; Torai Khan, Hamza Khan.

SULTAN KHEL.—A section of Hamza Khel, Gandab, Halimzai, Mohmands.

SULTAN KHEL.—A section of Hamza Khel, Kamali, Halimzai, Mohmands. Headman; Ajmir Khan.

SULTAN KHEL.—A minor fraction of Aka Khel, Ismailzai, Daulatzai, Malizai, Bunerwals.

SULTAN KHEL (2,400; Panjkora, Dir).—A sub-division of Sesads, Malizai, Yusufzais.

SULTAN MUHAMMAD.—A section of Musara Khel, Ashazai, Iliaszai, Bunerwals.

SULTANAI (240).—A sub-division of Shabi Khel, Alizai, Mahsuds.

SULTANZAI (140).—A sub-division of Yakubzai, Manuzai, Sheranis.

SULTANZAI (90).—A section of Natozai, Dumar, Sanzar, Kakars.

SUMLA KHEL (120; Black Mountain).—A division of Deshiwal, Swatis. Headmen; Idhar Ali, Saman.

SURAB KOR.—A minor fraction of Fatima Kor, Sharagh Khel, Kaddam Khel, Feroz Khel, Mashi Khel, Mannia Khel, Hassan Khel, Mitha. Khan Khel, Kuki Khel (4,500), Afridis. Gar.

SURAN KHEL.—A sub-division of Babakri, Sipah (1,200), Afridis. Samil. Headmen; Niaz, Karim, Iran, Gul Muhammad.

SURAT KOR.—A section of Ziauddin (200), Budai, Zakha Khel, Afridis. Samil. Headmen; Mir Usman, Nurzai, Gulistan, Pahlwan, Yar Shah, Dauran, Sandan.

SURBAT KHEL.—A section of Kulla Khel, Malikdin Khel, Malikdin Khel (4000), Afridis. Samil. Headmen; see Bakhmali Khel.

SUR DODI KHEL (Bannu District).—A minor fraction of Dodi Khel, Khandar Khan Khel, Hathi Khel (2,000), Shin Khel, Ahmadzai, Darwesh Khel Wazirs.

SURI (80).—A section of Sarangzai, Harun Khel, Sanatia, Kakars. Headmen; Saleh Muhammad, Anwar.

SURI PAO.—A sub-division of Kalut Khel, Samilzai, Tarkanis.

SURKHA KHEL.—A section of Ghaibi Khel, Babakri, Sipah (1,200), Afridis. Samil. Headmen; Akbar, Mauladad.

SURKHA KOR.—A sub-division of 'Kuz' or 'Khrappawal,' Burhan Khel, Pandiali, Mohmands. Headmen; Salo, Nasim Gul, Baz Mir, Lal Jan.

SURKH KHEL (15; Dera Ismail Khan District).—Nomadic, a minor fraction of Shadi Khel, Isot Khel, Mian Khel, Lohana, Pawindahs.

SWABAI.—A division of Mandal, Utman Khels.

SWATIS.—The original inhabitants of Swat, sometimes

called Dehgans, and according to some authorities, of Indian origin. Driven out of Swat and Buner by the Akozai--Yusufzais in the end of the fifteenth century, they emigrated eastwards, under the leadership of Saiad Jalal Baba, a son of the famous Pir Baba of Buner. Crossing the Indus, they settled in Tikri, Allai, Deshi, Nandihar, Pakli, Konsh, Bogarmang, Agror, Balakot, and Garhi Habibulla, north of Hazara, and their descendants are there to this day.

40,400

SWATIS (~~81,250~~;* Swat valley from Panjkora junction to Kohistan).—A term loosely applied to the Akozai—Yusufzai tribe.

T

TABBI KHEL.—A minor fraction of Hindi Khel, Tor, Jani Khel (1,000), Wali Khel, Utmanzai, Darwesh Khel Wazirs. Headman ; Malkun.

TAGHAL KHEL (20).—A minor fraction of the Rahimdad Khel, Abdul Rahman Khel, Sher Khel, Haibat Khel, Nana Khel, Bahlolzai, Mahsuds. Headmen ; Janbil, Band.

TAGHI KAI (50).—A section of Malik Dinai, Manazai, Alizai, Mahsuds. Headman ; Sahibgul.

TAHIR SHAH (6).—A section of Barim Khel, Amzoni, Mallizad, Dawaris. Headman ; Tahir Shah.

TAIB KHEL (300).—A subdivision of Amzoni, Mallizad, Dawaris. Headmen ; Wazirgai, Hathi Khel, Wanak, Said Akbar, Mokhsein.

TAIM KHEL.—A section of Bazid Khel, Jawaki (1,200), Adam Khel, Afridis.

TAIMUR KHEL.—A minor fraction of Gadia Khel, Tatar or Akhorwal (300), Hassan Khel, Adam Khel, Afridis.

TAJAL KHEL (110).—A section of Astanai, Shabi Khel, Alizai, Mahsuds. Headmen ; Shahzar, and Shahnir.

TAJBI KHEL (150).—A section of the Taru Khel, Boba, Dana, Battannis.

* These numbers do not include Gujars, Mians, and other *Fakirnama*.

Tajiks.—The name used throughout Afghanistan to denote any Persian speaking people who are neither Saiads, Afghans nor Hazaras.

Taju Khel (50; Dera Ismail Khan District).—Nomadic, a minor fraction of the Musazai, Sein Khel, Mian Khel, Lohana, Pawindahs. Headman; see Mian Khel.

Takhai Kor.—A minor fraction of Muradi Khel, Dalkha Kor, Dadu Khel Tarakzai, Mohmands. Headman; Achak.

Takhmal Khel.—A minor fraction of Nazar Khel, Star Ali Khan Khel, Sarki Khel, Madda Khel (1,600), Ibrahim Khel, Utmanzai, Darwesh Khel Wazirs.

Takhti Khel (Bannu and Shawal).—A section of Bakka Khel (1,000), Wali Khel, Utmanzai, Darwesh Khel Wazirs. Headmen; see Usman Khel and Khan Khel.

Takhti Khel (British territory).—A minor fraction of Budin Khel (100), Shadi Khel, Nasra Din, Kalu Khel, Ahmadzai, Darwesh Khel Wazirs.

Takhti Khel.—A sub-division of Umar Khel, Tatta Battannis.

Takor (Laman).—A division of Ismailzai, Utman Khels.

Talagh Khel.—A minor fraction of Kaddam Khel, Feroz Khel, Mashi Khel, Mannia Khel, Hassan Khel, Mitha Khan Khel, Kuki Khel (4,500), Afridis. Gar. Headmen; Mulla Wali, Khaza Khan.

Talim Khel.—A section of Zargun Khel (300), Galai, Adam Khel, Afridis.

Tal Khanzai (60).—A (Hamsaya) section of Shabozai, Dumar, Sanzar, Kakars. Headman; Salim.

Tamni (Herat).—A division of Sanzar, Kakars.

Tani Khel.—A minor fraction of Ghani Khel, Mir Hasani, Macha, Madda Khel, (1,600), Ibrahim Khel, Utmanzai, Darwesh Khel Wazirs.

Tanis (3,000; Southern border of Khost).—A tribe living between the Zadrans on the west, and the Gurbaz on east. Headmen; Khan Badshah. Chief village Dragi. About 100 families (Headman; Kaim) are settled amongst the Madda Khel Wazirs of the Kazha.

TAN KUSHI (30).—A section of Tarota, Idak, Tappizad, Dawaris. Headman; Ghulam Rasul.

TANZAI.—A division of Anjra Khel, Zmarais. Headman; Aku Khan.

TAOS KHEL (Bannu District).—A minor fraction of Pirba Khel, Hathi Khel (2,000), Shin or Sani Khel, Ahmadzai, Darwesh Khel Wazirs. Headman; Pilawar Khan.

TAOS KHEL (90).—A minor fraction of Sogi Khel, Muhammad Khel, Malakh, Mallizad, Dawaris. Headmen; Pirah Shah, Khan Muhammad Khan.

TAPAI (165)—A division of Khoidad Khel, Zaimukhts.

TAPIAI (504).—A division of Tappizad, Dawaris. Headmen; Baz, Mir Alam, Gul Ahmad, Fatteh Mir, Jumazan, Said Shah, Abdulla, Adil Shah, Isab Khan.

TAPPI.—Another name given to the Tapiai, Tappizad Dawaris.

TAPPI KHEL (82).—A subdivision of Badanzai, Shaman Khel, Mahsuds.

TAPPIZAD (2,333).—One of the two clans of Dawaris. Headmen; Talo Khan, Lalo Khan, Nazarband, Said Shah, Din Muhammad.

TARAKI (60).—A section of Yakubzai, Manuzai, Oba Khel, Sheranis.

TARAKIS (3,000; Ghazni and Kalat-i-Ghilzai).—One of the Pawindah trading tribes.

TARAKZAI or TARGHARI (3,210).—"Hamsayas" of the Sanzar, Kakars.

TARAKZAI (2,850).—One of the Mohmand clans. See note on page 46.

TARA KHEL (400).—A subdivision of Muia, Waraspun, Battannis. Headmen; Isof Khan (Khwad), Maidan Khan (Sarar), Maya Khan, (Maghzai).

TARAN (Saiads) (45).—Hamsayas of the (Western) Sanzar, Kakars.

TARAN KHEL.—A sub-division of Sarsa, Tatta, Battannis.

TARGADDA (40).—A minor fraction of the Khoidad Khel, Gidi Khel, Manazai, Alizai Mahsuds. Headmen; Shahib Dad, Kaim Shah.

TARGALI.—A minor fraction of Muhammad Khel, Hassan Khel (400), Mohmit Khel, Utmanzai, Darwesh Khel Wazirs. Headmen; Gulbat Shah.

TARGAM KHEL.—A minor fraction of Torsam Khel, Nazar Khel, Star Ali Khan Khel, Sarki Khel, Madda Khel (1,600). Ibrahim Khel, Utmanzai, Darwesh Khel Wazirs.

TARGHARI (3,210).—A Hamsaya division of the Sanzar, Kakars.

TARKI KHEL (30).—A section of Matti Khel, Galeshahi, Shaman Khel, Mahsuds. Headmen; Parang, Khana, Nizam Din.

TARI KHEL.—A sub-division of Shakhi Khel, Waraspun, Battannis. Headmen; Jandar (Chalak), Ahmad Khan (Fatteh Khan).

TARI KHEL.—A minor fraction of Tol Khel, Abdul Khel, Bora Khel (1,000), Utmanzai, Darwesh Khel, Wazirs.

TARINS.—A tribe inhabiting Peshin and Thal Chotiali. They are divided into Spin and Tor. The latter clan nearly all belong to Peshin.

TARKAI (30).—A section of Shamerai, Manazai, Alizai, Mahsuds. Headman; Pira Khel.

TARKA KHEL (30).—A minor fraction of Charkhil, Land, Malakh, Mallizad, Dawaris. Headman; Badani, Sultan, Mir Kazam.

TARKANI (or TARKALANI).—The name of the tribe inhabiting the whole of Bajaur. Headmen; Khans of Nawagai, Jhar, Khar, Pashat, Barwa.

TAR KHEL (Tartara).—A division of Mullagoris, a vassal clan of the Mohmands.

TAR KHEL.—A section of Kanizai, Kattagarm, Tatta, Battannis.

TARKIAL KHEL.—A section of Mughul Khel, Barmi Khel, Kamrai Khel (600), Afridis. Samil. Headmen; Anar, Bahadur Shah, Sifat Shah, Sheradin, Zardad, Mir Ali.

TARKI KHEL (20).—A section of Bibizai, Shati Khel, Alizai, Mahsuds. Headman; Mustafa.

TARKI KHEL.—A section of Usman Khel, Shanai (750), Budai, Zakha Khel, Afridis. Samil. Headmen ; Mehr Din, Bawar, Sultan Mir, Gul Shah.

TAROTA (184).—A sub-division of Idak, Tappizad, Dawaris. Headmen ; Israfil Idar, Ghulam Rasul, Daisal, Ram-ali, Fakir.

TARU KHEL (730).—A sub-division of Boba, Dana, Battannis.

TARU KHEL.—A section of Hamza Khel, Gandab, Halim-zai, Mohmands, closely allied to the Baru Khel. Head-man ; Hamid Gul.

TARU KHEL (10 ; Dera Ismail Khan District).—Nomadic, a minor fraction of Saiad Khel, Isot Khel, Mian Khel, Lohana, Pawindahs.

TARWIZAI (500 ; Shamil valley, Khost).—A clan of the Khostwals, also known as Turizai.

TASAN KHEL (200 ; Black Mountain).—A sub-division of Akazai, Isazai, Yusufzais. Headmen ; Dad Khan, Said Mian, Rahmat Khan, Sula Khan.

TASHI KHEL.—A section of Sharaki (200), Galai, Adam Khel, Afridis.

TATAR KHEL, or AKHORWAL (300 ; Kohat pass).—A sub-division of Hassan Khel, Adam Khel, Afridis.

TATOR KHEL (5 ; Dera Ismail Khan District).—Nomadic, a minor fraction of Shadi Khel, Isot Khel, Mian Khel, Lohana, Pawindahs.

TATTA (890).—A clan of the Battannis. Headmen; Bangi, Khushal Khan, Mir Azim, Kotta, Nawaz, Miani, Sher Khan.

TATTA KHEL.—A minor fraction of Madda Khel, Miamai, Kabul Khel (2,600), Utman-zai, Darwesh Khel Wazirs.

TATTAR KHEL (30).—A minor fraction of Idal Khel, Muham-mad Khel, Malakh, Malli-zad, Dawaris. Headmen ; Shahid Khan, Gulak.

TATU KHEL.—A minor fraction of Miwal Khel (760), Haibat Khel, Jawaki, Adam Khel, Afridis.

TAUS KHEL.—A section of Sen Khel, Gadaizai, Iliaszai, Bunerwals.

Taus Khel (35 ; Dera Ismail Khan District).—Nomadic, a minor fraction of Waruki, Sein Khel, Mian Khel, Lohana, Pawindahs. Headman ; see Mian Khel.

Tauz Khel.—A minor fraction of Bakhshi Khel, Madda Khel (1,600), Ibrahim Khel, Utmanzai, Darwesh Khel Wazirs. Headmen ; Gulli of Stara, and Alam Shah.

Tawla Khel (Bannu, Wana and Birmal).—A section of Sirki Khel (800 [400 in Wana]), Shin Khel, Ahmadzai, Darwesh Khel Wazirs. Headmen ; see Sirki Khel.

Tazi Khel (25 ; Mastura river).—A sub-division of Alizai (or Sturi Khel), Daulatzai, Orakzais, Samil. Shiah. Headmen ; Ghulam Muhammad, Muhammad Khan.

Temurzai (200).—A section of Sarangzai, Harun Khel, Sanatia, Kakars. Headmen ; Daoran and Mulla Arif.

Teri Khel (140).—A subdivision of Tapiai, Tappizad, Dawaris. Headmen ; Jumazna, Said Shah.

Tikriwals (400 ; Tikri valley, north of Agror).—Malkals and Ashtors are the principal sections in this valley, which also contains Swatis, Saiads, and Gujars.

Tila Khel.—A minor fraction of Mir Hasani, Macha, Madda Khel (1,600), Ibrahim Khel, Utmanzai, Darwesh Khel Wazirs.

Timar Khel (32).—A section of Gurbuzai, Darpa Khel, Mallizad, Dawaris. Headmen ; Kamrai, Khan Pir, Palali, Gul Nam.

Tira Khel.—A minor fraction of Mushakki, Macha, Madda Khel (1,600), Ibrahim Khel, Utmanzai, Darwesh Khel, Wazirs.

Tira Khel.—A section of the Ali Khel, Bobak, Dana, Battannis.

Tir Khel (60).—A minor fraction of the Ali Khel, Haidar Khel, Tor, Tappizad, Dawaris. Headmen ; Alif Khan, Amal Khan, Abu Samand, Mubati.

Titar Khel.—A minor fraction of Khan Khel, Takhti Khel, Bakka Khel (1,000), Wali Khel, Utmanzai, Darwesh Khel Wazirs. Headmen ; Khan Badshah, Khazan Khan, Mian Khel, Gulzamir.

TITTAR KHEL (30).—A section of Baran Khel, Chahar Khel, Shaman Khel, Mahsuds. Headman ; Hila Wazir.

TITTI KHEL (60).—A subdivision of Band Khel, Bahlolzai, Mahsuds. Headmen ; Sadda Din, Rahman.

TOCHI KHEL (30).—A minor fraction of Kiki Khel, Muhammad Khel, Malakh, Mallizad. Dawaris. Headmen ; Nidzamand, Amid, Wali Faiz, Gulla Khan.

TOGHLA KHEL.—A minor fraction of Dani Khel, Matkai, Malik Shahi (400), Wali Khel, Utmanzai, Darwesh Khel Wazirs. Headman ; Umar Khel.

TOIA KHEL.—A minor fraction of Bachagai, Tor, Jani Khel (1,000), Wali Khel, Utmanzai, Darwesh Khel Wazirs. Headman ; Mirbosh.

TOIB KHEL (55).—A minor fraction of the Sher Khel, Haibat Khel, Nana Khel, Bahlolzai, Mahsuds. Headmen ; Mir Ajab, Bare Khan, Malang Khan.

TOJI KHEL.—A minor fraction of Pira Khel, Jamal Khel, Malik Shahi (400), Wali Khel, Utmanzai, Darwesh Khel Wazirs. Headman ; Gulla Khan.

TOJIYA KHEL (1,600,—of whom 1,000 are in Wana).—A minor fraction of Bomi Khel, Nasra Din, Kalu Khel, Ahmadzai, Darwesh Khel Wazirs.

TOKHIS (1,500 ; Ghazni and Kalat-i-Ghilzai).—One of the Pawindah trading tribes.

TOLAB KHEL (30).—A minor fraction of the Kotar Khel, Abdul Khel, Langar Khel, Khoddad Khel, Gidi Khel, Manazai, Alizai, Mahsuds. Headman ; Sadamir.

TOLA KHEL.—A minor fraction of Mir Khan Khel, Asat Khel, Wuzi Khel (800), Mohmit Khel, Utmanzai, Darwesh Khel Wazirs.

TOLAZAI (West of Dera Ghazi Khan District).—A subdivision of Maghduzai, Ahmadzai, Balil Khel, Musa Khels. Headman ; Jamal.

TOLI KHEL.—A minor fraction of Musakki, Wuzi Khel (800), Mohmit Khel, Utmanzai, Darwesh Khel Wazirs.

TOL KHEL.—A minor fraction of Abdul Khel, Bora Khel (1,000), Mohmit Khel, Utmanzai, Darwesh Khel Wazirs.

TOR (1,328).—A division of Mallizad, Dawaris. Headmen; see Hassu Khel, Mullagan, Urmuz, and Musakki.

TOR (987).—A division of the Tappizad, Dawaris.

TORANG KHEL (60).—A minor fraction of the Lalli Khel, Abdullai, Aimal Khel, Bahlolzai, Mahsuds.

TORANG KHEL (80).—A minor fraction of the Torang Khel, Ladi Khel, Abdullai. Aimal Khel, Bahlolzai, Mahsuds. Headman; Khawaja Muhammad.

TORDALI (18).—A sub-division of Khaddi, Mallizad, Dawaris. Headmen; Pilawar Khan, Aghar.

TOR DODI KHEL (Bannu District).—A minor fraction of Dodi Khel, Khandar Khan Khel, Hathi Khel (2,000), Shin Khel, Ahmadzai, Darwesh Khel Wazirs. Headman; Nezam Khan.

TORI KHEL (2,670; A continuous belt of country outside, but parallel to our frontier from the Shaktu to the Kurram river and the Kaitu stream).—A sub-division of Ibrahim Khel, Utmanzai, Darwesh Khel Wazirs. Headmen; Ilias and Madd (Muhammad) Akbar are the leading men; for others see Shugai, Khushalai, Haibtanai and Dre Pillari.

TORI KHEL (68).—A minor fraction of the Shah Alam Khel, Kasim Khel, Chahar Khel, Shaman Khel, Mahsuds. Headmen; Shahzad, Miangul, Mamit.

TORI KHEL (12).—A minor fraction of Idal Khel, Muhammad Khel, Malakh, Mallizad, Dawaris. Headman; Niaz Muhammad.

TORI KHEL (Bannu District). —A minor fraction of Musa Khel, Hathi Khel (2,000), Shin Khel, Ahmadzai, Darwesh Khel Wazirs. Headman; Shah Tamoz.

TORI KHEL (70).—A section of Teri or Tori Khel, Tapiai, Tappizad, Dawaris. Headmen; Jumazar, Hassan Shah, Maghar Rahim. Sheikh Pir, Multan.

TORI KHEL.—Another name for Teri Khel, Tapiai, Tappizad, Dawaris.

TORI KHEL (15).—A minor fraction of Charkhil, Land, Malakh, Mallizad, Dawaris. Headmen; Kabir Shah, Umar, Nizam Khan.

TOR KHEL.—A section of the Mir Kulli Khel, Bazoti (500), Daulatzai, Orakzais. Samil.

TOR KHEL.—A section of Abdul Khel, Urmuz Khel, Sipah (1,200), Afridis. Samil. Headman; Daud.

TOR KHEL.—A section of Asad Khel, Mitha Khan Khel, Kuki Khel (4,500), Afridis. Gar. Headmen; Razai, Islam Din.

TOR KHEL.—A minor fraction of Aziz Khel, Shadi Khel, Bora Khel (1000), Mohmit Khel, Utmanzai, Darwesh Khel Wazirs.

TOR KHEL.—A section of Jani Khel (1,000), Wali Khel, Utmanzai, Darwesh Khel Wazirs. Headmen; Malkun, Pir Makhmad, Amaldad, Mirbosh, Shadamir, Kaimal and Gulbaz.

TOR (or BAZID) KHEL.—A minor fraction of Khazzar Khel, Star Ali Khan Khel, Sarki Khel, Madda Khel (1,600), Ibrahim Khel, Utmanzai, Darwesh Khel Wazirs.

TOR KHEL.—A minor fraction of Musakki, Wuzi Khel (800), Mohmit Khel, Utmanzai, Darwesh Khel Wazirs.

TOR KHEL.—A minor fraction of Said Khel, Umarzai (600), Shin Khel, Ahmadzai, Darwesh Khel Wazirs.

TOR KHEL.—A sub-division of Sheikh Ali Khel, Kamrai Khel (600), Afridis. Samil. Headmen; Mulla Amir Shah, Mulla Akhunzada, Sher Wali.

TOR KHEL (Bannu and Kurram).—A section of Umarzai (600), Shin Khel, Ahmadzai, Darwesh Khel Wazirs, Headmen; Jamal Din, Adal Khan, Alam Khan, Senian, Niazi, Fazal, Zaid Gul, Ghallai.

TOR KHEL (9).—A section of Alizai, Darpa Khel, Mallizad, Dawaris. Headman; Niazpare.

Torsam Khel.—A minor fraction of Nazar Khel, Star Ali Khan Khel, Sarki Khel, Madda Khel (1,600), Ibrahim Khel, Utmanzai, Darwesh Khel Wazirs.

Tor Sappar (350; a valley running from the Kohat road).—A sub-division of Galai, Adam Khel, Afridis.

Tor Tarins (2,000) Peshin*).—A clan of Tarins, divided into Harun Khels and Ali Khels. The divisions, etc., of the Tor Tarins are not separately indexed in this Dictionary.

* In addition some families of the Tor Tarins live with the Spin Tarins of Thal-Chotiali.

Tota Khel (Mahaban).—A section of Bazid Khel, Madda Khel, Isazai, Yusafzais. Headmen; see Bazid Khel and Madda Khel.

Toz Khel (160).—A section of Haidar Khel, Tor, Tappizad, Dawaris. Headmen; Gul Khan, Halim Khan, Asad Khan.

Trangani.—A sub-division of the Mekhiani, Spin, Tarins.

Tsalor Plara.—A minor fraction of Shati Khel, Wali Beg Kor, Gandab, Halimzai, Mohmands. Headmen Sherai, Zabat Khan, Gul Ahmad, Dawezai.

Tsu Kerai.—A sub-division of the Khoja Hawas Khel, Ali Khel (3,000), "Hamsayas" of the Orakzais. Gar. ⅛ Shiah.

Tughal Khel.—A division of Cis-Swat, Sanizai, Utman Khels.

Tukar Khel (90).—A section of Musakki, Tor, Mallizad, Dawaris. Headmen; Samand Khan, Hibat Khan, Wali Khan, and Tawabin.

Tura Khel.—A section of Sadin, Ilal Khel, Salarzai, Tarkanis.

Turangi (14).—A section of Alizai, Darpa Khel, Mallizad, Dawaris. Headmen; Ghazal, Gul Azam, Pir Azam.

Turangi Khel.—A minor fraction of Painda Khel, Manak Khel, Bakhshi Khel, Madda Khel (1,600), Ibrahim Khel, Utmanzai, Darwesh Khel Wazirs.

Turi Khel.—A minor fraction of Dod Khel, Mir Hasani, Macha, Madda Khel (1,600), Ibrahim Khel, Utmanzai, Darwesh Khel Wazirs.

Turi Khel.—A division of Mutakai, Utman Khels.

TURIS (6,100; Kurram).—A tribe of Shiahs, divided into two fractions, called respectively Ting Ghundi, and Sust Ghundi.

TURIZAI (500; Shamil valley, Khost).—A clan of Khostwals, also known as Tarwizai.

TURKI KHEL.—A minor fraction of Ghuli Khel, Ambar Khel, Mat Khan Khel, Kambar Khel (4,500), Afridis. Gar. Headman; Jamaldin.

TUTKAI KHEL.—A minor fraction of Mian Khel, Janakhori (800), Hassan Khel, Adam Khel, Afridis.

U

UDHI KHEL.—A sub-division of "Kuz" or Khrappawal, Burhan Khel, Pandiali, Mohmands. Headmen; Khan Mir, Muhammad Umar, Gulzar Shah.

UDREDUNKAI (Pipal).—This name is applied to those sections of the Dawezai and Utmanzai Mohmands, who, in contradistinction to the Kuchis, or nomad tribes, have fixed habitations in the Mohmand country.

UMAI KOR.—A sub-division of Kuz or Khrappawal, Burhan Khel, Pandiali, Mohmands. Headman; Lal.

UMAL KHEL.—A minor fraction of Mir Husani, Macha, Madda Khel (1,600), Ibrahim Khel, Utmanzai, Darwesh Khel Wazirs.

UMAR.—A section of Musara Khel, Ashazai, Iliaszai, Bunerwals.

UMAR BEG KHEL.—A sub-division of Shanai (750), Zakha Khel, Afridis. Samil. Headmen; Khanzad, Langur, Khandin, Said Khan.

UMAR KHAN.—A section of Musara Khel, Ashazai, Iliaszai, Bunerwals.

UMAR KHAN KHEL.—A section of Ali Karan, Mamuzai (3,500), Lashkarzai, Orakzais. Gar. Headman; Arsala Khan.

UMAR KHAN KHEL.—A sub-division of Alisherzai (3,000), Lashkarzai, Orakzais. Samil. Headman; Abbas Khan.

UMAR KHAN KHEL.—A sub-division of Malikdin Khel, Malikdin Khel (4,000), Afridis. Samil. Headmen; Darya Khan, Dauran, Yar Khan.

UMAR KHAN KHEL.—A minor fraction of Balli Khel, Shadi Khel, Bora Khel (1,000), Mohmit Khel, Utmanzai, Darwesh Khel Wazirs.

UMAR KHAN KHEL.—A minor fraction of Malik Shahi, Jani Khel (1,000), Wali Khel, Utmanzai, Darwesh Khel Wazirs.

UMAR KHAN KHEL (30).—A minor fraction of Miri Khel, Land, Malakh, Mallizad, Dawaris. Headmen; Khojai, Idali, Khoja Akbar, Nek Pirjad, Zarband, Fakir Shah.

UMAR KHAN KOR.—A section of Barkazai, Daulatzai, Malizai, Bunerwals.

UMAR KHEL.—A sub-division of Kakazai, Mamund, Tarkanis.

UMAR KHEL.—A minor fraction of the Marjan Khel, Utmanzai, Adinzai, Khwazazai, Akozai—Yusufzai Swatis.

UMAR KHEL (100).—A division of Tatta, Battannis. Headmen; Bangi (Mamli Khel) Sher Muhammad (Salemi Khel).

UMAR KHEL.—A section of Taru Khel, Muia, Waraspun, Battannis.

UMAR KHEL (Kharmana river).—A section of the Alizai, Musazai, Lashkarzai, Orakzais. Samil. Headmen; Said Ali.

UMAR KHEL.—A sub-division of Abdul Khel, Kuki Khel (4,500), Afridis. Gar. Headman; Mulla Lajbar.

UMAR KHEL.—A section of Masti Khel, Kambar Khel (4,500), Afridis. Gar. Headman; Muhammad Yar.

UMAR KHEL.—A section of Annai (1,000), Budai, Zakha Khel, Afridis. Samil. Headmen; Shahaba Din, Bolak, Arab, Bangai.

UMAR KHEL.—A minor fraction of Daulat Khel, Ghaib Khan Khel, Malikdin Khel, Malikdin Khel (4,000), Afridis. Samil. Headmen; see Daulat Khel.

UMAR KHEL.—A section of Sharaki (200), Galai, Adam Khel, Afridis.

UMAR KHEL.—A minor fraction of Sadda Khel (300) Isperka, Khalu Khel, Ahmadzai, Darwesh Khel Wazirs.

Umar Khel.—A minor fraction of Khizar Khel, Mintar Khel, Muhammad Khel, Hassan Khel (400), Mohmit Khel, Utmanzai, Darwesh Khel Wazirs. Headman; Kabul.

Umar Khel.—A minor fraction of Ali Khel, Khaddar Khel (770), Mohmit Khel, Utmanzai, Darwesh Khel Wazirs. Headmen; Salih Din, Nazarka, Zarak.

Umar Khel (150).—A section of Astanai, Shabi Khel, Alizai, Mahsuds. Headmen; Alif Shah, Khurri.

Umar Khel (150).—A minor fraction of Nikarrab Khel, Khoidad Khel, Gidi Khel, Manazai, Alizai, Mahsuds. Headmen; Badar Din, Muhammad Afzal, Salehin, Sari Band.

Umar Khel (205).—A sub-division of Nana Khel, Bahlolzai, Mahsuds.

Umar Kor.—A minor fraction of Sroh, Busha Khel, Kamali, Halimzai, Mohmands. Headman; Buland.

Umarzai.—A sub-division of Shamozai, Khwazazai, Akozai—Yusufzai Swatis.

Umarzai (Mastura, Khanki and Miranzai valleys).—A division of the Sheikhans "Hamsayas" of the Orakzais. Samil. Headman; Narulla.

Umarzai (600; Bannu and Razmak).—A sub-division of Shin Khel, Ahmadzai, Darwesh Khel Wazirs. Headmen; Pirmal Khan, Jamal Din, Alam Khan, Senian, Niazi, Fazal, Zaid Gul, Ghallai.

Umarzai (53).—A section of Zira Khel, Amzoni, Mallizad, Dawaris. Headmen; Amir, Malak Khan, Jumazan, Gulapir.

Umbar (Laman).—A section of Balo, Asil, Ismailzai, Utman Khels.

Umbara Khel.—A sub-division of Sultan-ka-Khel, Bar Ramizai, Akozai—Yusufzai Swatis.

Umla Kor.—A section of the Mir Ahmad Khel, Alisherzai (3,000), Lashkarzai, Orakzais. Samil.

Umrani (120).—A clan of the Jafar tribe.

Umr Khel (Agra, Chingai Shagai, etc.).—A sub-division of Shamozai, Ismailzai, Utman Khels.

UMRZAI (60).—A section of Sah, Yahia Khel, Sen Khel, Sheranis.

UMRZAI (213; Pawindahs; Dera Ismail Khan District). Nomadic, a section of Sein Khel, Mian Khel, Lohana, Pawindahs.

UMRZAI (45).—A division of Drigzai, Lunis. Headmen; Gulan, (Hamalzai), Dabai (Amranzai), Laban (Dungarzai), Kaim (Isafzai), Mihtar (Watarzai), Mohabat (Goramzai).

UMRZAI (969).—A minor fraction of Bulozai, Panizai, Harun Khel, Sanatia, Kakars.

UMRZAI MUSA KHEL (120; West of Dera Ghazi Khan).—A clan of Musa Khels. Headmen; see Shahozai, Pashezai, Jamalzai.

UMR KHEL (785; Kharmana river).—A minor fraction of the Mastu Khel, Khwaja Khel, Masuzai, Lashkarzai, Orakzais. Gar. Headman; Yusuf (?).

UMR KHEL.—A minor fraction of Mir Asan Khel, Babu Khel, Adinzai, Khwazazai, Akozai—Yusufzai Swatis.

UMR KHEL.—A section of Ibrahim Khel, Utmanzai, Bar Ranizai, Akozai—Yusufzai Swatis.

UMR KOR.—A minor fraction of the Hyatai Kor, Shah Mansur Khel, Dadu Khel, Tarakzai, Mohmands. Headman; Dawezai.

URAZAI.—A division of Alizai, Utman Khels.

URMAR KHEL (40).—A section of Malai, Shingi, Bahlolzai, Mahsuds. Headman; Mian Hassan.

URMAR KHEL (45).—A subdivision of Nana Khel, Bahlolzai, Mahsuds. Headmen; Jakhar; Khwajabaz, Shahzada.

URMARS (900).—A tribe of Saiads living among the Mahsuds. They have a language and customs of their own, and are probably descendants of the original inhabitants of the country.

URMUR.—A minor fraction of Balli Khel, Shadi Khel, Bora Khel (1,000), Mohmit Khel, Utmanzai, Darwesh Khel Wazirs.

URMUR (8).—A section of Taib Khel, Amzoni, Mallizad, Dawaris. Headman; Khangai.

URMUZ (180).—A sub-division of Tor, Mallizad, Dawaris. Headmen; Nizam Din, Kalim, Khiddar Khan, Alam Din, Kotan, Ghain Shah.

URMUZ KHEL.—A division of Sipah (1,200), Afridis. Samil. Headmen; see Keimal Khel and Abdul Khel.

USHTARANAS (900; hills opposite the southern most portion of the Dera Ismail Khan District).—A tribe of Pathans allied to the Gandapurs. They are divided into two clans, Gagalzais and Ahmadzais.

USMAN KHEL (1,060).—A minor fraction of Khudu Khel, Sadazai, Utmanzai, Mandan, Yusufzais.

USMANI KOR (Bohai Dag).—A sub-division of Maimana Khel, Khwaezai, Mohmands. Headman; Mir Waiz.

USMAN KHAN KHEL (40).—A section of Pathanai, Shabi Khel, Alizai, Mahsuds. Headman; Dinak.

USMAN KHEL (Upper Bohai Dag).—A division of Baezai, Mohmands. Headmen; see Isa Khel, Khuga Khel, Atamar Khel, Koda Khel.

USMAN KHEL.—A section of Hasan Khel, Gadaizai, Iliaszai, Bunerwals.

USMAN KHEL (500; Swat river, north-west of Malakand).—A division of Bar Ranizai, Akozai—Yusufzai Swatis.

USMAN KHEL (30).—A section of Tappi Khel, Badanzai, Shaman Khel, Mahsuds. Headmen; Sadrawan, Auli Shah.

USMAN KHEL.—A minor fraction of Takhti Khel, Bakka Khel (1,000), Wali Khel, Utmanzai, Darwesh Khel Wazirs. Headmen; Khojamir, Mozalmir, Islam Khan, Akmad Din, Sakam.

USMAN KHEL (British territory).—A minor fraction of Budin Khel (100), Shadi Khel, Nasra Din, Kalu Khel, Ahmadzai, Darwesh Khel Wazirs.

USMAN KHEL.—A sub-division of Shanai (750), Zakha Khel, Afridis. Samil. Headmen; Mihr Din, Bawar, Sultan Mir, Gul Shah.

USMAN KHEL.—A sub-division of Sikandar Khel, Kuki Khel (4,500), Afridis. Gar. Headmen; Mir Alam, Rahmatulla.

USMAN KOR.—A minor fraction of Khwaja, Khadin Khel, Ashazai, Iliaszai, Bunerwals.

USTA KHEL.—A minor fraction of Khwaja, Khadin Khel, Ashazai, Iliaszai, Bunerwals.

UTAM KHEL.—A section of Sultan Khel, Sher Gulla, Aka Khel (1,800), Afridis. Samil.

UTAZAI.—A division of Salar, Gaduns.

UTMAN (63).—A sub-division of Miram Shah, Tappizad, Dawaris. Headmen; Nakkar, Mongal, Parak Shah, Shabat.

UTMAN KHEL (Wana).—A minor fraction of Zalli Khel (3000), Bomi Khel, Nasra Din, Kalu Khel, Ahmadzai, Darwesh Khel Wazirs.

UTMAN KHELS (12,000; a stretch of country north-west of the Peshawar border).—A Pathan tribe, inhabiting a large tract of country which extends across the hills bordering the Peshawar valley, and includes the country west and south-west of the junction of the Swat and Panjkora rivers.

UTMAN KHEL (2,000; Upper Zhob and Bori valley).—A division of (Southern) Sanzar, Kakars.

UTMAN KHEL (400 to 600; Mastura river and Ublan pass).—A division of Daulatzai, Orakzais. Samil.

UTMAN KHEL (10).—A minor fraction of Charkhil, Charkhil, Land, Malakh, Mallizad, Dawaris. Headman; Landai.

UTMANZAI (12,000; Kurram river, Dawar and Shawal).—One of the two clans of Darwesh Khel Wazirs.

UTMANZAI (335; Mahaban) —A division of Mandan, Yusafzais.

UTMANZAI (500; 'Bar' and 'Kuz' Yakhdand).—One of the affiliated Mohmand clans. They are divided into "Kuchi" and "Udredunkai." Headmen; Badshah, Muhammad Ali Khan, Shamshai, Muhammad Abbas, Amirbaz (Bar Yakhdand), Umar, Islamdin, Lal Kaim, Wali Muhammad, Nasim (Kuz Yakhdand). See note on page 40.

UTMANZAI.—A sub-division of Adinzai, Khwazazai, Akozai—Yusafzai Swatis.

UTMANZAI (800; Left bank of Swat river).—A division of Bar-Ranizai, Akozai—Yusufzai Swatis.

W

WADER (Kunar river.)—A division of the Safis, who are a vassal clan of the Mohmands.

WADIN KHEL.—A minor fraction of Khazzar Khel, Star Ali Khan Khel, Sarki Khel, Madda Khel (1,600), Ibrahim Khel, Utmanzai, Darwesh Khel Wazirs.

WAHAB KOR.—A small, broken sub-division of Gandab, Halimzai, Mohmands, who are closely allied to the Rasul Kor.

WALAI KOR.—A minor fraction of Asaf Khel, Dalkha Kor, Dadu Khel, Tarakzai, Mohmands.

WALAINAI (29; Thal-Chotiali).—A division of Rakanwal, Lunis. Headmen; Ali Umrzai, Mir Khan.

WALA KHEL.—A minor fraction of Sardi Khel, Bakka Khel (1,000), Wali Khel, Utmanzai, Darwesh Khel Wazirs. Headman; Rasul Shah.

WALAK KHEL.—A minor fraction of Dosalli, Wuzi Khel (800), Mohmit Khel, Utmanzai, Darwesh Khel Wazirs.

WALI BEG KOR (820).—A sub-division of Gandab, Halimzai, Mohmands.

WALIDAD KHEL.—A minor fraction of Hilal Khel, Keimal Khel, Urmuz Khel, Sipah (1,200), Afridis. Samil. Headmen; Gul Salim.

WALIDAD KHEL (348).—A minor fraction of the Ladi Khel, Abdullai, Aimal Khel, Bahlolzai, Mahsuds.

WALIDAD KHEL.—A division of Mutakai, Utman Khels.

WALIDAD KHEL.—A minor fraction of Zakho Khel, Jatakhori (800), Hassan Khel, Adam Khel, Afridis.

WALIDAD KOR.—A minor fraction of Mamun Kor, Kandai, Isa Khel, Pandiali, Mohmands.

WALIGAI (Bannu District).—A minor fraction of Musa Khel, Hathi Khel (2,000), Shin Khel, Ahmadzai, Darwesh Khel Wazirs. Headman; Adam Khan.

WALI KHEL (60; Kharmana river).—A minor fraction of the Ash Khel, Khwaja Khel, Masuzai, Lashkarzai, Orakzais. Samil. Headman; Nijah.

WALI MUHAMMAD KOR (800; Loe Shilman with Wazir Kor and Hassan Kor).—A section of Shah Mansur Khel, Dadu Khel, Tarakzai, Mohmands. Headmen; Ghulam Kadir, Adam, Nasro, Narai, Fazl Din.

WALLI BEG KHEL.—A minor fraction of Ahmad Beg Khel, Mohib Khel, Shekhai, Anmai (1,000), Budai, Zakha Khel, Afridis. Samil. Headmen; Akbar Din, Aliakai, Mohiuddin.

WALLIBEG KHEL.—A subdivision of Mat Khan Khel, Kambar Khel (4,500), Afridis. Gar. Headmen; Sher Khan, Hamid, and Nurai.

WALLI DAD KHEL.—A section of Kulla Khel, Malikdin Khel, Malikdin Khel (4,000), Afridis. Samil. Headman; see Bakhmali Khel.

WALLI KHEL.—A minor fraction of Ali Khel, Sheikhmal Khel, Kambar Khel, Kambar Khel (4,500), Afridis. Gar. Headmen; Miro, Ali Khan, Gauhar, Feroz.

WALLI KHEL.—A section of Asad Khel, Mitha Khan Khel, Kuki Khel (4,500) Afridis. Gar. Headman; Wadan.

WALLI BEG KHEL.—A minor fraction of Fatteh Khel, Miri Khel, Pakhai (1,000), Budai, Zakha Khel, Afridis. Samil. Headmen; Akbar Din, Aliakai, Mohiuddin.

WALLI KHEL (35).—A minor fraction of Mirdad Khel, Abdul Rahman Khel, Sher Khel, Haibat Khel, Nana Khel, Bahlolzai, Mahsuds. Headman; Mianji.

WALLI KHEL.—A minor fraction of Mirghat Khel, Basi Khel, Kamal Khel, Sahib Jan, Aka Khel (1,800), Afridis. Samil.

Walli Khel (5,000).—One of the 3 great divisions (*viz.*, Mohmit Khel, Ibrahim Khel, and Walli Khel) of the Utmanzai clan of the Darwesh Khel Wazirs. Headmen; see Kabul Khel, Malikshahi, Bakka Khel and Jani Khel.

Walli Khel.—A section of Pakhai (1,000) Budai, Zakha Khel, Afridis. Samil. Headmen; Kamran, Kadin.

Wand Gharai.—A sub-division of Landi Khel, Sipah (1,200), Afridis. Samil. Headmen; Sher Muhammad Khan, Gul Salim.

Wani Khel (Bannu District).—A minor fraction of Kundi, Pirbu Khel, Hathi Khel (2,000), Shin Khel, Ahmadzai, Darwesh Khel Wazirs.

Wanuchi (307).—A division of Spin, Tarins. Headman; Ismail.

Wara (or **Wur**) (3,000; Wattelai valley).—A division of the Mamund, Tarkanis.

Waraspun (1,030).—A clan of the Battannis. Headmen; Saidal Ahmad Shah.

War Durbi Khel.—A section of Durbi Khel, Kambar Khel, Kambar Khel (4,500), Afridis. Gar. Headmen; Muhammad Sher, Khwaja Ali, Yaro, Nurai.

Wargare (100).—A division of the Dana, Battannis. Headman; Gula Khan (Maruf Khel).

War Gharra.—A minor fraction of Karra Khel, Ghaibi Khel, Babakri, Sipah (1,200), Afridis. Samil. Headmen; Lalgul, Purdil, Shah Kalim.

Waria Khel (33).—A sub-division of Ahmad Khel. Oba Khel, Sheranis.

Warria Khel.—A section of Ali Khel, Bobak, Dana, Battannis.

Warika (12).—A minor fraction of Ahmad Khel, Zira Khel, Amzoni, Mallizad, Dawaris. Headman; Shandai.

Warkam Khel.—A section of Aib Khel, Salarzai, Iliaszai, Bunerwals.

War Khel.—A minor fraction of Dreplara, Paindai, (940), Nasruddin, Zakha Khel, Afridis. Samil. Headmen; Chikkun, Tamas, Anwar, Nazr Din.

WAROJAI (110; Black Mountain).—A division of Deshiwal, Swatis. Headman; Hazrat Shah.

WARO USMAN KHEL.—A subdivision of Usman Khel, Bar Ranizai, Akozai—Yusufzai Swatis.

WARRUKAI.—A minor fraction of Idia Khel, Jani Khel (1,000), Wali Khel, Utmanzai, Darwesh Khel Wazirs. Headmen; Zargai and Sheikh Majid.

WARUKA ALI KHAN KHEL.—A name sometimes applied to the Niamat Khel, Khwaja Ahmad Khel and Jambal Khel minor fractions of the Mian Ali Khan Khel fraction of Sarki Khel, Madda Khel (1,600), Ibrahim Khel, Utmanzai, Darwesh Khel Wazirs. Headmen; Maddi and Sheikhnur.

WARUKI (125; Dera Ismail Khan District.)—Nomadic, a section of Shin Khel, Mian Khel, Lohana, Pawindahs.

WASUL KHEL.—A section of Paindai (940), Nasruddin, Zakha Khel, Afridis. Samil. Headman; see Paindai.

WATAR (26).—A minor fraction of Bar Kaum, Hassu Khel, Tor, Mallizad, Dawaris. Headmen; Baki, Badrang.

WATI KHEL (60).—A minor fraction of Miri Khel, Land, Malakh, Mallizad. Dawaris. Headmen; Muhammad Akbar, Kaim Khan, Alam Shah, Jawahir Shah.

WATIRAI (25).—A minor fraction of Aghzan, Zira Khel, Amzoni, Mallizad, Dawaris. Headmen; Shah Murad, Aziz Khan.

WATIZAI (510).—A division of Mamuzai or Muhammadzai, Zaimukhts.

WAZAR KHEL.—A minor fraction of Mir Khan Khel, Asat Khel, Wuzi Khel (800), Mohmit Khel, Utmanzai, Darwesh Khel Waziris.

WAZAR KHEL (35).—A minor fraction of Kiki Khel, Muhammad Khel, Malakh, Mallizad, Dawaris. Headmen; Tirob, Kutti Khan.

WAZI KHEL (90).—A minor fraction of Shammal, Hassu Khel, Tor, Mallizad, Dawaris. Headmen; Madda Khel, Gul Hassan, Mir Kazam,

Wazir Khel (9).—A minor fraction of Ali Khel, Barim Khel, Amzoni, Mallizad, Dawaris. Headmen; Bakhtamir, Piya Khan.

Wazirgai (160).—A minor fraction of Khamar Khel, Gidi Khel, Manazai, Alizai, Mahsuds.

Wazirs (41,530).—A large tribe of Pathans, who inhabit the hill country to the west of the Trans-Indus Frontier from the Kurram river near Thall, to the Gomal pass. They are divided into 5 main branches—The Darwesh Khel, *viz.*, Utmanzai 12,600 and Ahmadzai 11,960; the Mahsuds 10,048; the Gurbaz; the Laili; Headmen; see the above clans.

Wazir Kor (300).—A section of Shah Mansur Khel, Dadu Khel, Tarakzai, Mohmands. Headmen; Kazi, Haji, Shahbaz, Amin Shah, Saiad Muhammad, Daraz, Raza Khan.

Wilayat Kor.—A minor fraction of Sangar Khel, Yusaf Khel, Isa Khel, Pandiali, Mohmands.

Wochak Khel (40).—A minor fraction of Mitha Khel, Badiwai, Khadi Khel, Shaman Khel, Mahsuds. Headmen; Jamal, Shabnir.

Woruke (350).—A division of the Dana, Battannis. Headmen; Morad Khan (Kesu); Mehr Khan (Senzai); Adil Shah and Ali Gul (Maissizai.)

Wujji Khel (40).—A section of the Malai, Shingi, Bahlolzai, Mahsuds. Headman; Muhamad Ashraf, Khan Bahadur.

Wujji Khel (80).—A section of the Haidrai, Chahar Khel, Shaman Khel, Mahsuds.

Wuzi Khel (800; Khaisora and Kaitu).—A sub-division of Mohmit Khel, Utmanzai, Darwesh Khel Wazirs. Headmen; Bozi, Wazir Khan, Nakir Khan, Niyaz Gul, Kaloni, Jama Gul.

Y

Yaghi Kor.—A minor fraction of Sroh, Busha Khel, Kamali, Halimzai, Mohmands. Headman; Buland.

Yagi Khel; see Tor Sappar.

Yahia Khel, or Hezai, (115).—A sub-division of Ahmad Khel, Oba Khel, Sheranis.

Yahia Khel (167).—A division of the Chuar Khel, Sheranis.

Yahia Khel, or Hezai (690).—A division of Sen Khel, Sheranis.

Ya Khel.—A section of Babu Khel, Adinzai, Khwazazai, Akozai—Yusufzai Swatis.

Yakubi Khel (Goshta).—An offshoot of the Sargarrai Kor, Khadi Khel, Khwaezai, Mohmands. Headmen; Jamal, Nadir Shah, Mian Jumma Khan.

Yakub Khel.—A section of Ghaibi Khel, Bahram-ka-Khel, Bar Ranizai, Akozai—Yusufzai Swatis.

Yakub Kor.—A minor fraction of Ranra Khel, Shati Khel, Walibeg Kor, Gandab, Halimzai, Mohmands. Headman; Ahmad.

Yakubzai (256).—A sub-division of Manazai, Oba Khel, Sheranis.

Yar Ali Khel.—A division of Kamrai or Kamar Khel (600), Afridis. Samil. Headman; Azam Din.

Yaran Khel.—A section of Sheikhmal, Kambar Khel, Kambar Khel (4,500), Afridis. Gar. Headmen; Muhammad, Sher, Khwaja Ali, Yaro, Nurai.

Yardil Kor.—A section of Kadai Kor, Gandab, Halimzai, Mohmands. Headmen; Shah Jehan, Nawab, Musa Khan, Gulai, Yad Muhammad, Niamat.

Yargul Khel.—A section of Pabbi Khel, Kambar Khel, Kambar Khel (4,500), Afridis. Gar. Headmen; Sherai, Sher.

YAR KHAN KHEL.—A minor fraction of Kasim Khel (250), Kimat Khel, Jawaki, Adam Khel, Afridis.

YAR KHAN KHEL.—One of the sub-divisions of the Mamozai, Mishtis (3,000), "Hamsayas" of the Orakzais. Samil.

YARKULLI KHEL.—A sub-division of Bazoti (500), Daulatzai, Orakzais, Samil. Headman ; Baznur.

YAR MUHAMMAD KHEL.—A sub-division of Karna Khel, Malikdin Khel (4,000), Afridis. Samil. Headmen ; Azim Din, Samand, Sharit Din.

YAR MUHAMMAD KHEL (25).—A minor fraction of the Sharri Khel, Kasim Khel, Chahar Khel, Shaman Khel, Mahsuds. Headmen ; Badarkai, Kamardin, Kakar.

YARU KHEL.—A section of the Yarkulli Khel, Bazoti (500), Daulatzai, Orakzais. Samil.

YASIMZAI (140).—A section of Karmozai, Ahmad Khel, Sen Khel, Sheranis.

YASIMZAI (60).—A section of Umrzai, Dumar, Sanzar, Kakars.

YASINZAI (809).—A sub-division of Isa Khel, Sanatia, Kakars. Headmen ; Pirak and Mulla Hotan.

YAR KHEL.—One of the sub-divisions of the Mamozai, Mishtis (3,000), "Hamsayas" of the Orakzais. Samil. Headman ; Ali Sher, Kambar.

YUNAS KHEL.—A section of Bosti Khel (150), Galai, Adam Khel, Afridis.

YUSAF KHAN KHEL.—A division of Salarzai, Tarkanis.

YUSAF KHEL.—A minor fraction of Eash Khel, Annai (1,000), Budai, Zakha Khel, Afridis. Samil. Headmen ; Hawassu, Mirdad, Bazai.

YUSAF KHEL or ISA KHEL (Danish Kol).—A sub-division of Isa Khel, Pandiali, Mohmands.

YUSAF KHEL.—A sub-division of Kakazai. Mamund, Tarkanis.

Yusaf Khel (Dir).—A section of Painda Khel, Sesada, Malizai, Yusufzais.

Yusufzai (73,000*).—A great group of Pathan tribes which includes those of the Black Mountain, the Bunerwals, the Swatis, the people of Dir and the Panjkora valley, and the inhabitants of the Yusufzai plain in British territory. They all claim descent from one Mandai, his son Yusaf, and grandson Mandan. From Yusaf's four sons, Isa, Musa, Mali and Ako are descended, respectively, the Isazais, Iliaszais, Malizais and Akozais: Ako was also the progenitor of the Ranizais. The Utmanzais are descended from Mandan.

Z

Zabar Khel (North-east of Buner).—A minor fraction of Musa Khel, Makhozai, Nasozai, Iliaszai, Yusufzais.

Zado.—A minor fraction of Madak, Bada, Asil, Ismailzai, Utman Khels.

Zadrans or Jadrans (9,000; Spalgun valley, Khost).—A tribe of Khost, bordering the Kazha Madda Khels of the Tochi. They lie between the Ghilzais on the west and the Tanis on the east. Headman; Babrak.

Zaffar Khel (35).—A section of Nana Khel, Tapiai, Tappizad, Dawaris. Headmen; Khamid, Dawogar, Pir, Mir Alam Khan.

Zafiran Kor.—A minor fraction of Hyatai Kor, Shah Mansur Khel, Dadu Khel, Tarakzai, Mohmands. Headman; Abdullah.

Zaid Khel (6).—A sub-division of Khaddi, Mallizad, Dawaris. Headman; Ajam.

Zaimukhts or Zaimushts (3,500; country between the Zawaghar range, Kurram river, and Miranzai).—A tribe of Pathans, divided into Kheidad Khel, or Eastern Zaimukhts, and Mamozai, or Western Zaimukhts. Samil.

* This number, Bellew's estimate, is probably considerably under the mark.

ZAKARIA KHEL (140; Black Mountain).—A sub-division of Hasanzai, Isazai, Yusufzais. Headmen; Najim Khan, Zabbar Khan.

ZAKARIAZAI (300).—A section of Mareghutzai, Kebzai, Sanzar, Kakars. Headman; Bangar.

ZAKARIYA KHEL.—A minor fraction of Khojal Khel (600), Shadi Khel, Nasra Din, Kalu Khel, Ahmadzai, Darwesh Khel Wazirs. Headman; Amin Khan.

ZAKAR KHEL.—A minor fraction of Drepillari, Tori Khel (2,670), Ibrahim Khel, Utmanzai, Darwesh Khel Wazirs. Headmen; Keily.

ZAKARZAI (7).—A division of Rakanwal, Lunis. Headmen; Mekh, (Saiadanzai), Guldad (Rahmanzai).

ZAKHA KHEL (4,500; Khyber, Bazar, Bara and Maidan; *i.e.*, diagonally across the whole Afridi country).—One of the most important of the 8 Khyber Afridi clans. Samil. Headmen; Khwas Khan and Wali Muhammad (both deposed by Government in 1898, but since reinstated); and their nephews Gulnam and Sultan Jan.

ZAKHBEL (150).—A (Hamsaya) section of Umrzai, Dumar, Sanzar Khel, Kakars. Headman; Aulia.

ZA KHEL (Girdi Kats, Kabul river; Unai pass, Afghanistan).—A sub-division associated with the Dawezai Kuchis of the Mohmands. Headman; Azamdin.

ZAKHO KHEL.—A section of Janakhori (300), Hassan Khel, Adam Khel, Afridis.

ZAKKU KHEL.—A sub-division of Sikandar Khel, Kuki Khel (4,500), Afridis. Gar. Headmen; Nazir, Guljai, Taus, Said Gul.

ZAKORI (130; Dera Ismail Khan District).—Nomadic, a section of Sein Khel, Mian Khel, Lohana, Pawindahs.

ZAKRI KHEL (30).—A minor fraction of the Mitha Khel, Badiwai, Khalli Khel, Shaman Khel, Mahsuds. Headman; Haiyat Khan.

ZALLI KHEL (3,000; 2,000 in Wana).—A minor fraction of Bomi Khel, Nasra Din Khel, Kalu Khel, Ahmadzai, Darwesh Khel Wazirs.

ZAMANI KHEL.—A minor fraction of Shpalkai Khel, Zargun Khel (300), Galai, Adam Khel, Afridis.

ZAMAN KHEL (Bannu District).—A minor fraction of Ali Khel, Musa Khel, Hathi Khel (2,000), Shin Khel, Ahmadzai, Darwesh Khel Wazirs.

ZAMAN KHEL.—A minor fraction of Makki Khel, Kattia Khel, Hassan Khel, Mitha Khan Khel, Kuki Khel (4,500), Afridis. Gar. Headmen; see Makki Khel.

ZAMAN KHEL.—A section of Musa Khel, Kuz Sulizai, Baizai, Akozai—Yusufzai Swatis.

ZAMAN KOR (Danish Kol).—A minor fraction of Rajai Khel, Yusaf Khel, Isa Khel, Pandiali, Mohmands.

ZAMIA KHEL.—A section of Masti Khel, Kambar Khel, Kambar Khel (4,500), Afridis. Gar. Headmen; Fakir, Gulistan, Gul Shah, Rahmat.

ZAMURI KHEL (80).—A minor fraction of Wazirgai, Khamar Khel, Gidi Khel, Manazai, Alizai, Mahsuds. Headmen; Gulzadia, Ghaizal.

ZAMUR KHEL.—A section of the Yarkudi Khel, Bazoti (500), Daulatzai, Orakzais. Samil.

ZANA KHEL.—A section of Mali (or Muli) Khel, Salarzai, Iliaszai, Bunerwals.

ZANGI KHEL.—A section of Ghaibi Khel, Babakri, Sipah (1,200), Afridis. Samil. Headman; Darya Khan.

ZANKA KHEL (Mastura river, at its source).—A division of the Ali Khels (3,000), "Hamsayas" of the Orakzais, Gar. ⅓ Shiah. Headman; Khalid Khan.

ZARA KHEL (14).—A section of Boya, Tappizad, Dawaris. Headman; Gulab.

ZARGAR (6).—A sub-division of Khaddi, Mallizad, Dawaris. Headmen; Khoja, Muhammad Khan.

ZARGAR KHEL (15).—A minor fraction of Kharmach Khel, Nazar Khel, Aimal Khel, Bahlolzai, Mahsuds. Headman; Malo.

ZARGAR KHEL (16).—A minor fraction of the Nikarrab Khel, Khoidad Khel, Gidi Khel, Manazai, Alizai, Mahsuds. Headman; Utman.

ZARGAR KHEL.—A minor fraction of Sarmast Khel, Badi Khel, Dardoni, Wuzi Khel (800), Mohmit Khel, Utmanzai, Darwesh Khel Wazirs. Headman; Wazir Khan.

ZARGAR KHEL.—A minor fraction of Umar Khel, Ali Khel, Khaddar Khel (770), Mohmit Khel, Utmanzai, Darwesh Khel Wazirs.

ZARGAR KHEL (18).—A subdivision of Boya, Tappizad, Dawaris. Headman; Gulbat Khan.

ZARGAR KHEL (20).—A section of Malli Khel, Idak, Tappizad, Dawaris. Headman; Walli Hassan.

ZARGUN KHEL (300).—A subdivision of Galai, Adam Khel, Afridis.

ZARIF KHEL.—A minor fraction of Durar (300), Khusrogi, Nasruddin, Zakha Khel Afridis. Samil. Headman; see Bucha Khel.

ZARIF KOR.—A section of Kani Khel, Kasim Khel, Tarakzai, Mohmands. Headmen; Shamshere, Adam, Dadshah, Ajun.

ZARI NAI.—A minor fraction of Haibtanai, Tori Khel (2,670), Ibrahim Khel, Utmanzai, Darwesh Khel Wazirs. Headman; Lal Khan.

ZARIN KHEL.—A minor fraction of Mashi Khel, Mannia Khel, Hassan Khel, Mitha Khan Khel, Kuki Khel (4,500), Afridis. Headmen; Kolak, Sherai, Khairulla, Zarin.

ZARIN KHEL.—A minor fraction of Mian Khel, Jana Khori (800), Hassan Khel, Adam Khel, Afridis.

ZARMAR KHEL (18).—A minor fraction of Karimdad Khel, Abdul Rahman Khel, Sher Khel, Haibat Khel, Nana Khel, Bahlolzai, Mahsuds. Headmen; Shahwardin, Mamindar.

ZARO KHEL.—A section of the Aimal Khan Khel, Zanka Khel, Ali Khels (3,000), "Hamsayas" of the Orakzais. Gar. ½ Shiah. Headman; Madar.

ZARRAK KHEL (8).—A minor fraction of Walidad Khel, Ladi Khel, Abdullai, Aimal Khel, Bahlolzai, Mahsuds. Headman; Ghab Din.

ZARRIB KHEL (160).—A minor fraction of the Shamak Khel, Abdullai, Aimal Khel, Bahlolzai, Mahsuds. Headman ; Tarkai.

ZARRI KHEL (115).—A sub-division of Chahar Khel, Shaman Khel, Mahsuds.

ZEBA (20).—A section of the Sah, Yahia Khel, Sen Khel, Sheranis.

ZERAKKI (203).—A division of Mallizad, Dawaris. Headmen ; Shahzada Haibad Khan, Gulapir, Ahmad Khonar, Rozam Shah, Ghain Shah, Pir Muhammad, Masal, Dodi, Bandi, Said Akbar, Salamai, Nabat Shah, Khataki, Saidulla Jan, Badrang.

ZERDAST KHEL.—A minor fraction of Sherga Khel, Utmanzai, Adinzai, Khwazazai, Akozai-Yusufzai Swatis.

ZER KHEL.—A minor fraction of Kambir (or Kambo) Khel, Aib Khel, Salarzai, Iliaszai, Bunerwals.

ZHAO KHEL (88).—A sub-division of Tapisi, Tappizad Dawaris. Headmen ; Isab Khan, Ahmad, Gulab Din, Ahmad Shah, Sheikh Amin, Zariband.

ZIAUDDIN (200).—A sub-division of Budai, Zakha Khel, Afridis. Samil. Headmen ; Mir Usman, Nuzai, Gulistan, Pahlwan, Mir Azam, Mabrez, Amir Shah, Yar Sher, Sherdan, Dauran, Yar Baz, Said Khan, Yar, Ghulam.

ZIKRYA KHEL (Mastura river). A sub-division of the Mani Khel (1,000), Muhammad Khel, Orakzais. Gar. Shiah. Headman ; Ali Jan.

ZIMMU.—A minor fraction of Aib Kor, Shaikh Khel, Aib Khel, Salarzai, Iliaszai, Bunerwals.

ZIRAI (10).—A minor fraction of Shadi Khel, Lar Lorai, Land, Malakh, Mallizad, Dawaris. Headman ; Fakir Muhammad.

ZIRA KHEL.—A minor fraction of Mad Khozhai, Khaddar Khel (770), Mohmit Khel, Utmanzai, Darwesh Khel Wazirs. Headman ; Pir Muhammad.

ZIRA KHEL (247).—A sub-division of Amzoni, Mallizad, Dawaris. Headmen; Malik Khan, Muhammad Alam, Garwal Khan, Ghulam.

ZIRA KHEL (15).—A sub-division of Banda, Tappizad, Dawaris. Headman; Ayaz Khan.

ZIRKIZAI (West of Dera Ghazi Khan District).—A sub-division of the Hamzazai, Balil Khel, Musa Khels. Headman; Lashkar.

ZMARAIS, MIRZIS, or MIZRIS (130; Dera Ismail Khan frontier).—A small tribe claiming descent from the ancestor of their neighbours the Musa Khels, with whom they are very friendly. Headman; Sardar Hakim Khan.

ZOHRA KOR.—A minor fraction of Zaman Khel, Makki Khel, Kattia Khel, Hassan Khel, Mitha Khan Khel, Kuki Khel (4,500), Afridis.

ZOLI KHEL (14).—A section of Atman, Miram Shah, Tappizad, Dawaris. Headman; Shabah.

ZOLIZA KHEL.—A minor fraction of Muhammad Khel (700) Isperka, Kalu Khel, Ahmadzai, Darwesh Khel Wazirs. Headmen; Jan Nur Muhammad, Shah Kamran.

ZUBAIR KHEL.—A minor fraction of Musa Khel, Makhozai, Nasuzai, Iliaszai, Bunerwals.